John J. Egan
Walter J. Burghardt, S.J.
Richard Gielow, C.M.

Extraordinary Lives

Thomas W. Cummings, S.J.
Michael A.
Thomas M.
Richard W.
Arnold Weber
William
William J.
Leonard
John Mackey
Michael W. Warfel
Jack D. Barker
Louis A. Sigman
Ned J. Blick
Andrew J. Umberg
Donald J. Goergen, O.P.
James A. Krings
Raymond B. Kemp
Robert L. Marciano
John F. Carney
Michael Sheehan
Thomas C. Brady
Charles Ferrier
John D. Sheridan
Francis J. Smith
Gregory Ramacher
Daniel J. Ward
Theodore M. Hesburgh, C.S.C.

Extraordinary LiVES

thirty-four priests tell their stories

FRANCIS P. FRIEDL

REX REYNOLDS

AVE MARIA PRESS Notre Dame, Indiana 46556

International Standard Book Number: 0-87793-656-0

Printed and bound in the United States of America.

Library of Congress Cataloging-in-Publication Data

Friedl, Francis P.
     Extraordinary lives : thirty-four priests tell their stories / Francis P. Friedl, Rex Reynolds.
               p.   cm.
        ISBN 0-87793-656-0
        1. Catholic Church--United States--Clergy--Biography. 2. Catholic Church--Clergy--Biography.   I. Reynolds, Rex (Rex V. E.)   II. Title.
BX4670.F74   1998
282'.092'273--dc21
[B]   98-3985
                                                                       CIP

Contents

FOREWORDS 7

Virgil C. Dechant
    Supreme Knight, Knights of Columbus 7
Raymond F. Mohrman
    President, Serra International 8

PREFACE 9

I. LIGHT A LAMP 13

Priests in Special Ministries

- John J. Egan 14
- Walter J. Burghardt, S.J. 24
- Richard Gielow, C.M. 30
- Charles A. Gallagher, S.J. 38
- Gerard S. Sloyan 47

II. TAKE NO PURSE 53

Priests in Religious Communities

- Steve Doyle, O.F.M. 54
- Juan Rivas, L.C. 62
- Thomas W. Cummings, S.J. 68

III. LET DOWN YOUR NETS 75

Priests in Parishes

- Michael Heras 76
- Thomas M. Anglim 81
- Richard W. Moyer 87
- Arnold Weber, O.S.B. 93
- William Trienekens 99
- William J. Bausch 105

IV. LOOK AFTER MY SHEEP 115

Priests Who Became Bishops

- Leonard J. Olivier, S.V.D. 116
- John Mackey 123
- Michael W. Warfel 131

V. OTHER SHEEP I HAVE 141

Priests From Different Faith Traditions

- Jack D. Barker 142
- Louis A. Sigman 148

VI. COME AFTER ME 155

Priests Who Conquered Self-Doubts

- Ned J. Blick 156
- Andrew J. Umberg 162
- Donald J. Goergen, O.P. 167
- James A. Krings 177

VII. I HAVE BEEN IN DANGER 187

Priests Who Survived Unusual Difficulties

- Raymond B. Kemp 188
- Robert L. Marciano 199
- John F. Carney 207
- Michael Sheehan 218

VIII. GET UP AND GO 221

Priests Who Changed With New Insights

- Thomas C. Brady 222
- Charles Fortier 228

IX. THAT YOUR JOY MAY BE COMPLETE 235

Priests Who Would Do It All Again

- John V. Sheridan 236
- Francis J. Smith 246
- Edward Ramacher 252
- Patrick J. Waite 255
- Theodore M. Hesburgh, C.S.C. 261

AFTERWORD 269

ACKNOWLEDGMENTS 270

ABOUT THE AUTHORS 271

Forewords

A book on the priesthood—rather, a book on priests reflecting on the whys and wherefores of their own priesthood—is much needed today, when many who are called by God to the priesthood are not answering the call.

The Knights of Columbus have been promoting vocation awareness and encouraging and supporting vocations to the priesthood for years through our ongoing vocation program. We have zeroed in on the concept that "families are the seedbed of vocations." Indeed, many of the life stories in this book bear that out.

But it can also be said that priests themselves—good, holy, happy priests—recruit new priests by their presence, example, and joy in their vocation. This too is amply illustrated in *Extraordinary Lives*.

A proud tradition of the Knights of Columbus is that we stand in solidarity with our priests. In light of that, let me recapture a reflection I made in 1993 to our annual convention, explaining why we so stand:

> The priesthood is, somehow, transcendent; the priesthood is mystical; the priesthood is something unique to be revered by those of us called to other stations in life.

> Yet priests stand at the center of our faith experience. In some special way our lives are intertwined with theirs, going back to our baptism when, in the pouring of the waters of salvation, we entered into a spiritual relationship with the one who welcomed us into the Mystical Body of Christ.

This book is about such priests, and we are indebted to them, just as we are indebted to Msgr. Friedl and Rex Reynolds for helping us to see Christ through these "other Christs."

May the Lord send many more laborers into the harvest!

VIRGIL C. DECHANT
SUPREME KNIGHT
KNIGHTS OF COLUMBUS

It has been documented that religious vocations are fostered primarily by the example of someone serving in the priesthood or religious life, and the explicit suggestion from another that the young person consider such a ministry.

There is a need for successful and happy priests to tell the stories of their lives. *Extraordinary Lives* records the stories of thirty-four priests and their call to the ministerial priesthood. They share with us the values of their vocation. These accounts are edifying, stimulating, joyful, sincere, and often humorous. They are as unique as the individuals, and are always interesting and inspiring.

Extraordinary Lives allows young people to hear the story of how God's call manifested itself in the lives of a variety of priests. Today, more than ever, people are looking for spiritual guidance and need to see priests as religious and holy individuals.

In *Extraordinary Lives* we receive a glimpse of how a few priests feel about their vocations, their call by God, and how they reacted to that call. We find who influenced them—their family, teachers, priests, and friends. This is not a novel, but a collection of stories about commitment to the priesthood and the joy of being a priest. It offers encouragement to those who may be considering the priesthood and tells of the blessings of priesthood: preaching the Word, celibacy, love for God, care for people, and, above all, the gift of Eucharist.

Serra International is an organization whose primary objective is the promotion of vocations to the ministerial priesthood and vowed religious life. As Serrans we know the importance of having young people hear the stories of how priests received their calls. But how do we get this information to them? *Extraordinary Lives* endeavors to be an instrument to help in the fulfillment of this challenge.

RAYMOND F. MOHRMAN
PRESIDENT
SERRA INTERNATIONAL

Preface

No one disputes that the Catholic priesthood is in a state of crisis, but many disagree with the gloomy predictions of some that the priesthood as we know it is ending. Father Bill Bausch writes in *Take Heart Father* (Twenty-Third Publications, 1991) that these signs "are all pointing, not to demise, but to rebirth. And in this rebirth we are chosen to be midwives." Distinguished theologian Bernard Häring writes:

> A distinction must be made between crisis as a manifestation of decadence, and crisis as a sign of growth (or an opportunity that allows new growth). Ten years after the Second Vatican Council, a Spanish-born priest who had served in Latin America wrote, under my direction, a doctoral dissertation on the undeniable crisis in priestly life. He concluded that this crisis could very well turn out to be a crisis of growth, if priestly formation and spirituality are understood and developed within the framework of the council's *Pastoral Constitution on the Church in the Modern World* (*America*, 21 September 1996, p. 19).

The Chinese have a similar approach. The characters for crisis are a combination of two characters, *wei* (danger) and *qi* (hope or opportunity) as listed here.

DANGER   OPPORTUNITY

The crisis facing the priesthood can lead in either direction, and judging from the wonderful men whose stories are told in this book, it seems more likely that the shortage of priests presents us with an opportunity for growth, for change, and for a breakthrough in the work of bringing about God's kingdom.

During the recent barrage of negative reporting about priests, who could have foreseen the outcomes of two national surveys conducted in 1994—one by the *Los Angeles Times* and the other by the National Federation of Priests' Councils? These surveys present a picture of the priesthood quite at variance with books and articles which portray priests as disagreeing with the Pope, disliking their bishops, wanting to marry, and inclined not to choose the priesthood if they had it do to over again.

In July and September of 1994, Father Andrew Greeley, a priest of the Archdiocese of Chicago and a professor at the University of Chicago and the University of Arizona, wrote two articles for *America* drawing conclusions from the surveys mentioned above ("A Sea of Paradoxes," July 16, 1994, p. 6 and "In Defense of Celibacy?" September 10, 1994, p. 10). Greeley found results which run counter to the image too often portrayed of the American Catholic priesthood. His conclusions were:

> 1. *The much discussed morale crisis in the priesthood does not exist.*
> 70% say they would definitely choose to be a priest again;
> 20% say they would probably do so.
> 2. *Celibacy does not seem to be the problem that it is often alleged to be.*
> Only 4% say they would definitely marry if the Church approved.
> 3. *Priests are generally satisfied with the quality of their work performance.*
> 4. *Most priests give Church leadership moderately high marks.*
> 83% approve the job performance of Pope John Paul II;
> 72% approve the job performance of their own bishops.

We, the authors of this book, one a cleric and one a layman, believe that it would be worthwhile to explore in greater detail what happy priests think about their vocation. We believe that such a work will be useful particularly for men who may be thinking about a vocation to the priesthood, as well as for those parents, priests, religious, and others who might be able to support and influence such choices and to reaffirm priests already laboring in the vineyard. The result is *Extraordinary Lives.*

For this book, we traveled to all parts of the United States and even outside of its boundaries and interviewed more than forty priests. Their stories were so interesting and rich that the work of conducting and transcribing the interviews was easy compared to the pain we experienced in selecting only thirty-four stories and then reducing the manuscripts by more than 75,000 words for publication. We ended up choosing a variety of priests of different locales—sixteen states, Washington, D.C., Canada, and New Zealand; of different jurisdictions—ten are members of religious congregations, twenty-four are diocesan priests; of different ages—sixteen were ordained before 1960, the others since; and of different ministries—pastors, associate pastors, bishops, administrators, specialists, activists, and former Episcopalian priests.

The reader is cautioned not to assume that what is presented here is any attempt to define priesthood or even what any one of the priests would pen if he were to write his autobiography.

To stimulate and advance the interviews, we prepared a set of questions which attempted to cover various aspects of priesthood. Some of the interviewees followed the line of questioning more than others. Because of the nature of the topics discussed and the similarities in the lives and works of the priests, a number of focuses for this book were possible. We decided on one that highlights the variety of jobs and skills, as well as the satisfaction and joy, found in the priesthood.

The narratives are sometimes surprising, sometimes what we might expect, but never ordinary. These are truly extraordinary stories by ordinary men engaged in essential and challenging work, stories that reveal how deep runs the desire and satisfaction of serving Christ by serving others.

The reflections of these men lift a veil on the priesthood, giving all of us—clergy and lay people alike—an opportunity to hear priests speak frankly about their lives, both their ups and their downs. We learn that holy water does not flow in their veins, that they, like all of us, face life with doubts, difficulties, and discouragement, and that hope in Christ lifts them up each day.

We may wonder why men would voluntarily enter and continue a life without a spouse, foregoing the natural desire to have progeny. We may also ask what possible values celibacy might have, whether or not it is an outdated detriment for priests in bringing God to people and people to God. Every priest whom we interviewed addressed the issue forthrightly. To avoid needless repetition, we chose not to print all the comments; instead we selected those which were typical or which added another dimension to the topic. We can report that not one priest expressed a desire to marry even if the requirement were lifted, and that every single priest said in one way or another that celibacy means much more than an idle requirement. At the same time, their insights into the future of celibacy are thoughtful and arresting.

Always, both explicitly and between the lines, the grace of the Holy Spirit is evident in these stories. We marvel at how these men can open up and discuss the innermost workings of their hearts and minds. Their stories are touching and edifying, packed with practical spirituality.

One of the titles proposed for this book was "Climb a Tree." A story in Luke's gospel tells how Zacchaeus, a wealthy tax collector from Jericho, unable because of his diminutive stature to catch sight of Jesus in the crowd, climbed a sycamore tree to better see Jesus as he passed by. Every priest is a Zacchaeus. Priests are men with a variety of talents who, in the words of Fr. Francis J. Feeney, "climb a lonely drawbridge [and] mount a narrow stair" in order to have an unimpeded view of Jesus. *Extraordinary Lives* describes the results of their climb.

If no one were to read these stories, we think our efforts would have been worthwhile merely for our own edification and growth. By publishing them, we trust you, too, will glimpse the positive lives of these priests and the opportunities presented by this crisis in the Catholic priesthood.

MSGR. FRANCIS P. FRIEDL
. REX V. E. REYNOLDS

I. Light a Lamp

Priests in Special Ministries

N̲O ONE LIGHTS A LAMP AND PUTS IT IN SOME
HIDDEN PLACE OR UNDER A TUB, BUT ON A
LAMP-STAND, SO THAT PEOPLE MAY SEE IT WHEN
THEY COME IN.

–LUKE 11:33

*Almost every priest wants at some time to be a pastor,
either in his own country or in the mission territories, but
because of special needs of the Church or unusual
charisms, a surprising number of priests have been
assigned to or have chosen other tasks. And they found,
often to their own astonishment, that these ministries
developed latent or unsuspected talents which they were
able to offer to the Church. If their gifts had not been uti-
lized, we would be much the poorer. The five priests in this
section testify how their unexpected ministries have
enriched and complemented their lives.*

John J. Egan
Chicago, Illinois

Monsignor Jack Egan was born in New York City and grew up in Chicago. He was ordained in 1943 for the Archdiocese of Chicago.

Any priest, politician, or public servant who lived in the Midwest in the fifties and sixties could not have escaped meeting this human dynamo who emerged from the South Side of Chicago to fight the battles of minorities and to promote programs geared to make the laity—especially married couples—aware of their mandate to the apostolate by virtue of their baptism. Monsignor Egan was to become so famous that when someone referred to "Jack" in a discussion of parish programs or of social activism, it was understood that you were talking about Monsignor Jack Egan.

Monsignor Egan draws fire from those who disagree with his programs and respect from those who see vision and charity in his work. The scholarly Notre Dame Professor of Christian Ethics Richard A. McCormick, S.J., writes of Egan, "In the American Catholic church we look for leadership. We cannot demand that every pope be a John XXIII, every bishop a Helder Camara. We cannot demand that every theologian be a Karl Rahner, every priest a Monsignor Jack Egan, every Christian activist a Dorothy Day. . . " ("Authority and Leadership: The Moral Challenge," America, *July 20, 1996, p. 17). As you feel the excitement in Monsignor Egan's work, ask yourself where the Church would be today if he had not been on the scene and had not undertaken the tasks he describes.*

The deep faith of my family, especially my father, caused me to think about the priesthood. My father was very religious. Every morning I would see him kneel at a chair in the kitchen before he went to work. I later learned that he attended daily Mass at old Saint Hyacinth's. That impressed me. I first had a desire to study for the priesthood when I was in eighth grade. Several classmates and I wanted to join a missionary society. Surprisingly, my father stopped me from enrolling. He said, "You are too young to know your own mind. You are getting a scholarship at DePaul. Take it." I went to DePaul High School and later to DePaul University.

In 1935 I was working for the payroll department of the Chicago Motor Club. I began to wonder if there weren't a better way to help people. I went to see Father Ray O'Brien, the spiritual director at Quigley Seminary, and O'Brien invited me to attend Quigley that fall.

Then came a terrible disappointment. My father refused to accept my wish to study for the priesthood. He told me I should be a lawyer. But I had made up my mind, and I was stubborn. My father didn't speak to me for six months. I remember getting on the bus and heading for Quigley that first morning with a heavy heart. Yet that day also brought me a great deal of joy, because I knew I was beginning to fulfill an ambition that was crowding out everything else in my life. It was only after my father's death that my mother told me that he had once been a Christian Brother but dropped out before final vows. His resistance to my entering the seminary stemmed from a fear that what he thought of as his failure would be replicated in my own case.

I was not a good student, but my father's objections made me work all the harder. It was a terrible struggle. One day I asked two fellow seminarians who were very good students to tutor me. They accepted the challenge. Through their coaching I was able to pass my exams. From then on it was easier—a little easier.

After ordination I worked for many years with community organizations. We tried to bring together the people of a particular community to look at the problems they faced and to develop a bond among them so they would be able to accomplish together what they could not do individually. We worked to develop programs that would enhance their lives, improve their living conditions, and give them a sense of dignity. We helped them face up to the forces—political, economic, and cultural—that were preventing them from achieving goals for themselves and for their families. I was really the go-between for Saul Alinsky, the famous organizer of neighborhood self-help groups, and the Archdiocese of Chicago.

While I worked closely with community organizations, I was not really an organizer myself. I was a facilitator and a stimulator. I encouraged people to organize. My job was to help people have a vision of what could be. Then I would walk with them while they were organizing. I have done that kind of work all my life—in Cana, Pre-Cana, and Family Life programs. To promote and encourage those programs, I developed personal relationships with pastors, priests, and lay people of many dioceses, especially young married and engaged couples. I spent literally all day and night getting people involved. Once a priest said to me, "Jack, you are not too smart, but you do know how to pick people, to develop leaders." That is true. I am not exceptionally bright, but I do know how to judge people and have the ability to encourage them to go a little further than they would ordinarily go.

I had been working in the Cana Conference movement in the middle fifties when I met Saul Alinsky. I began to work with Saul and learned that his programs were applicable to what I was doing in Cana. He would insist that each of us write a daily report on what we had done. On Friday, he would gather the reports, go over them in detail, analyze and criticize them, and stimulate our thinking on how the efforts of one day related to those of another.

Saul was an interesting historical figure. He had tremendous talent for planning and organizing. Yet in time all of his groups fell apart, while those of Ed Chambers, another skillful organizer of that day, are still operating. Why the difference? In each of his groups, Chambers developed exact accountability procedures and a thorough evaluation program. Those two procedures gave stability and permanence to Ed's organizations. A third factor was this: Ed installed an organizer in each program. Saul didn't train enough organizers. As long as he was with the group it functioned well;

when he left, with no accountability and no organizer the group would fall apart.

I persuaded the new archbishop of Chicago, Cardinal Meyer, to gather the priests together and start the Organization of the Southwest Community. He gave pastors permission to use parish funds for the project. My jobs were to visit all the pastors, to get them to commit money, and to hold at bay the various hate groups that wanted to keep African-Americans out of the neighborhood. The organization was almost totally white.

On the other hand, Woodlawn, a similar organization, was the first of mainly African-American members in the country. Monsignor Vincent Cooke and I persuaded Cardinal Stritch, then archbishop of Chicago, to give $150,000 during the first three years of that organization. Other funds were donated by the First Presbyterian Church and by foundations.

Another organization that I helped form was the Pacific Institute on Community Organizing, on the West Coast. It is still going. Still another organization is the Industrial Area Foundation. Alinsky and I together developed in a Polish neighborhood a group known as the Northwest Community Organization, with goals similar to the other groups.

Of course the inevitable happened: all that work led to heart attacks in 1962, 1980, and 1988. Perhaps I worked too hard.

I think that in this country the Hispanics and the African-Americans are the groups most in need of priests today. The need and the opportunities today are among the minorities. We should be sending our finest priests to serve them, to care for their spiritual life, to walk with them in their quest for jobs, health benefits, retirement, and housing. We have to encourage them by developing leadership among them through organizations. A lot of Asians are coming to Chicago, and we aren't doing nearly enough for them. In my early days, the work of the priest was with immigrants—the first generation Irish, Polish, and Germans. We have a new immigrant class today, the Asians, Hispanics, and African-Americans. We should concentrate our best efforts with them. They have suffered greatly and still suffer from discrimination.

My first experience with Cardinal John Cody, in retrospect, demonstrated for me the value of obedience. I first met the cardinal when he appointed me pastor of Presentation Parish in January, 1966. At that same time, he told me he didn't think the Office of Urban Affairs, which I directed, was doing much.

This remark hurt me very much because my staff and I had been working hard daily with the Jewish synagogues and Protestant churches in the city to structure community organizations and to help solve the multitude of social problems affecting the people of Chicago, particularly the poor.

The cardinal asked me if it was acceptable for me to take the pastorate in this all-black neighborhood on the west side of Chicago. I countered and asked, "Is this what *you* want?" He replied in the affirmative. "Then it is acceptable to me," I told him.

What his motivation was, I was not quite sure. I learned later that the cardinal had told Father John Fahey that there was a group of troublemakers in the archdiocese, and that the cardinal meant to "trim their sails."

I apparently was the first of the troublemakers. I was followed by Monsignor Daniel Cantwell, Monsignor William Quinn, Father Jake Kilgallon, and Father Gerard Weber—all of them were sent to large black parishes as pastors. They were four of the finest priests we had in the diocese. That time was the beginning of the Association of Chicago Priests.

Even though I was elected to the first board of the ACP, I had nothing to do with the initial organizing of it. That was done superbly by Father Jack Hill and Father Patrick O'Malley.

Now to the point of this story.

Because I was obedient in accepting the assignment to Presentation Parish, I had the opportunity to live and work with the black people of Lawndale for the next five years, an experience which I badly needed and which was most fruitful spiritually and psychologically.

With the duties of being pastor and my later duties as the fourth chair of the ACP, my physical health was becoming impaired. Around this time, I met Father Theodore Hesburgh, the distinguished president of the University of Notre Dame, at O'Hare one day. He greeted me and then said, "Jack, you look terrible." I told him I was exhausted from my many duties. He invited me to come to Notre Dame for a year to rejuvenate myself. I asked him to write a letter of invitation, which he did in great detail. I presented it to the cardinal as soon as I received it. Although he objected to my leaving the archdiocese for a year, by the end of an hour's conversation he told me he would not stand in my way.

What followed next were thirteen productive years of work with the Catholic Committee on Urban Ministry and the Institute for Pastoral and Social Ministry at Notre Dame.

When I felt that my work at Notre Dame was finished, I appeared before the Priests Personnel Board in the archdiocese and told them I would be returning to Chicago. They seemed overjoyed and told me to wait until the new archbishop was in place.

I had known Cardinal Bernardin for some twenty years before he came to Chicago. He graciously made me the Director of the Office for Ecumenism and Human Relations in the archdiocese, a position I held for four years.

When I became seventy-years-old, I moved on to DePaul University where I still happily serve.

All these blessings came to me because of my obedience to my superiors.

Despite all my other faults, I think I can honestly say that my father taught me well, and I have never disobeyed a request or an order by any superior in my fifty-five years as a priest. And it all "paid off" in some constructive work and a very happy life as a priest.

Commitment is important in the priesthood, as it is in marriage. But the issue of permanent commitment to the priesthood is an interesting and open question. Our whole tradition of priesthood used to be based on the supposition that men would live to be about fifty years of age. I am seventy-nine. Should the priesthood be permanent? I have read some of the discussions about approving the concept of a temporary priesthood. Actually we are doing that right now with the laicization of clergy. Still, there is a great value for society in the permanent commitment made by priests and married couples. I do think it is an issue that needs study, discussion, and prayer if we are to solve the priest shortage problem. I am saddened by the fact that many dioceses are planning for priestless parishes, while our whole theology emphasizes the eucharist as the very center of our spiritual lives. Are we now going to deprive people of the eucharist because of a disciplinary question? That is a serious matter that calls for careful exploration. Otherwise, very soon North America will be facing the same situation that now exists in South America.

I don't have the answer to the shortage of vocations, but there is one Person who does have the answer and that is the Holy Spirit. And if we do our best, in good time the Holy Spirit, together with the priests of the Church, will renew the Church as it has been renewed in every dark period in history.

I come from a generation where the commitment of employer to employee and employee to company was considered very important. My father used to brag that he worked forty-nine years for the Chicago Motor Coach Company. Loyalty to the company was a high priority. That has all changed now. A working person might go through three or four work changes during a lifetime. Commitment to an employer is no longer there. With all the downsizing that is going on, the same is true for commitment by the employer. And even people who are getting married often shrink from the idea of a permanent commitment. A young fellow once said to me, "Marriage is one thing . . . but a commitment?" Whether it is important to society or not, I have made a permanent commitment to the priesthood and intend to keep it.

I have had some crises in my life. One of them came in the middle of all my organizational work. I was in a state of turmoil, not sure what direction my life should take in the future. I had some concerns about my vocation. I was working with young couples who were happily married. Their lives seemed so appealing, and I went to see Father Charlie Curran (the psychologist, not the theologian). He was a non-directive counselor who had studied under Carl Rogers. I spent ten days at his home in Columbus under his direction. He helped me sort out the questions that were plaguing me. When the ten days were over, I felt totally clean. It was a magnificent experience, a turning point in my life. As I look back, I see the single life as having been a blessing for me. That doesn't mean I would recommend it for all priests. It is a gift which the Church should cherish and there should always be a celibate clergy. But it is not for all.

From the time that Charlie counseled me, he and I were very close. I got him a teaching post at Loyola University. I also organized a weekly program of classes in counseling, taught by Curran, for the priests of the archdiocese. More than two hundred priests participated. Curran also developed a training center for counselors at the Dominican sister's Sinsinawa Mound near Dubuque, Iowa.

One day Charlie's secretary called to say that Charlie was dying. I dropped everything, flew to Dubuque, and drove to the Mound. He was jaundiced, in great pain, and obviously going fast. We sat and told stories about our life together. He thanked me for all I had done for him and vice versa. We prayed together and blessed one another. I said, "Charles, I won't see you again alive. Is there anything you want me to do, something you want me to remember?" He looked at me and said, "Jack, you are Irish and from time to time you are going to feel you didn't do enough with your life. But never forget all the good that you have done." Those were his last words to me. He died three days later. He did for me what no other counselor or psychiatrist could have done. At one point he gave me back my life, and at the end of his life he renewed me again.

My life as a priest has been supremely happy. My only real disappointment has been my lack of spiritual development. I would like to be a holier person, yet don't seem to have the courage and ability to bring about the changes I need to make at this stage of my life. But I keep trying.

To balance that defect, I have experienced incredible joy in having so many opportunities to help people who need consolation and hope. It has also been a joy to work with community organizations and with labor and civic groups, to help improve the life of the poor in our communities. Sometimes I look back on the work I have done and wonder whether it was worthwhile, because at times things seem worse than when I started to help. One day I confided this concern to Monsignor William Quinn. He said, "Jack, don't forget that you showed up. You gave the Church the opportunity to be present where things were happening. Had you not been there, the Church would not have been present." I guess that expression "just showing up" has been around for a while. I am not sure who said it first; maybe it was Saul Alinsky. Perhaps it was Woody Allen. More likely it was Moses.

Now that I am approaching octogenarian status, I often reflect on the question, "Have I made a difference because I showed up?" That is a question better answered by someone else. Yet I do feel my life has been worthwhile and that I have made a difference in my little portion of the world. I made a difference among the minority communities that I helped organize and in my interfaith work with Jews and Protestants. I think my work in Pre-Cana and Cana made a difference in thousands of Christian families. I know I made a difference in the lives of those who participated in the work of the Catholic Committee on Urban Ministry at the University of Notre Dame, as well as the Institute of Pastoral and Social Ministry, also at Notre Dame, in which I trained a whole generation of priests, sisters, and laity in the social teachings of the Church. I made a difference with the priests of the archdiocese when I helped them form the Association of Chicago Priests. I made a difference in the lives of the people in Presentation parish where Cardinal Cody had sent me for exile.

One small example of someone I helped in that parish: About twenty-five years ago, I had a conversation with an African-American teenager on the basketball court across from the Presentation rectory. I encouraged him to finish high school and make something of himself. In 1980 I was about to have my first heart operation. A distinguished looking man came into the room and stood beside my bed. He told me his name and reminded me of that day on the basketball court. He said he had seen in the paper that I was to undergo surgery and wanted to visit me to thank me for what he had become. "I did finish high school because of your recommendation; also college. Then I became an architect, and now I work for one of the finest architectural firms in Chicago." That one experience answers the question about making a difference in the lives of others.

I would have to say that the happiness that comes to a priest in the service of people is absolutely unparalleled in any other ministry. Just consider the opportunities the priest has in baptizing a child, assisting a dying person, presiding at a funeral and above all, consecrating the eucharist. To want to experience those joys is not enough reason for seeking ordination. When I was a young priest, people revered you just because you were a priest. Today they respect you for what you are and what you do, for your competence, your zeal, your generosity, love, kindness, and compassion. The oils of ordination are still important, but they are not enough.

I encourage young men to consider the priesthood. I tell them that it is the most wonderful vocation in the world for this reason: no other vocation demands and makes use of all the talents and gifts a person can bring to their vocation. I was not a good student and I think my father's objections to my entering the seminary made me work all the harder to continue even when my grades were poor. Hard work and staying in the priesthood has allowed me to "show up" when someone needed me.

Today the priest is so badly needed by people. If he is competent and caring, people will flock to him for help.

Walter J. Burghardt, S.J.
Washington, D.C.

Mention the name Burghardt to any priest and he will say, "Do you mean the preacher?" Often called the dean of American preachers, Father Burghardt is famous for his precise, carefully crafted homilies. He has published twelve collections of homilies plus a widely read text, Preaching, The Art and the Craft.

Since 1991 he has offered to clergy of the United States and abroad "Preaching the Just Word," a project of the Woodstock Theological Center in Washington, D.C. The five-day retreat/workshop integrates personal prayer with reflection on sacred scripture, the social teachings of the Church, contemporary culture, homiletics, and liturgy.

Usually we idealize the pastor as the man for all seasons for all people, but even the best pastor can benefit from the skills of the priest who has the opportunity to bring another lamp to the faith communities he serves. Enter Father Burghardt.

Father Burghardt was born in Manhattan in 1914 and was ordained in 1941 while a member of the Society of Jesus. He is a senior fellow at the Woodstock Theological Center.

My parents, immigrants from Gallipean, part of the Austrian-Hungarian Empire, were quiet people. Some have told me their whole lives were centered on my brother and me. I didn't realize that was true until later. My father was a laboring man who worked on a horse-drawn milk wagon. We had little money, but we never felt deprived of anything. Both my father and mother had a high sense of justice, by which I mean if we said we were going to do something, by heaven we had better do it. When finally I told my father I wanted to be a Jesuit, all he said was, "If that is what you want to be, be a good one."

My brother and I attended Saint John the Evangelist parish school on Fifty-fifth Street in New York City. We had a group of remarkable priests there. Not only were they good priests, but they were easy to talk to, especially one long dead, Father Francis X. Shea, who off and on would stop me on the street to visit with me and ask me if I wanted to be a priest. My earliest sense of vocation came from those fine men. I don't recall ever wanting to be anything but a priest. We went to Xavier High on the west side. I was impressed by the Jesuits who taught there, some of them priests, others scholastics. They had an unusual combination of qualities that appealed to me. They were both intelligent and friendly. They played handball and basketball with us. So, looking back, my first thought of the priesthood came from my grade school. The desire to be a Jesuit came from Xavier High.

I was at Woodstock from 1946 to 1974. When it closed, we moved to New York City, setting up a relationship with the Union Theological Seminary. In 1974 I was invited to come to Catholic University, where I taught patristics until 1978. Then, weary of the impedimenta that accompanies teaching—blue books, exams, committee meetings—I accepted an invitation from Father Timothy Healy, president of Georgetown University, to be Theologian-in-Residence. I stayed in this position until 1990. I was allowed to write my own job description, and it was simple: I did what I wanted to do and was paid for it. I could still move around the country, giving lectures and addresses, without exams to correct. Also, I was able to put serious time into my preaching, which was becoming an increasing priority for me. It was then that I started to think of publishing my homilies on a regular scale. I had previously published two books of homilies. Since then I have published another ten.

Early in my priesthood, I began to develop a keen interest in preaching. A most moving experience was giving the *Tre Ore* at Saint Michael's in Buffalo. That consisted of nine homilies. The first was an introduction, then seven homilies on the seven last words of Jesus, and a concluding sermon. It was a wonderful experience to preach three hours on the passion of Christ.

My most recent book is from Yale University Press, *Preaching the Just Word*. It grew out of the 1994 Lyman Beecher lectures on preaching at Yale Divinity School. The book sustains a thesis of mine that preaching is the most obvious and stimulating way to spread the Church's social gospel. The Yale Press sent the manuscript to William Sloane Coffin, a noted Protestant minister. He loved it but said, "Look, you are going to get a lot of criticism if you don't add a section dealing with three contemporary problems: assisted suicide, ordination of women, and gays and lesbians." I valued his criticism and insights, so I added a fourth chapter on those social issues, a chapter that will in turn probably provoke its own criticism.

For me a big disappointment in the priesthood lies in the ineffectiveness of so much of our preaching. We have a captive audience, and by and large that audience is not being fed. What an opportunity! And so often we lose it. Preaching affords enormous opportunities for good. I get letters from people all over the country who thank me for something they read in one of my books of homilies. One example: the wife of a senior government official sometimes called her husband at the office when he was faced with a decision on a key issue. She would say, "Listen to this," and read something from one of my books. Preaching can be very influential.

The opportunity for effective preaching has become even greater and in a sense, perhaps more oppressive after the *Newsweek* article in which Ken Woodward printed Baylor University's list of the twelve most effective preachers in the English-speaking world. To be the only Catholic on the list is a bit scary, especially in terms of the status of Catholic homilists.

The consistent and growing reaction of people to my preaching has been a big surprise to me. What an unending source of wonder that people in every walk of life tell me how something they heard or read in one of my presentations has given them a new direction, a new hope, a new joy. Preaching is not an easy task. It takes me altogether, including the research I do, about forty to sixty hours to produce what I call an acceptable homily. Those hours of preparation aren't spent just sitting down at a typewriter. I take the experiences of the past week. I try to speak to the needs, the joys, the hopes and the fears of the congregation. That, by the way, is the basic message of our Preaching the Just Word workshops.

A uthority is one of the problems we all must face—not only we who are ordained, but every Christian. It has been a problem for me in the practical order. I have seen it abused and have seen the effect it can have on priests. In 1968 Cardinal O'Boyle of Washington summoned forty-eight priests of his archdiocese who had expressed opposition to *Humanae Vitae* and ordered them to recant or face suspension. More than half left the priesthood. At the same time I was in the Archdiocese of Baltimore and had expressed reservation on the absoluteness of the prohibition. Cardinal Shehan wrote to each of us who had questions and asked, "Will you find it possible in preaching, in the confessional, and in counseling to present the doctrine of *Humanae Vitae* as the official doctrine of the Church?" I said, "Of course. I would not think of doing otherwise." Those two methods of exercising authority are light years apart.

Humanae Vitae is really the only authority issue in the theological area that has presented me with a serious difficulty. That was because I was convinced from actual experience that there should be exceptions in this area. One moral theologian has a pertinent example of a woman he knows for whom each pregnancy became more and more life threatening. After eleven children she had a hysterectomy. She was called anti-life. Later she and her husband adopted three more children. Sometimes we have tunnel vision.

A problem often mentioned for priests is the idea of permanence. In my day when Catholics entered the priesthood or matrimony, we took it for granted that it was permanent. John Haughey has a book with a pertinent title, *Can Anyone Say Forever?* Abstractly, people would agree that permanent commitment is a good thing. In the practical order, many would say it is unlikely, if not impossible. Today a boss is not committed to employing anyone for a lifetime. No wonder employees are no longer committed to their firms. And I wonder, in marriages, how many partners have the same view of commitment that the Church expects of them.

It seems to me that one of the reasons why so many have left the priesthood, or if not, have had serious problems in recent years, is that they have identified priesthood with functions—with consecrating the bread and wine, with forgiving sins—something only they and not the laity could do. What helped me greatly was to get away from functions. I still recognize their importance, of course. They are a part of my priesthood. My point is: no matter what I am doing, as long as I am responding to what the Church is asking of me at this particular moment, I am engaged in priestly work. That is how we can explain the priest teaching a class in chemistry or political science. Not that we somehow put Christ into chemistry or political science, but that we do what the Church wants us to do at this moment in her history and mission. Thus every action of mine is priestly, with two possible exceptions: sin and sub-par golf.

So many of my contemporaries have left the priesthood. What keeps me in? My answer is, I have never found anything in life more attractive to me than the priesthood. It was that way in the beginning. It still is. There have been times of course when I would have liked to have a family. Each night I go to bed alone and at times experience a loneliness that is built into the priesthood. Yet that has not been a serious problem for me. Through travel, preaching, and lecturing, I have gathered an awful lot of friends and they have been a salvation for me. Another thing that has helped me a good deal is living in a Jesuit community. Jesuit existence has been vital to my priesthood. I would find living alone as a parish priest rather constricting. The combination of living in community and being able to exercise my gifts in varied ways has made my life fulfilling. In the final analysis I still say that I have never found anything approaching the priesthood for an attractive, satisfying life.

I think the priesthood offers a wide variety of opportunities for using one's skills. For instance, how did I get into the Preaching the Just Word project? My scholarly field was patristics, the early Christian theologians. I was managing editor of *Theological Studies* under John Courtney Murray, S.J., from 1946 to 1967. When Murray died in 1967, I became editor-in-chief and so was connected with the magazine for forty-four years, until 1990. Then, at seventy-six years young, what was I to do with the rest of my life, something that would make use of my particular competencies as I saw them—communication, lecturing, preaching, writing? This project, Preaching the Just Word, has turned out to be an effort to improve justice preaching.

In 1991 Ray Kemp, a diocesan priest ordained in 1967, was assigned by Cardinal Hickey to assist in developing my project on preaching. Father Kemp is fantastic with both priests and laity and an extremely competent coordinator for the project. We have had more than sixty of these five-day workshops in Australia, Jamaica, Canada, and in twenty-two states. The project has been a great success, and our schedule is pretty well filled out for the next two years.

A wonderful aspect of the last six years is that Preaching the Just Word is one of those projects where everything I have done or been in the past has been integrated. I am aware of the gifts God has given me that are effective in helping people to become better persons, better Christians, to love the Church more. Even in this time of crisis, I believe that as a priest I am able to give something to the world that I could not do in any other capacity.

For me this has been a remarkable life to live. And only God's grace makes it possible.

Richard Gielow, C.M.
Independence, Missouri

Richard Gielow is a member of the Congregation of the Missions, more commonly known as the Vincentians. Vincentians are secular priests bound by the simple vows, plus a vow of stability. Originally named the "Lazarists" from the College of Saint Lazare, the home of the Vincentians, the worldwide Congregation of the Missions was founded by Saint Vincent de Paul in 1625 to give missions and to educate the clergy. Their third calling is education, especially of those preparing for the priesthood. At one time in the history of this country, any diocesan priest ordained west of the Mississippi and south of Nebraska was trained by the Vincentians. Now the Vincentians are involved in mainly pastoral ministries, except for three universities which they operate—DePaul in Chicago, Saint John's in New York City, and Niagara in Niagara Falls, New York.

Father Gielow was born in La Salle, Illinois, in 1943 and was ordained in 1970. He now heads the home mission team of the St. Louis Province in Independence, Missouri. What sort of challenges does a priest face in traveling from parish to parish? His account tells of rabbit tracks in the snow, the challenge of starting a Marian shrine in the Rockies, and the glow from his great love of the eucharist.

I am five minutes older than my twin brother, Bob. He was born with a broken arm and always claimed I broke it trying to get out first. When I was growing up, our teachers were the Daughters of Charity, founded by Saint Vincent de Paul. Our parish priests were Vincentians. The sisters and the priests were the strongest influence on my vocation. My parents always encouraged my attraction to the priesthood, but never pushed. One priest in particular stands out, Father Charlie Saunders, our parish associate, who is still living. He did everything I thought a priest should do. He was our coach. He turned the basement of our grade school into a boys' club, with a soda fountain, pinball machines, shuffleboard, boxing ring, basketball court, and every imaginable kind of game for kids. It was open on Wednesday nights. A quarter got you in, but first you had to attend the Miraculous Medal Novena.

I had a wonderful childhood. We were poor, but never lacked anything we needed. In those days it was so easy to choose the priesthood as a vocation. I decided to go to a high school seminary in Lemont, Illinois, run by Vincentians. The recruiter didn't tell me my twin brother had signed up, nor did he tell my brother about me. In the fifties twins dressed alike and were expected to act alike. We had to fight for our own identity. Had I known Bob was going to the Lemont Seminary, I would have signed up just about anywhere else to show my independence. After graduating from eighth grade, I asked Bob where he was going to high school. He said he was going to a special school. "You don't mean Saint Vincent's?" He said, "Yeah." And I said, "You can't do that. That's where I'm going." He wouldn't give in, nor would I, so we went together.

When I was a junior at Lemont, I was thrown out of the seminary. I was supposed to go to my spiritual director on a specific date, but postponed it. Father Schulte, the superior, told me to pack my bags and get out. I told him I couldn't because I had a vocation. He said, "You are gone." I went to my spiritual director, Father Trapp. I cried. I pleaded. He sent me back to Schulte, who finally relented and let me stay. After I was ordained in 1970, the first person to visit me was Father Schulte. He asked me to hear his confession.

I went to college in Perryville, Missouri, and there got into trouble again. As dean of students I asked the rector, Father Ed Riley, to let a group of students go to St. Louis for a day. We had a great time. Some of us went to see the Cardinals, others took a tour of the town. We all went to a restaurant and had a drink, which, of course, was strictly forbidden. Father Riley found out about it and excoriated me. Years later he said to me, "Dick, I don't think I would ordain anyone today who didn't get into some trouble in the seminary."

After college I went to the Deandreis Institute of Theology in Chicago, run by the Vincentians. Up until that time my decision to be ordained was a little cloudy. I did think seriously of marriage, but finally in second-year theology I made at least a preliminary decision to go ahead. While yet a year away from ordination, I went to Father Trapp, who had saved me from getting kicked out of high school. I told him, "I have all this wonderful theology, but I'm not sure if I could ever put it across to people." Trapp gave me my first challenge to be a good preacher. He said to me,

> Let's deal first with the problem of getting the message across to people. When we teach the faith to people, we are dealing with mystery. But if you decide to be a priest, make it as simple as you can for them. Touch their hearts, not their minds. We attribute creation to the Father, redemption to the Son, and the love between them is the Holy Spirit. That love is very strong today, and that is what guides the Church; that is what will guide you.

Still today I can recall how impressed I was with the simplicity of his words, the validity of his approach to preaching.

But of all people, lay and cleric, my dad was my best homiletics professor. Not long after we were ordained, he said to Bob and me,

> Sons, I didn't make it through high school. Your grandfather died, and I had to stay home and take care of your grandmother. Let me make one thing straight. I have made a lot of sacrifices, and so did your mom, so you two could go to Catholic schools. We lost you after grade school when you left home. Your community has spent hundreds of thousands of dollars on your education. When I go to church on Sunday, I don't care what Moses and Aaron and all those people did. When you get in the pulpit, talk from your heart to ours. Don't worry about our heads; touch our hearts.

My father's second piece of advice was, "Get them out in an hour." And the third was, "Take care of the sick and the elderly, and you'll never have to worry about your priesthood."

At the end of 1982 when I finished my term as rector of the seminary in Kansas City, my superior, Hugh O'Donnell, now provincial in Taiwan, said to me, "Dick, you have some gifts in preaching; I would like you to consider joining the home mission team." I was honored and jumped at the chance. Of my twenty-five years as a priest, the last fifteen have been the most rewarding, joyous, happy, spiritual years of my life. I have been able to do things of which I would never have dreamed. My twin brother, Bob, formerly athletic director at DePaul University, lives in Lemont and joined our mission team in 1987. We are good friends and give five missions a year together. One of the most moving experiences in my priesthood came when I was celebrating my silver jubilee. As Bob and I walked down the aisle together he turned to me and said,

> On behalf of the community present, and on behalf of the Church, I want to thank my twin brother for his love of the eucharist. I can't think of anyone more qualified to be provincial of our province. But I will beg the Lord not to ever let it happen, because that would take him away from the work he is doing.

His words just blew me away.

I am always on the lookout for vocations and include a talk on the priesthood as part of every mission. One evening in Omaha I told the people I considered myself a very lucky man. After the mission a kid came up to me and said, "Father, why do you say you are a lucky man?" My answer was that I get to do what I love to do. "What do you mean by that?" I responded:

> Well, how many people today get to do exactly what they enjoy doing and even feel God has called them to do that job? That is what has happened in my life. And when people see me doing these things, they praise God. Remember the line in the gospel of Matthew, when Jesus said, "You are the light of the world and the salt of the earth?" How lucky can you be when you are doing what you enjoy most, and because you are doing it, people praise God? Jesus lets me be salt and light. Do you know why Jesus called his disciples salt? No? Don't you like salt on your French fries? Without salt they would be

tasteless. Jesus wants us to make things taste good for people. And happy priests can do that.

From the standpoint of the Vincentian mission, I might be expected to say that the most important thing a priest does is to preach. I am aware of the bishops' statement and that of Vatican II telling us that the primary function of the priest is to proclaim the word of God, but I see our priestly priorities in a different light. Eucharist is central to me and preaching enhances eucharist. I see the celebration of eucharist as not being limited to forty-five minutes. It is an ongoing celebration. And so my preaching in the pulpit or in the classroom is simply an extension of eucharist. Yes, preaching comes first in order of importance, but eucharist is the most sacred thing I do.

The belligerence and the stridency of dissent in the Church today have saddened me. And yet I do believe those things don't affect the vast majority of our Catholic people. When people come to a mission, I see in them a hunger to be closer to Jesus. Most of them aren't interested in all that stuff that the media reports as being so earth-shaking. If we want to find out the real depths of a person's spirituality, we will find it in the sacrament of reconciliation. I am simply awed by the experience of being God's instrument of forgiveness. It has given me insights into the human condition I would never have found any other way; it has been a wonderful privilege to be in touch with people at the deepest level, to see their beauty and their goodness.

One of my favorite stories about mission work happened at Saint John Vianney's in Bettendorf, Iowa. After the Wednesday night session a ten-year-old boy came up to me and said,

"Father, what about all this mission stuff? I'm not sure I believe there is a God."

"Why would you say that?"

"My mother is so sick; she has cancer, and is dying. If there is a God, how could he do this to her?"

My heart went out to the boy. I prayed to the Lord to give me the right thing to say. Finally I held up my three fingers and said,

"Do you ever see little prints in the snow outside your house that look like this?"

"Sure, those are rabbit tracks."

"Do you ever see the rabbits?"

"No, they come in the night and are usually gone before I get up in the morning."

"But you do know the rabbits have been there?"

"Yes."

"OK, tell me this, does your mother love you?"

"She loves me more than anything."

"How about your dad?"

"Sure, he does too."

"How do you know your dad loves you?"

"He does a lot of cleaning and cooking and stuff."

"How about your brothers and sisters, do you fight a lot?"

"Yeah, we used to, but not since my mom got sick."

"How about your math teacher in school?"

"I'm not doing very well in math, but she stays after school and helps me."

"All those are God tracks. You can't see God, but you know he is there, because his tracks are all around you."

That night I prayed for the boy. Saturday night after the mission he met me again, and said, "I'm not ready to tell you I believe there is a God, but I promise you I will look for some more God tracks."

I had an unusual experience at Medjugorje. People kept asking me when I was going to go there, and for three years I fought against it. Finally I went. I didn't want to go on a tour, so I decided to go with the secretary from a parish where I was helping out and her daughter. It was pouring rain during Mass one morning in Medjugorje. I was asked to be one of the communion distributors outside the church because of an overflow crowd. When I got to the door someone came up with an umbrella to protect me and the hosts. Outside I saw a group of students from the University of Kansas. These weren't old-fashioned Catholics. They weren't right-wingers. These were Jayhawks, who stood in the rain for more than an hour to receive communion. I went up to one of them later and asked him why he did this. He said, "Father, it's difficult to tell my peer group on the campus where my heart is; over here, it's easy." I make no statement about the validity of Medjugorje, but I do say that the faith is alive and well there, and that people everywhere still believe in and love God.

In Pueblo in 1988 I was giving a homily on the feast of the Assumption. Near the end of the homily I said,

> You people in Colorado claim to be living in God's coun-
> try. I am from Kansas City. When you hear the word
> *Kansas*, you think of nothing but a drab, dead state. Just
> for the record, back in the Midwest we have shrines to
> the Blessed Mother everywhere. I don't see many here in
> the West.

After Mass a guy came up to me and said, "When you are ready to do something about a shrine out here, call me." I decided to take him up on his offer. I told the people that all I wanted from them was a piece of property. The man who had given me the idea said he would put up $25,000. That was a start. The pastor, Father Schwaab, a Benedictine, wasn't convinced and said he needed a sign. A few months later, when I was in Medjugorje, my secretary taped a talk given by Father Jozo to the Americans. He said, "I understand that you people in America have shrines. In fact you have all your chairs in a circle, and for eight hours a day you sit and watch this shrine." It dawned on me that he was talking about television. He passed out pictures of the Blessed Mother and said, "I don't want you to tear down that shrine. I want you to go home and build another one." My secretary took the tape to Father Schwaab. He listened, watched, nodded, and said, "We will build the shrine." As of today, the parishioners have given $302,000 for the shrine. It was built and is now featured in the Southern Colorado Tour Guide.

The requirement of not being married has been a problem off and on with me. When I was younger, I had close relationships with women, not in a sexual way, but certainly in an exclusive way. And the tensions of having female friends in a culture that is quick to judge is always a problem. I had some good spiritual directors to help me through that period. I know that I couldn't be married and do the kind of mission work I am doing now. If I were married, my wife and kids would be the most important things in my life. If my kid had a volleyball game or a little league game, I would be there, not at a mission or a day of recollection. Marriage may work for others. It could not work for me. I don't really believe celibacy is the prime deterrent for vocations today. A study conducted by the Center for Applied Research in the Apostolate (Georgetown University, Washington, D.C.) reported that the number one obstacle is parents. I think the number one problem is lack of encouragement to a priestly vocation. We shouldn't blame everything on celibacy.

If we are going to increase vocations, we need to tell the world how happy we are. During missions I tell the young men, "I am over fifty years old. It has been a great life. Obviously you like what I do, or you wouldn't be here tonight. I'd like you to think of taking my place when I get a little older." Their eyes light up, and a few of them have accepted my invitation. I tell them how much they are needed and also tell them that I have gotten more recognition, affirmation, and acceptance since I was ordained than I could ever have imagined. And that respect has increased, not decreased in recent years. There seems to be a different and very deep respect for those newly ordained today because of the realization that they are taking on a tough job in difficult, painful times.

Charles A. Gallagher, S.J.
Elizabeth, New Jersey

Father Chuck "Please don't call me Charles" Gallagher was born August 18, 1927 in Garrison, New York, and was ordained in 1960 as a member of the Society of Jesus.

Father Gallagher is an incredible man, known all over the world as Father Marriage Encounter. He is a master at developing and promoting new programs, many of them spin-offs from Marriage Encounter. He is a prolific writer, with fifty books and manuals to his credit. The encounter movement began in Spain, but it was Father Gallagher who, almost single-handedly (a fact he is quick to deny) turned it into a revolution that has swept the United States and reached more than fifty countries. He is a legend among married couples. When he speaks at national conventions, he is given the largest assembly hall to accommodate the thousands who know him personally and want to hear him again.

Together with his ministry to married couples, Father Gallagher's love for the priesthood is obvious. He currently operates the Matrimonial Renewal Center in Elizabeth, New Jersey.

During my childhood the parish was the center of everyone's social life. There were dances and Catholic Youth Organization activities of every kind. Monsignor McMahon, our pastor, was an extraordinary priest, an intelligent and powerful man. He was way ahead of his time. He brought priests from England to give Lenten courses in the parish and had a drama society that put on a passion play every year, as well as other plays with spiritual topics, so that teaching in the parish was not restricted to the pulpit. He ran a great school, and I attended it for four years. What a marvelous group of sisters taught us!

All of us kids in the parochial school went to Mass and communion daily. Sister Mary Antoine, my teacher, was a wise woman. She told us that what separates the men from the boys is going to Mass and communion on Saturday. Pretty smart, making it a macho thing for us! Mother went to Mass daily. My father worked at night as foreman of the mailers at the *Daily News*. He too often went to daily Mass. Priests were invited over for dinner, and they were never criticized. Not that my parents were naive; they just loved priests.

All the experiences our family had of Church were positive. The Church was the center of our lives. When I was a teenager and going to dances, if someone asked me where I was from, I wouldn't say, "Washington Heights," but, "Our Lady of Lourdes," and I would expect the girl to give me the same information, telling me what parish she was from.

Ours was known as a vocation parish. We had more first Masses every June than we had weddings. The conversation on Sundays was always about one of the parish boys who was in the seminary. He belonged to the whole parish, and when he was ordained, the *whole* parish attended his first Mass. All of this was a great stimulus for a fellow to think about being a priest. The lessons of faith were being taught by the faithful as much as by the priests.

When I was perhaps ten years old, I was walking down the street throwing a ball against the buildings. I passed an Irish cop twirling his stick. He looked at me and said, "Well now, you look like a nice boy. Have you ever thought of being a priest?" I said nothing, but from that time on I couldn't get the idea out of my mind.

Wanting me to have male teachers, my parents sent me to All Hallows, an Irish Christian Brothers School. I had a happy time there. The brothers were wonderful. There was a lot of caring, all of them wanting us to do well. Then I went to Regis High School, run by the Jesuits, and began to think about becoming a priest. The teachers at Regis were kind to me and I felt close to them, especially to Father Tom Burke, a very holy but down-to-earth man. He loved sports, and he was a man of faith and of prayer. He was the student counselor but never enforced discipline. We used to claim that if he passed a building that we were burning down he would say,

"Nice fire, boys." But if anyone was fooling around in the church, he would become an avenging angel.

During high school I found my dates at daily Mass. I know I wasn't supposed to look around in church, but I cheated. I allowed myself the privilege of seeing some of God's beauty. We were taught to make a visit to church before and after a date, so when we picked up a girl for a date we went first to the church. Sounds strange today; it wasn't then.

When I told my mother I wanted to be a Jesuit, she reacted as I thought she would: she cried. I am sure in her mind she already had me in vestments, giving blessings right, left, and sideways. My father reacted differently. He got very serious. "That is wonderful. I am proud of you." But then he looked at me right down to my soul and said, "If you are going to be a priest, make sure you are a good one." That was a revelation to me. He was aware of priests who didn't follow the call too well, but that didn't stop him from loving priests. And he wasn't caught up in the honor that came to a family by having a priest. He was more concerned with what the Church was getting.

Jesuit training for the priesthood takes thirteen years, including time for teaching as a scholastic. My assignment to teach was at Canisius High School in Buffalo. After our third year of theology, we were ordained subdeacons on Thursday, deacons on Friday, and priests on Saturday. As I lay prostrate in the sanctuary, I prayed for one favor: *just let me not be irrelevant*. The next day I had my first solemn Mass at Saint Ignatius, where I had attended Mass so often as a student at Regis High School. One of the special joys of that day was when twenty of the kids I taught at Canisius hitchhiked from Buffalo to come to my first Mass, including one guy who was still in his tuxedo from the prom! I was so moved by that. And I shall never forget the wonder of the moment of consecration. I almost didn't want to say the words, feeling unworthy of speaking them, yet knowing this is what the Lord and his people had called me to do.

From 1961 to 1967 my assignment was to the boys' retreat house in Monroe, New York. The house was begun at the time of the Korean conflict to prepare kids for the army by one of the greatest priests I ever knew, Father John Magan. Later, Father Walsh turned it into a summer camp for poor boys from the Lower East Side with four retreats each week. The buses that came to pick up those who were going home would bring in a new crowd. These tough city kids would come there belligerent and disagreeable. Before they left they would be crying before the crucifix.

In 1968 a great change took place in my life. I was working with the Christian Family Movement, which ran a national convention every two years at Notre Dame. A friend asked me to conduct a seminar on the formation of a Catholic conscience. While I was there, she came and told me she had just attended another seminar called Marriage Encounter. "It needs a priest. They are going to put on a weekend in New Jersey. Will you go?" I did and I was tremendously impressed by how that program reached out to married couples. That weekend was something that I wanted very much for my people, and so we put together a team, wrote some talks, and scheduled an Encounter weekend for the very next month.

We gave that weekend at Saint Andrew's, my old novitiate. We had only five couples, but they were marvelous. I still remember this huge man who played football in college. On Sunday he was sitting in a conference room, pounding a table, with tears streaming down his cheeks. He kept saying, "But I hurt her; I hurt her, and I promised to love her." If nothing else did, that experience sold me on Marriage Encounter.

After that first weekend, in November of 1968, we gave others. By March of 1970 we were up to four a month. In April, we did six weekends, all in the Long Island area. Then we flew to Sioux Falls and Buffalo and gave weekends in those areas. They were one shot deals. We didn't have a plan, but we kept growing. About that time we decided we didn't have the right to restrict the program to Catholics, so we began to reserve one seat out of four for those of other faiths.

The simple reason for not going beyond the "one in four plan" was that we wanted to talk about the sacraments and other Catholic topics. We couldn't do that if the majority of the couples were of other faiths. About 1971 we helped the Jewish expression of Marriage Encounter get started. Our policy was to help any religious expression that wanted the weekend to begin on their own. We trained their teams and gave them money and supplies. There was not yet a national board, just a Long Island board. Team training began that year, and we put a whole new emphasis on the difference between feeling and judgment, a key concept in the presentations.

Toward the end of 1971 we began to formalize our plan. We said, "Let's take the ten most Catholic cities in the country and target Marriage Encounter weekends there for the next two years." It was just miraculous. Marriage Encounter grew like a weed.

Encounter is a conversion experience. We can't really be effective with people without a conversion experience. Just the intellectual stuff doesn't do it. Strangely enough, the Encounter weekend wasn't a conversion experience for me personally, not in the sense of what happened to Saint Paul on the road to Damascus. But gradually, over a period of time, it did change my whole priesthood.

A remarkable phenomenon of Christian life is the link between the sacramentality of marriage and priestly celibacy. Across the spectrum of Christian churches the two ways of expressing sexual love are intertwined. Only those churches that practice and revere celibacy (Orthodox, Anglican, and Catholic) uphold the marital relationship as one of the special signs of Christ's presence in their midst.

The churches of priestly celibacy go even further in perceiving the relationship between a Christian man and woman as sacred and pleasing to God. These churches proclaim that the love of believers is more than marriage. The marital love of the faithful is not looked upon as a private relationship merely to be supported and encouraged by the church community. Matrimony is essential to the understanding of the message of Jesus for the whole community of the faithful, married and unmarried. This sacrament reveals the inner nature of the church as the chosen and beloved of Jesus.

It is hardly accidental that the sacramentality of marriage is unique to the churches of priestly celibacy. There is an eschatology in both. Both call for a death to self. Both live a life beyond immediacy. Both reflect the glory of the other. The absolute permanence of marriage is an awesome mystery, a puzzle in a world without celibacy.

Around 1973 I got out of leadership in Marriage Encounter and started the Pastoral and Matrimonial Renewal Center. My purpose was to develop programs involving relationships that could be used in the Church at large. We began with a fourteen-session marriage preparation program for juniors and seniors in high school. It was called "Matrimony: Jesus Invites Us to Love." Thousands of students made this program, mostly through the encouragement of couples who had made the Encounter weekend. Next we developed Evenings for the Engaged and Engaged Encounter. The Evenings program involved six nights of presentations given by a married couple to five or six engaged couples. It was held in homes. That program is still going. Then we developed Barnabas, a program for single young adults. That was followed by the Parish Renewal, Parish Healing Weekend, Parish Family Weekend, Celebrate Love, and Celebrate Love Parish Evenings (with a series of 19 *Celebrate Love* books). All told there were fifty programs and books. Parish Renewal was a powerful experience. When I worked with Marriage Encounter, I took everything I knew about the Church and applied it to marriage. When I worked with Parish Renewal I took what I knew about marriage and applied it to the Church. It caused people to fall in love with the Church. I trained about six thousand priests to give the weekend course. At the end of one course an elderly priest came up to me with tears in his eyes and said, "I feel you ordained me a priest. I had almost given up."

There is so much talk today about temporary commitment. There is no such thing. Long-term commitment is the only kind of commitment that is possible. I think it is nice that people make a pledge to work with things like the Jesuit Volunteer Corps for a year, but I wouldn't call that a commitment. To me a commitment is like marriage. A man doesn't commit himself to a woman for the next three months or two years. A marriage commitment has to be total and permanent. I made a permanent commitment to the priesthood; for me there was just no other way. I don't think it was an accident that I had the parents God gave me, that our pastor was Monsignor McMahon, that my counselor was Father Burke. It was no accident that the people of Our Lady of Lourdes were thrilled with those being ordained.

I think the role of the priest today is to be a father. Some of our priests are ministers, some are teachers, some are administrators, some are pencil pushers, others are preachers. Our vocation, our calling, is to be a father. By that I don't mean paternalism. And I am not talking about being in charge. The first thing a father does is to give life. Secondly, he enables. The mother calls the child to be part of the family, the father calls the child to accomplishments. Of course the mother also encourages the kids to do well, but it is more important for her that they be close to the family. For the father, being close isn't good enough if the kid doesn't produce. Similarly, the main role of the priest is to discover the capabilities of his parishioners, to call them forth, and to enable them to exercise their talents. So the real test of a priest isn't "Am I living up to my potential?" but "Are my people living up to their potential?"

There has never been a time when I wanted to be anything other than a priest. It has been a wonderful life, but as in every life there have been problems. One of the joys and even a surprise in my priesthood has been seeing the fidelity of the laity to the priest. With all the changes in the Church and all the disillusionment because of priests who have failed, the laity have never failed us. They come to us with the statement of Peter, "Lord, to whom shall we go?" That fidelity is there because of the eucharist and because we represent the eucharist. The fellow I talked about who regretted how he had treated his wife, once said to me,

> You have such an advantage that I don't have. I think I love the Church as much as you and that I am as talented as you. But from the time you get up in the morning till you go to bed, you are involved in advancing the kingdom of God. I can't do that. I have to earn a living.

The privilege the Church has given me is that I can be full time.

One of the downsides in the priesthood is the loss of so many of my priest friends. The long black line is gone. Thirty-three men were ordained with me. This year two will be ordained at our seminary.

And you know how much I love kids. The awful thing is that with all the scandalous things that some priests have gotten into, I don't dare hug a kid today. These priests have not only hurt the Church; they have hurt me.

One idea I would like to see implemented is this: In every parish we should set up a council of people on the basis of their holiness and their devotion to the Church. One of their roles would be to discern who should be invited to be a priest for that parish. Let the people in the pews select this group. This council would meet often in prayer and decide whom they should ask. Then they would go to a boy and say, "In the name of Our Lady of Lourdes (or whatever is the name of the parish) we invite you to be a priest for us." If the kid says, "I don't have a vocation," the council will say, "Yes, you do. We just told you that you have one. You are free to say yes or no, but don't say you don't have a vocation." It wouldn't be wise for this group to go around asking every kid they meet to be a priest; that would be meaningless. If I were a bishop, I would go to a parish that has not produced a priest and tell them, "Give me a seminarian in the next five years or I will close this parish. If you are not producing priests you are not fulfilling the commandment of the Church to support your pastor."

I would also like to tell men what a wonderful time it is now to be a priest. With all the scandals, our people still love us and are faithful to us, even though we have not always been faithful to them. One thing has amazed me: I am just a meat and potatoes Irishman, nothing extraordinary, but because I am a priest, I am taken far beyond anything I could ever do on my own. It is awesome to recognize the fact that I am allowed to be significant in the lives of so many people merely because I am a priest.

Gerard S. Sloyan
Hyattsville, Maryland

Father Gerry Sloyan is Professor Emeritus in Religion at Temple University and Distinguished Lecturer in the School of Religious Studies at the Catholic University of America. He is unique among the clergymen whose stories are told here. While his early days in the priesthood involved parochial work, and while his talents were ideally suited to administration, his background prepared him for a different type of life. He is a dedicated academic, an intellectual, a perpetual scholar. Throughout his life he has been deeply involved in teaching, research, religious studies, writing, and ecumenism. Moreover, he delights in sharing his public ministry through participation in sacred liturgies.

Father Sloyan was born in the Fordham section of the Bronx in 1919 and was ordained for the Trenton diocese in 1944. Two of his four sisters entered religious communities.

The priests of the parish of my youth were large figures, starting with the pastor who took a deep interest in the life of the parish school. Father John B. McCloskey was from a town in south New Jersey where anti-Catholic prejudice ran as deep as in the rural south. It made him an apologist for the faith through education. Not only did he see to it that the twelve-grade school was staffed by the best and the brightest Sisters of Mercy he could cajole out of the Reverend Mother, but he would report from the pulpit on every Catholic school victory he knew of, be it in a science fair in Kansas or in a spelling bee in Ohio. The visibility and accessibility of priests and their way of life was important in projecting the priesthood as an attractive calling. I saw priests as living human lives, as part of the culture.

The assistant pastors assigned to my parish were athletic types. On the whole, the priests were an attractive group of men. It was not long before I decided I wanted to be one of them. In fact, I can't remember a time when I didn't. As my desire to become a priest grew, my only fear was that I was not good at sports. I played them all, but badly. The only one I became good at was swimming and diving, a non-competitive sport at my level. Most of my youthful energies went into the Boy Scouts. I thought that if I did become a priest, I could put my scouting skills to use in the priesthood.

I was awarded a tuition scholarship at Seton Hall College, conducted by the priests of the Archdiocese of Newark. The next two years were an eye-opener. I learned that one could be a diocesan priest and, at the same time, a man of books and learning. Up to that point my priest role models had every virtue, but they did not preach or teach especially well. From the beginning of college, my desire to become a priest coincided with my interests in the intellectual life.

The United States was in World War II as the order of my subdiaconate approached. I began to be unsure of my vocation. I thought that my faith wasn't strong enough for me to serve as the spiritual leader of people or to preach to anyone but myself. I had a visit with the seminary spiritual director, a man universally respected. When I voiced my fears and told him I was considering joining the army, he was dismissive. He said, "Gerry, you would make a rotten soldier but a good priest. Forget it." I did. The final year in the Theological College at Washington's Catholic University put all such ideas out of my head. The students there were an interesting crowd. I lost my timidity and forged ahead.

The seminary formation we received was intensely pastoral. We were never allowed to forget that there was work to do in the parishes of New Jersey or whatever dioceses the students came from. Our priest teachers, almost to a man, helped out in the parishes on weekends. The spiritual director, who was a professor, would frequently say, "Boys, it's a lonely life; you need to know how to recreate wisely. Stay in touch with your priest friends. Take your day off and your vacations with some of them."

We knew, of course, that he was talking about the single life, but I learned there was more to it than that, more than simply not having a wife and family. I wasn't long in the priesthood before it became clear that I needed ways to cope with many long hours on my own. Reading is the best use to which I can put my spare time. It expands my mental horizons and greatly benefits the people who have to listen to me preach. Additionally, anything active and out-of-doors is a good antidote to a life that can easily become sedentary.

My bishop received a request from the rector of the Catholic University of America for my services in a religion department that taught undergraduates and also offered graduate degrees. The bishop agreed to the request, and forty-seven years later I am still writing in chalk on a blackboard. I spent seventeen years at Catholic University. During four of those years Vatican II was in session. During the Council and the years immediately following, I was kept busy barnstorming the country to explain what the Council's documents were teaching. It was exciting work, but much more important to me was my teaching of hundreds of college students, brothers, sisters, and lay people, military chaplains, and priests from many dioceses and religious congregations. Teaching is pastoral work without the hurly-burly of the parish. As far as parish life goes, I have heard confessions and presided at the eucharist in parish churches on Sundays for much of my life. Yet, I have seldom been engaged in the care of the sick and dying. I am the poorer for not having that opportunity of serving.

After my Washington teaching days, I spent the next twenty-five years in the religion department at Temple University. Temple is a state-related institution of the Commonwealth of Pennsylvania where I was generally known to my students as Doctor Sloyan. Occasionally, in the mid or late semester, an undergraduate would approach the desk after class and with a strange look on his face say, "I was talking to a priest in my parish the other day. . . ." I would know immediately that the student had mentioned my name and one of the local Philadelphia priests had blown my cover.

The Temple years brought me in close contact with many Jewish and Muslim graduate students and, among the Protestants, some Mennonites and Brethren church members. A number of men and women from the Reconstructionist Rabbinical College, situated close by, would take two degrees concurrently. They were among my best students of whose dissertations I directed. The Muslim students came largely from Pakistan, South Africa, Malaysia, India, Indonesia, and Nigeria. They had all been teachers in their home countries and were well-educated. I felt a special bond with them, not only because of the similarities of Christianity to the teachings of the Holy Qur'an (something that came as a surprise to them), but because their medieval theologians and the Catholic schoolmen spoke the same language. We had the entire Aristotelian philosophic tradition in common. In common with the Protestant seminary graduate students, we had only the Bible and Saint Augustine read through Lutheran and Calvinist lenses.

The Bible was my academic specialty, especially the New Testament. The African-American students knew the text of the Bible well, the white Protestant and the Catholic students not as well. The Jewish students knew their scriptures as the rabbis had taught them, namely midrashic. Just as Christians often teach the Bible in the light of theological developments that derive from it, so Jews teach the Torah through homiletic elaborations in the form of stories that illustrate the text.

Off the Temple campus I was kept busy by several bilateral dialogues between teams of Catholic and Protestant theologians and clergy. The dialogues were sponsored by the United States Catholic Bishops and various churches. I was fortunate enough to be a part of three successive dialogues with the United Methodists and one with several reformed churches, chiefly Presbyterian but also Dutch and Hungarian Reformed. Much more memorable, probably because it went on for eight years and resulted in several close friendships, was my appointment as an observer to the Commission on Church Order of the nine member Churches of the Consultation on Church Union—now renamed the Church of Christ Uniting. Those ecumenical conversations (many of which continue today) between other communions of the East and West are doing something, if slowly and silently, to reduce tensions and increase understanding. Hopefully they will also diminish the scandal of a divided Christianity, a scandal both to those within and those outside the Christian faith.

In all of these activities, my seminary education in philosophy, theology, and the worship forms of the Roman rite stood me in good stead. While it was somewhat narrow, it was nonetheless rich and varied compared to that of some ecumenical dialogue partners. Many Protestant theologians had a certain envy for the spiritual formation programs of Catholic seminaries. They would speak in praise of the prayer life of Catholic priests who were expected to be leaders in prayer the rest of their lives.

That Roman Catholic priests do not marry was a fact so well known as not to be remarked. It is a matter of infinite curiosity at certain levels, deplored by some and applauded by others. But participants in theological conversations know that the single life, just as married life, has its pluses and minuses. Fidelity to either commitment, whether in Christian ministry or totally apart from it, is a marvel of God's grace.

One continuing contact I have had with people of a non-Christian religious orientation has been with Jews. This has come chiefly through long-term service on the board of the Philadelphia (later the Interfaith) Council on the Holocaust. My membership in that Holocaust Council has been ongoing for fifteen years. It has brought me to a realization of the way that ordinary Jews look at Christians. The attempt of some Christians to eliminate Jews *totally* from all lands under Nazi control was the fruit of a long-term Christian antipathy. I deem myself fortunate to have learned of this common Jewish view first-hand through survivors of some of the death camps and adult children of survivors. The fact that I am a priest of the Catholic church has always been a part of the subtext of any relationships with Jews, whether for good or ill.

What has most defined the priesthood for me, and what I always took delight in, is the ability to play an active part in the Church's public liturgy every day. The office of presider at the holy mysteries, the possibility of laying bare the riches of the scriptures in this context, has been the joy of my youth and continuing middle age. To be part of the ritual act with all the grace and beauty with which the Church has endowed it, to be a leader of the people in prayer, is more than I could have hoped for as I prepared for the priesthood.

Ours is an imperfect Church in an imperfect world. But there is great happiness available to anyone who lives one's life in the body of Christ. Priesthood is a public role in the Church. For that reason, anyone who is an intensely private person in today's parlance should not aspire to it or be ordained to it. Neither should he who has no taste or talent for liturgical celebration. To be useful as priests, we need the capacity for a wide variety of friendships which are the perfection of human love.

The priesthood is a wonderful way of Christian life, and I commend it to anyone who thinks he has the requisite characteristics and inclination. "Yes," he might say, "but I keep falling in love. In fact, I am in love right now." So was I, several times over the years. Luckily for the women, nothing ever came of it.

II. Take No Purse

Priests in Religious Communities

Take no purse with you, no haversack, no sandals.

—Luke 10:4

When Christ sent the seventy-two disciples out to evangelize communities that he was to visit later, his instructions included the words quoted above. Today two types of priests carry on the work of the original seventy-two disciples. Diocesan priests are attached to a particular geographic region. They serve under a bishop, promise him obedience and make a promise of celibacy. They are provided a residence, food, and a modest salary. Other priests are not diocesan but belong to a religious community or order. They serve under a superior known as a provincial in a wider region called a province. They take perpetual vows of poverty, chastity, and obedience. These religious take no personal possessions according to their vow of poverty, relying on their community to meet their financial needs. Throughout this book are a number of religious, identified by the initials after their names. Here follow the stories of three men who reflect on their communities, why they serve in them, and the joys associated with carrying no purse.

Steve Doyle, O.F.M.
Boston, Massachusetts

Father Steve Doyle was born in Philadelphia on August 12, 1934. He was ordained March 27, 1962, for the Order of Friars Minor (Franciscans). His home base is the Saint Anthony Shrine in downtown Boston.

Father Doyle is a remarkable man. He doesn't run with the pack. He is a confident, determined, and goal-oriented man with many talents. He uses each of them extremely well for the benefit of others. He has guided over eighty trips to the Holy Land, sharing his insights and inspiring all who accompany him. If anyone can make the histories of Israel and Christianity come alive in the land where those faiths were born, it is Father Steve Doyle. No one has a better entrée to the Holy Places. He knows the languages. He is a scripture scholar with consummate knowledge of the Judaeo-Christian story. And, since the Franciscans supervise nearly all of the shrines in the Holy Land, he has only to make a phone call to find the doors of hospitality and information swinging wide open.

Each religious community has its own spirit. The spirit of the Franciscans has played a significant role in the Church for centuries. That joyful, caring, loving spirit is evident in the reflections of Father Doyle.

I came from a dysfunctional family, and I suspect that my going to the seminary was partly an escape. My father was an alcoholic—a mean alcoholic. The way he treated my mother and the children caused us kids to leave home when we came of age. All of us except me either got married or entered the Marines. I went to the seminary.

Actually, there was more behind my wanting to be a priest than running away. The idealism of an Irish Catholic family and its tremendous respect for the priesthood were the two springboards for my interest in becoming a priest. There were always a lot of priests around our house, and they were models for me. And the Sisters of Saint Joseph who taught us were magnificent women. But even with such a background, I don't think I had a vocation when I entered the seminary. It was in the seminary where I found my vocation.

I had never met a Franciscan, so I can't really say why I applied to them. Anyway, I was accepted by the Holy Name Province of the Order of Friars Minor to attend their minor seminary. I was only fifteen. At the minor seminary I found companionship, the blossoming of spirituality, and the first real happiness of my life. During my last year, I was informed that I wouldn't be allowed to enter the novitiate because of my dysfunctional family. I protested and the decision was reversed.

Our prefect of studies asked us what we would like to do after ordination. Although my seminary years were wonderful, the classroom experiences were less so. I realized that if someone didn't do something about the horrible theological training we were given in preaching, spirituality, and biblical studies, our schooling would continue on the same dreadful level. And so I volunteered to go on for graduate studies. I was asked to get a licentiate in theology at Catholic University and to teach apologetics the following year in the very seminary I had just left.

After graduating with a licentiate and working during the summer at the Church of Saint Francis, New York, I looked forward to going back to Washington to teach. Suddenly the assignment list came out. I was sent to the Buffalo diocesan seminary to teach Old Testament (which I had never studied) plus biblical Hebrew, biblical Greek, and, when a priest became ill, the history of philosophy. Before the semester began, the rector said he had a problem with the course on preaching; two Dominicans had refused to teach it. Would I also teach that course? From that time until I quit teaching a couple years ago, I taught both scripture and preaching, a great natural combination.

I had always wanted to study scripture, but had pushed the thought away because the training was so difficult. I would have had to become acquainted with nine languages to get a degree in Scripture: first, the languages the Bible was written in, Hebrew, Greek, and Aramaic; then the two languages into which the Bible was first translated, Syriac and Latin; also the modern languages in which biblical studies occur, German, French, and English; and finally, when I got to the Biblical Institute in Rome, Italian in order to get along and to ask my confreres to pass the bread at meals. Fr. Roland Murphy, a Carmelite at Catholic University, gave me good advice: "Get your language requirements done in the States. Otherwise you might get to Rome and study Hebrew from a French grammar, taught in Latin by a Polish professor. People who take that route have a lot of trouble." His advice was sound. Because of his counsel, I finished in one year, a record time. Usually it takes three years.

I did my licentiate in scripture in Rome, staying at our friary. The living conditions were absolutely medieval, but there was a joyful spirit among the friars and I had a wonderful time. I almost didn't make it. When I was preparing my oral exams, my provincial came to Rome. I spent considerable time with him and had little time to study for the exams. A German Jesuit had taught us one course for an entire year on the seventeenth chapter of Genesis. I thought surely the examiner wouldn't ask about that chapter, so I didn't review it. But a Genesis 17 question he did ask, and I did poorly. Finally he said, "Father, I don't think I can pass you. Go out, clear your head for a while, then try again." I did. When I finished the second time, he gave me a "Vix Six," which means barely passing. I often relate this story to my seminary students and tell them, "When you minister to God's people, no one will ask you what grades you got in seminary. They will ask, How well can you preach?' 'How well can you minister?' 'How kind are you, how gentle?'"

When our novitiate was reopened in Brookline, Massachusetts, the faculty, who used a team approach, needed a theologian. I accepted their offer. It was an exciting time to work on the training of young Franciscans. It was a time when the order was coming back to the spirit of our founder and the charism that we were not a clerical order, but primarily brothers. We discovered that community itself was our most important attribute and that it overflowed into ministry. We were to be the Church in miniature. Our goal was to become a community of people living in love, praying together, and celebrating God's love for us. This is what we tried to witness to the men coming to join us.

About the same time I was invited to become a professor of sacred scripture and biblical preaching at Pope John XXIII Seminary for delayed vocations. It was an extraordinary experience to see older men who had to make major sacrifices to come and serve the Church. They were willing to give up lucrative positions, pensions, homes, and families to follow Jesus. I taught them the beauty of God's word.

After seventeen years at that assignment, I decided it was time to move on, so I accepted an offer to become assistant to the rector at Tantur, the Ecumenical Institute just outside Jerusalem. When I left Tantur, I spent a couple months running an adult education course in an English-speaking parish in Tokyo for people from various countries. In every one of my assignments, I seem to have learned something new. In Japan I believe I grew in my ability to open up to people and to show them kindness and understanding. When I was ordained in 1962, I thought my job was to dispense the sacraments. Later I learned that I was to be a sacrament. People have to see Christ in the priest. We have to live such an intimate spiritual life with Christ. We first have to be a sacrament, then we can dispense them.

I returned to the Saint Anthony Shrine in Boston, and since then have tried to satisfy the hunger of God's people for his word by preaching and by giving retreats and workshops on the word of God.

A relatively new book, *The Image of God, a Biography,* shows how the image of God has changed in scripture over the course of time. In a similar way, my image of priest has also changed. When I was first ordained, canon law was the primary rule. We judged our actions to be legal or illegal. The one who enforced the law had to be either a divine state trooper or a judge. The Franciscans helped me change that image. They are renowned as confessors because of their gentleness, kindness, and understanding. They made me see that is what God is like, and the way I had to be. The charism and life of Francis has molded my self-image. When I hear confessions and find people with a guilt complex, I tell them the wonderful thing about God is that he has a lousy memory. As soon as you confess, God forgets it, and wants you to forget it.

Commitment is not a top-of-the-line commodity today. I made my commitment when I took solemn vows in 1959. I wrestled with the decision. I asked myself if I could do it. The answer that came was the one that came to Jeremiah and others when God asked them to do something impossible. They said they couldn't do it. God said, "Good. If I thought you could do it, I wouldn't have asked you. You can do it only because I am with you." Every day I realize I can keep my commitment only because God is with me. Some of us are called prophetically to show the world that commitment is both possible and valuable. When I marry people I worry whether it will last. For some of them, I hope, one of the things that will keep them together is the example of how I have kept my vows.

Some look at the decline in church attendance and at the secularization of people and wonder whether the Church is failing. Not at all. The Church is a community of love, but she is often tempted by idols, and needs to be evangelized over and over again. Prophets are people who remind the institution what it was established for. The contemporary Church needs prophets.

Sure, the Church has failed, many times. But so have I, so I can't complain. I have failed in being self-centered, wanting to be in charge. I have failed out of laziness and pride. Like Jesus, I have been tempted in every way. Some temptations I have gone through well, others not so well. But I can always go back to the fact that the whole process of being a Christian means allowing Jesus to be Lord of my life. I often say a prayer of Saint Paul, one of the briefest and finest in the Bible: "Jesus is Lord." When I can say that and mean it, I know the Holy Spirit is with me.

When the Holy Spirit is with us, we can do almost anything. We can beat the odds. There are times when I have accomplished things that almost frightened me because I knew that alone I couldn't do them. I once counseled a woman who for twenty-five years was afraid to talk to a priest. A year later she wrote to me and said her whole life had changed. There is no way I could do that on my own. I've said a word in the confessional that I didn't think was important. However, it was so grace-filled that the person later came back and told me how much that meant to him. The power that God works through a priest is incredible.

To maintain contact with the Lord, we priests must develop our spirituality. I don't think it's a matter of working through some set of exercises. Rather it is being faithful and responsive to the Lord. A married couple has to spend time with one another; priests have to spend time with God. God is our commitment. We must be careful not to become so busy that we miss out on the one thing people really want. They want to meet God through us.

Have I ever had any doubts? Yes, I had one difficult assignment that brought doubts. And I guess every celibate regrets at some point not having a family. Sometimes I feel I am the odd man out. Community resolves that issue for me, the friars and priests who support me in so many ways with their trust, love, and concern.

For many, celibacy has been a stumbling block. It has been a help to me, and, I believe, to the people I serve. It has freed me up to be available. I spend an amazing amount of time on pilgrimages to the Holy Land, biblical conferences, and preaching. It would be difficult for me to do that if I were married. It is possible that the elimination of the requirement would help some priests in their work. Celibacy may have been a long tradition of the Latin church, but not of the universal Church. Yet I look on it as a positive thing. It may develop that celibacy will be the practice of those who live in religious communities. Those in the religious life have a community to support them, something generally missing in the diocesan ministry.

Still another problem that has to be faced not only by priests, but by every living person, is authority. Obedience to the bishop sticks in the throats of a lot of us. Bishops are good people, but they, too, need to be evangelized. A young priest recently told me that he believed it was totally wrong to criticize the Holy Father. Not at all! Criticism of papal authority has been with us from the beginning, and do you know who was the first to do that? Christ himself. He had just made Peter his successor, the Rock. When Christ told the apostles he would be a suffering Messiah, Peter, the first Pope, said, "You are wrong; you won't have to do that." And then comes the first dissent against papal authority: "You, Peter, are a Satan." So, sometimes there is an obligation to criticize. If it is simply nit-picking, saying authorities can't do anything right, I don't buy that. But if there is a reason to criticize, which means to be prophetic, it must be done so there can be a brake to misguided authority.

Everyone seems to have a solution to the decreasing number of vocations today, though none of them is working. I have heard some say the problem arises from a world that is negative, cynical, selfish, and secular. There may be some truth to that judgment, but it is too easy to point the finger at others. Maybe we should take a closer look at ourselves and see if we are models that would encourage men to join us. One of the things that keeps men away is the identity crisis among priests. When we ask a man to go to the seminary, we are telling him, "I want you to become like me." But if we don't know who we are, they will say, "Why should I become like you? Who are you, anyway?" And we answer, "I'm not sure, but we are having a meeting on Friday to figure it out."

I'm not really distressed by the drop in vocations. Historically the situation from the 1920s to the 1960s was a fluke. Never before in history did we have such a blossoming of vocations. We were ordaining priests to teach kids math in high school. One of the reasons for the drop in vocations is the fact that the laity are finding their roles and priests are getting rid of the barnacles in their lives.

At this point we are at an in-between situation. What the Church needs right now is prophets who will criticize. Yves Congar, the theologian, was a prophet and, for a while, suffered for being one. He was forbidden to write and to speak. Yet he loved the Church, and never gave up on it. In the days of the Council, he became a *peritus*; he was even made a cardinal by John Paul II. The Church never apologizes; they just give you the red hat. Two other great theologians, Teilhard de Chardin and Lubac also suffered but did not give up on the Church. Nor did they tear it to pieces. It has been often said they were loving critics, and they criticized lovingly.

One of the things that makes it so rewarding for me to be a priest is the gratitude of people who are affected by my twenty-five years of teaching and preaching. I was not trained well in preaching. I had to develop my talent with the help of God's grace. After I have preached well, and after I have celebrated liturgy well, it is so encouraging and affirming to have people walk up to me and tell me that because God spoke through me, their lives were affected. That makes me feel my life has been worthwhile. It makes me realize I have made a difference, that I have become a sacrament.

Shortly after this interview, Father Doyle was greeted by a gentleman who approached him near the Saint Anthony Shrine and said, "I just want to tell you that for some years I have attended your Mass at the Shrine. You celebrate the liturgy with such reverence. Your homilies are marvelous. They have meant a great deal to me." When the man went on his way, Father Doyle turned and winked. He didn't need to say "I told you so," but he could have.

Juan Rivas, L.C.
El Monte, California

Father Juan Rivas was born in Guadalajara, Mexico. He was ordained for a relatively new order, the Legion of Christ. Radiating efficiency, he is a handsome, trim young man, who dresses in full regimentals. His love of the priesthood and his loyalty to the Holy Father open a window into the spirit and purpose of a little-known community.

Several articles have appeared recently in the media about the Legion, some critical of their intensity and style and labeling them as radically conservative. This man does not seem to fit the mold. He is orthodox, somewhat conservative, but hardly old church. His father did not want him to become a priest at all because he thought the Church had changed too much since Vatican II and considered the Legion too liberal.

Father Rivas has his office in El Monte, California, the location of the Radio Missions of the Legion of Christ.

Since it is a relatively new and modern congregation, let me begin with a few words about my religious community, the Legion of Christ. Our founder, Father Marcial Maciel, grew up during the time of the Cristeros War. [*The Cristeros were the Catholic fighters in Mexico who took up arms when peaceful means to defend the Church had failed.*] He entered the seminary in 1936, and in 1941 perceived a call to found the Legion of Christ. The Legion began in Mexico, was approved by Pope Pius XII, and moved to Rome in 1950. The center of our formation is the person of Jesus Christ. Jesus is the model of what a priest should be. We are deeply rooted in devotion to the eucharist and to the Blessed Virgin. We are also faithful to the pope. We are a worldwide organization. Our main apostolate is the formation of lay leaders, and our mission is to transform the world through the gospel. In the United States we work in ten dioceses. Our apostolates include missions, schools, family and youth centers, retreat houses, formation courses for diocesan priests, and radio and television outreach. We use all the means that the world offers to spread the gospel.

My earliest education began with the Jesuits in Guadalajara, Mexico. During this time I was introduced to devotion to the Blessed Mother through the Legion of Mary. My young life was divided between studies and sports. I studied engineering at the Public University of Guadalajara, and played a good deal of racquetball. Once a priest came to our parish, speaking about the missions, and I was both attracted to that calling and fearful of accepting. I told the Lord, "If you want me to be a priest, you have to do everything. I'm not going to move a finger." And he did. My mother invited a priest who was a member of the Legion of Christ to come to our home for a visit. At our first acquaintance he asked me to consider becoming a member of the Legion. I saw that as a sign, and so I passed quite naturally from the Legion of Mary to the Legion of Christ.

At that time, we did not have a seminary in Mexico, and so I went to Salamanca, Spain, for my studies. After three years there, I went to Rome to study philosophy and theology at Thomas Aquinas University. I was ordained on the vigil of Christmas in 1982. When the Holy Father became pope in 1978, I served his Mass. When he was shot in 1981, I was there.

After ordination I came to work in the United States, trying to help Catholics, especially Hispanics, who are joining sects. Someone has estimated that fifty thousand Hispanics join these groups every year. Mostly through providence, I began a radio program to try to win them back to Catholicism. I am also trying to do some TV programs. However, using radio and TV amounts to nothing if we do not have a message. Our message is the rich doctrine and experience of the Church. We try to communicate the splendor of the truth.

Our center actually has two names. One is *Hombre Nuevo*, which means the New Man. That is what Jesus is portrayed as in the gospel. Our formal, published name is the Catholic Multimedia Center. We use audio and video in our broadcasts and call our radio program the Radio Missions. We broadcast daily at 11:30 a.m. We also broadcast in Laredo and for Mother Angelica's shortwave station. I send my tapes to those outlets. We currently broadcast on ten radio stations in the United States, thirty in Central America and Mexico. Presently we have no television stations in the U.S., but expect to use that medium in the future. Because of the commitment of our congregation to the Holy Father, and also because of my personal devotion to him, I promote his Wednesday talks over the radio. Each Friday we also have a special program about him.

In our programs we preach, teach the Catholic faith, and answer letters of people who seek help in their personal and faith lives. One lady wrote to ask whether she could have an abortion. A physician had told her she would probably die if she did not have the abortion. I reminded her she would have to answer to God about what she chooses. She decided against the abortion and gave birth to a beautiful, healthy child. Another letter came from a family that had joined a fundamentalist group. I sent them copies of my tapes about the truths of our faith. The entire family came back to the Church. I try to teach the joy of being Catholic and explain the splendor of our faith. My programs have helped many recover their faith.

Preaching is my life. My radio and TV programs are essentially preaching. And when I do help out in parishes, I give the homily. We priests have to be very careful in our preaching. We have a confined audience. They have to be there, though they don't have to listen. We could learn from our Protestant brothers and sisters; if they don't preach well, a committee terminates their contract. We are always tempted to give our listeners fast food. If we do that long enough, their stomachs will revolt, and they will turn us off. When I talk on the radio, I ask myself, "Am I feeding them or am I just entertaining them?" When I give a weekend homily, I realize what a precious opportunity I have to get out the message of Christ. I go deeply into the gospel, and I don't avoid the tough topics—heaven, hell, abortion, homosexuality, how to live a Christian life.

I think what attracts young men to our seminaries is our spirituality, which centers on Jesus, the eucharist, and the Blessed Mother. Our apostolate is challenging, the formation of lay leaders. Our job is to train lay people and get them involved in the world. We have no priests in parishes, except for an occasional arrangement whereby a pastor offers us a place to live. I am the only member of my community in this area working in the field of media. Our work arrangement, using radio and TV, enables each priest to cover a lot of ground. We live in community whenever possible. I live with two Irish priests who are in campus ministry.

The group that needs special attention today is our youth. When the pope visited Denver, the world was astonished at how much the young people love the Church and how much they want to work for the Church. The media, assuming that the young people were there against their will, and if prompted enough would reveal their animosity toward the Holy Father, kept asking them leading questions of a negative nature about the Denver Congress, the Church, and the Holy Father. They found it virtually impossible to get a single hostile quotation from the thousands there. Young people have so much energy. Look at my staff here; they are all young; they work hard, often stay after working hours till 8 or 9 p.m. Most of my work goes toward the formation of young lay persons.

Young people by nature are drawn to ideals. If we present to them a vocation that calls for love of Jesus and Mary, fidelity to the pope, and challenging apostolates, if we present to them a picture of what the priesthood is really like, not just a profession but a vocation that calls for total commitment of the heart, they will respond. I often talk about vocations when I visit the universities. When a young man says he is thinking of the priesthood, I tell him to give Jesus a chance in his life. Will he find happiness in the priesthood that he might not find elsewhere? I relate my own experience. I was studying engineering. I liked sports. In the Legion I found the opportunity to develop my whole personality, my intelligence, all of my human qualities. In this calling you can become all that you are capable of being. I am a happy priest. I don't say that there are no troubles, that I have no weaknesses. There are plenty of them. But I have never been happier than I am now.

I thank God every day for my vocation, and pray every day that he will give me perseverance to continue. My calling is such a tremendous gift that I have a hard time understanding a priest leaving the ministry. A priest leaving causes me such pain, and when I see the many Catholics who have abandoned their faith I sometimes wonder whether they might have stayed if the priests they knew had persevered.

We priests have a special role to fill in this life. Basically it comes down to the sanctification of souls. Some priests may become involved in professional fields that could be appropriately handled by lay professionals. We have to be professionals in the field of spirituality, in preaching the gospel, in preaching the love of Christ.

I believe that a priest has a call to reflect the importance of commitment to the world. For me, commitment means perseverance in doing what I should be doing in the life I have chosen, the life God has pointed out to me. The problem of lack of commitment comes when you aren't practicing what you are. When married people live like unmarried people, unmarried people live like the married, there will be unhappiness, boredom, and a lack of perseverance. A priest who also is not doing what is a priest is called to do will be unhappy. Ultimately, of course, that perseverance, that commitment, is a grace of God.

I have experienced down sides in my life as a priest, but I would rather think of them as mountains to climb. For example, when I began this work, I had a TV program. After one year the person who was supporting the project could not help any longer. I was faced with the choice of doing nothing or starting something new. So I began these radio programs with $200 in my pocket and with trust that help would come.

And it did. In only seven years we have built this beautiful center from nothing. The next mountain for me to climb will be starting a TV station.

When I think of chastity, obedience, and poverty, I must admit there are difficulties. They are mountains not easily climbed. Nature seems to speak out against those things. But when I have faith, I can deal with all of them. I see celibacy as a very special gift. Jesus chose it, so did Saint Paul and Saint John. I don't look at it as refusing to love anyone; just the opposite: it directs me to love more people with more strength and to live unattached to them. The task of the priest is to put his heart so completely into his apostolate that there can be no loneliness, no further needs.

Because there are more sheep for every pastor, more souls to be cared for, this is the best time to become a priest. The field is wide open, the opportunities are limitless. We are at the brink of the third millennium, and we need brave hearts for the mission in front of us.

Thomas W. Cummings, S.J.
Denver, Colorado

Since its beginning in 1540, the Society of Jesus has been a prominent religious order in the Church. Jesuits have participated in the actions and passions of the modern world as missionaries, teachers, professors, parish priests, writers, confessors to kings and popes, retreat masters—in short, anything the Holy Father asks of them. To accomplish their missions, Jesuits are required to undergo a long and rigorous training in both academics and spirituality. The spirit of the Jesuits, their scholarly approach to bringing the kingdom of God to the world, can hardly be grasped from the story of one man. Yet, Father Cummings, one of twenty-five thousand Jesuits, presents well the pride these men have in their order.

Father Tom Cummings was born in South St. Louis and after the usual thirteen-year training in the Society of Jesus, was ordained in 1969 for the Missouri Province. He has been president of two prestigious Jesuit high schools and now teaches at Regis University in Denver, Colorado, and serves as dean of one of the residence halls.

None of my near ancestors was Catholic. My mother was Episcopalian and became a convert to Catholicism. My father was born into a Catholic family by a circuitous route. His father taught Greek, fell in love with the liturgy of the Roman Catholic Church, and converted. His mother entered the Church thirty years later. Faith in our family was never a burden, but a gift. However, neither of my parents had any Catholic education. They would ask us kids to teach them what the sisters taught us in school.

I attended a Catholic grade school in South St. Louis, staffed by Sisters of Saint Joseph of Carondelet, who were a strong influence in my life. When we were near the end of our grade school years, my father said, "You have now had eight years of Catholic education; I want you to go to public high school as your mother and I did, so you can face the real world." Sister Daria Joseph was our eighth grade teacher, a real tough nun, and a superb educator. She said that my twin brother Terry had talent, so we all connived to have him take the entrance exams at the local Jesuit school, Saint Louis University High. He won a scholarship, and my father said that since it was free he should go ahead and take it. I didn't want to be separated from Terry, so I convinced my father to let me enroll with him. I did, and was one of eighteen from our class of forty-five who entered the Jesuit priesthood. Another ten became diocesan priests.

I had three great loves in my life: swimming, gymnastics, and dancing. I dated a lot in my junior and senior years and had a wonderful relationship with a girl whose family I am still close to. During my last year in school, I signed up for the senior retreat, and within a few hours I was beginning to feel a call to the priesthood. One evening I skipped out of the retreat; I was going to sneak off the grounds and call my girlfriend. It was snowing heavily that night. I passed a statue of the Blessed Mother, to whom I always had a special devotion, and stopped in front of it, perplexed and even angry. I said to her, "Would you please tell your Son to quit bugging me? Don't you realize I am in love with this girl?" Then suddenly, with a clarity that even today amazes me, the realization came to me that if I could be in love with such a wonderful girl, what must the God be like who made her? The thought overwhelmed me, and I stood there by the statue for two hours. From that time on I was convinced that Mary's Son was calling me to the priesthood.

I entered the Jesuits, and to my surprise, my twin brother decided to study for the diocesan priesthood. I'll never forget the day we told our parents. They were shocked. They loved and respected priests, but as so often happens with the best of parents, they wanted their children to be successful in the secular world. Yet, they took it well, and at my first Mass, among all his Protestant friends, my father gave me a special blessing as I began the Mass and whispered to me, "This is my beloved son in whom I am well pleased." After two years Terry left the diocesan seminary and married.

I look back with awe at the self-sacrificing commitment that my parents made to one another and to their children. When I was dating, I fought the decision to become a priest. I wanted to marry and have children. I went to see Father Johnny Doyle, an irrepressible, wiry little Irishman, and told him I didn't think I was cut out to be a priest. He said, "It takes exactly the same commitment, energy, and virtues of compassion and love to be a good priest that it takes to be a good husband and father. But once you make that commitment, either to marriage and parenthood or to the priesthood, the challenge begins." That made sense to me. I gave up the thought of giving new life in order to give a new quality to life. I think the latter is both a tough and worthwhile challenge. Anyone can give new life, but to give a new quality to life is real fatherhood. And by the way, I insist on students calling me "Father." It took me thirteen years to earn that title, and hearing it reminds me how precious those young people are to me. I am trying to give their life a whole new quality, a new vision, a new energy.

I see preaching as an extension of my teaching role. I put a lot of time in preparation. The students listen carefully, they are critical, they affirm so easily when they like what they hear. The frightening part of preaching is the demand of personal holiness on the part of the preachers. In some ways we have to be the word before we represent it. That is both humbling and terrifying. Christianity is more caught than taught.

During my forty years as a Jesuit, mostly in education, the priesthood has taken a lot of new turns. In the 1950s we talked about the pedestal priest: father knows best; father knows the truth. He had social prestige then. We went through the period of the hyphenated priest: the priest-teacher, the priest-administrator. Today, we are more conscious of the priest as servant-leader. We can't deny the leadership role—especially as presider of the eucharist—that has not changed and never will. But really the priest today is a servant.

There is one special grace in the priesthood that I have often experienced. Something wonderful happens, and I know it happened through me but not because of me. It might be someone returning to the Church on his or her deathbed or the reawakening of young parents who have slipped a little; then I see the wonder of faith in their eyes as their daughter or son receives first communion. So many times things happen in the presence of a priest that go beyond who we are. The Jesuit theologian Teilhard de Chardin once said that a priest has the power from God to consecrate every person and every thing he touches. In a way that expresses the core mystery of the priesthood.

I remember being with a fellow priest, my best friend, when he was dying. His name was Pat Lawless. We entered the Jesuits together. Just prior to his appointment as principal of Rockhurst High School, he developed cancer. The doctors over-radiated him, and I went through the last stages of his death with him. I have never experienced anything so painful, but at the same time so rewarding and so touching. He was in a coma for three days. His body was actually getting cold as he neared death. I held him and began to recite in Latin the words of our vows. His lips opened and he repeated them with me, word for word. We shared together in his last moments the depth of our priestly commitment.

As I reflect on my life, I treasure the times when I seem to have helped a young man to gain maturity. I have a book on my shelf with about three hundred thank-you notes from students I taught. I will share one with you. I was given a farewell party when I left Rockhurst High School, and I asked the students to help with details of the cooking, serving, and cleanup. About 2:00 a.m. I received this note from one of them:

> I would like to thank you, Father, for allowing me to be a part of your farewell dinner and to thank you for the many times you have served us. Once again your phenomenal talk inspired us and set new dreams in my head

for my senior year. Suddenly I have realized that my senior year is not about a 4.0 GPA or a state tennis title or an award for loyalty or love. It is about building a future with my classmates and with other people. Last night you thanked us for giving you so much energy in life. In turn I would like to thank you for teaching me what it means to mature into a Christian, Catholic, caring, loving young man, with the help of all those around me. I have heard that in giving you receive. Last night I gave my time, but I received from you some great dreams. Soon I would like to share them with you.

Today that young man is a Jesuit priest.

Of course there are down times in the life of a priest. One of them is sporadic loneliness. That hit me hard when my twin brother died. I saw the immense love with which his wife treated him during his last two years. She slept on a couch next to his hospice bed every night. She held his hand. Every fifteen minutes she would turn him over and she would minister to his every need. I thought to myself, as a priest I will never experience that kind of love and concern. Yet I know that loneliness doesn't come only to a celibate. I know many married people who have bouts of loneliness. When it happens to me, I try to move from loneliness to a creative aloneness with God as my companion.

I have had other dark moments. I won't ever forget my first anointing in New York. A young Puerto Rican teenager committed suicide with a shotgun. I pulled back the cover to administer the sacrament and there was no face there to anoint. I have had crises with my faith. Those crises are good for me, because they prepare me to help students understand their own moments of doubt and darkness. If I didn't have those moments myself I wouldn't know what they are talking about.

We Jesuits take the vows of poverty, chastity, and obedience. Poverty isn't easy. Still, that's not the hardest one to handle. The vow of obedience is the hard one, though there is a deeper spiritual aspect to the vow that makes it easier. It is really a vow of mobility. We have to be ready at any time of our life to be uprooted from friends and move to a new location.

As a man in a religious community, I see celibacy in a different context. I freely took a vow of perpetual chastity, and it is not the same thing as celibacy. It is a commitment of unconditional purity before God. Celibacy follows simply as a consequence of that vow. If tomorrow the pope allowed priests to marry, I could not, because as a religious order priest I am still bound by my vow of chastity, which is broader than celibacy and includes it. Almost every religious culture has a kind of primacy of priesthood. In every culture there are different strata, different levels within the priesthood. For example even in some Christian denominations, if you are a bishop, you do not marry or if your wife dies, you do not remarry. I would like to see the situation in which some priests remain unmarried by choice, but others (such as in mission countries where loneliness is a critical issue) could marry. That is historically inevitable.

In all the concern about increasing the number of priests, I don't think our motive should be to prevent the so-called burnout among the brethren. I think it is crucial for a priest to learn to set boundaries in his life. I try to be a generous person. I want to help anyone who needs help, but I am not the savior. Burnout is not inevitable, no matter how few the priests.

On the personal level, I want to say that one of the reasons we aren't getting enough vocations is that we priests are not joyful enough. We don't publicly share our gratitude for the gift of priesthood. And we need to share our spirituality. I work closely with gifted young men and women who seem to have a vocation. In fact, I was appointed Vocation Promoter on this campus—not director, but promoter. And it amazes me how God is working among young people. I did nothing except announce my appointment, and already I have dealt with about twenty students who wanted to talk about a vocation. Of those twenty, twelve are very interested. All of them are either college graduates or nearing graduation. One is a lift operator in Vail, a *cum laude* from Boston College, who is going to spend three days of Holy Week with the Jesuits. Another, who is a recent convert, is a former college fullback. Still another is at the Air Force Academy. I inspired none of them. They simply came to me. Perhaps it was because I try to be a joyful priest. I tell them all the difficulties, and I ask them, "Do you understand the problems of celibacy, loneliness, and priestly exhaustion?" The tougher I make it sound, the more they want it. For those raised in the traditional Catholic environment, priesthood is a presumption, not a privilege. It's like the air we breathe. There are priests around, and the students expect to see a priest when they need one. The students on secular campuses often have to fight for their faith. I am wondering if a few more gifted priests shouldn't be placed on those campuses. Although they already have two diocesan priests in residence, administrators at a university in the Midwest have invited some of us to consider being there as resident theologians and as "listening priests." It is an exciting invitation.

When I was ordained, it was harder to make a difference in society, because there weren't so many critical problems. Every priest today has an opportunity literally to change the world. I tell young men thinking of the priesthood that this is a wonderful age to be a priest because we live in a society with a faith that is countercultural, even for some of our fellow priests. Yes, I tell them about the men who have left; I think it is good for them to see that this is not an occasion for anger on our part, but of loyalty and love and forgiveness. These young people are plenty feisty; they want to reverse the current image of the priesthood. They have a reserve of goodness in them that is overwhelming.

III. Let Down Your Nets

Priests in Parishes

WHEN HE HAD FINISHED SPEAKING, HE SAID TO SIMON, "PUT OUT INTO DEEP WATER AND LET DOWN YOUR NETS FOR A CATCH." SIMON ANSWERED, "MASTER, WE WERE HARD AT WORK ALL NIGHT AND CAUGHT NOTHING; BUT IF YOU SAY SO, I WILL LET DOWN THE NETS." THEY DID SO AND MADE SUCH A HUGE CATCH OF FISH THAT THEIR NETS BEGAN TO SPLIT. SO THEY SIGNALLED TO THEIR PARTNERS IN THE OTHER BOAT TO COME AND HELP THEM. THEY CAME, AND LOADED BOTH BOATS TO THE POINT OF SINKING.

—LUKE 5:4-7 (*REB*)

A theme that runs through most of the stories in this book is that a call to the priesthood is perceived as a call to service in a parish, to be a pastor. At times some people may think that other ministries in the Church are more glamorous and possibly more important than serving as pastor of a flock. But the parish priest is the fundamental priest. He is the one who has constant contact with and leads and develops the community of faith. He is there day after day, week after week. He is there to baptize, to offer reconciliation, witness marriages, comfort the grieving, bury the dead, participate in our daily lives. The parish priest is our most immediate conduit from God and his Church. The stories of the following six men tell of some of the ways the lives of parish priests are fulfilling.

Michael Heras
Corpus Christi, Texas

Monsignor Michael Heras was born in El Paso, Texas. He attended the North American College in Rome and was ordained in 1984 for the Diocese of Corpus Christi, Texas, where he is now pastor of Our Lady of Perpetual Help.

Monsignor Heras has, within three years, rebuilt a distressed parish into a thriving Christian community. Since his arrival, the parish has doubled in size and the school has grown substantially. His parishioners say he is not simply their pastor; he is their friend. Activities flourish. On an average evening every building in the compound is full of people studying scripture, attending prayer meetings, or working on environmental decorations for the season.

To discover a pastor who has success in building and forming a community is not difficult. To discover a pastor who devotes every minute of his day to his work is not unexpected. To find a pastor who is happy in his work is not surprising. In the story that follows, we find a pastor with all these qualities and one whose joy inflames his parishioners. The feedback that Monsignor Heras receives from his flock energizes him daily.

My upbringing was very Catholic. We were introduced to Jesus, Mary, and the saints at an early age. We always had prayer in the home and never missed Mass. A picture of the Sacred Heart in the bedroom of my parents was so compassionate and loving that it seemed to bless our house. It now hangs in the rectory to remind me of those days when I was growing up. From the time I was five years old, I wanted to be a priest. I used to say Mass for the kids on our block, using bread and Kool-Aid. I would even hear confessions. I attended Christ the King School in Corpus Christi, and I think I knew from the time of fourth or fifth grade that God was calling me.

The hardest time I had in the seminary was trying to overcome the opposition of my father. He was embarrassed, confused, and angered by my vocation to the very day of my ordination. Why? I think it was a cultural thing, and the older I get the more I understand it. He wanted to have grandchildren. He seemed to think I was being manipulated and coerced, without goals of my own. My mother was, at best, cautiously supportive. Even to the end, she would ask, "Are you happy?" So there was never all-out support from her. That left a cloud over my seminary years. I said to them, "I can't live my life for you, and you can't live my life for me." Yet the lack of support made my decision very difficult. I realized this had better work and that I had better give it all I could. What if I came to the point where I needed their love and support in the priesthood and didn't have it? That forced me into a special kind of spiritual life.

My father refused to go to my ordination. In fact he locked the front door of our house to try to keep my mother and brother from going. They had to sneak out the back way. Nor did my father come to the church on Father's Day, when I celebrated a Mass of thanksgiving. It was a difficult time for me. After only a year and a half I was made pastor of Immaculate Conception in Gregory, a small city north of here. The people of the parish began to work on my father. They prayed for him. They invited him to their gatherings. They got him involved in the Saint Vincent de Paul Society. Little by little he became more tolerant. He wouldn't talk to me, but I would talk to him. I would say, "Dad, I do love you. Why won't you talk to me?" Slowly but surely he began to warm up.

Then came that November day that I will never forget. I woke up too late to shower. My hair was a mess. I had an administrative council meeting. Bishop Gracida called me out of the meeting and said, "Michael, you have been a faithful priest, loyal to me and to the Holy Father, and you have worked hard. We just received word that the Holy Father has named you a monsignor." I was stunned. The investiture took place at my parish on December 8, the feast of the Immaculate Conception. My father attended that Mass, received communion, knelt, and prayed. And he smiled. Five months later he was dead. Recently I have had some very difficult managerial situations, not personal, but delicate issues. I believe my father is interceding for me to help me make the right decisions in those cases. I am so grateful today for his change of heart.

When I was asked to come to Our Lady of Perpetual Help, there was a problem in the parish, but I wasn't sure what it was. About 1,100 families were registered, but only about 1,500 people attended weekend Masses. The school was in financial straits. There were suits against the parish personnel. The parish had a debt of $633,000. And people were leaving in droves. There were only four Masses on the weekend. The school had lost thirty-five families the previous year. It was a place a pastor tries to avoid, but I found it a challenge. Although this is a predominantly Spanish-speaking parish, there was nothing being offered for Hispanics.

Today we have seven Masses on the weekend, and we added a whole retinue of ministries and activities for Hispanics. Nearly 2,500 families are registered, and close to 4,000 people attend Mass. Parish revenue has risen by $110,000 a year, and the debt has been reduced by 30 percent. We have been able to make major improvements in the plant. The school is in the black, and we are receiving new students every year. We have enough income to help out other parishes. For example, we asked our people to help a parish destroyed in the Oklahoma City bombing. We wound up giving that parish $5,000, plus food, candy, and clothes.

Our main work in the parish is with families. We have youth groups studying sacred scripture. We are careful to work with them without weakening family unity and family ties. Vocations come from families, just as the Holy Family produced the first vocation. Vocations will begin to increase again if we continue to promote strong, healthy families.

I have had some rough times in my priestly work, but the support of my people has more than made up for it. Their patience, kindness, gentleness, generosity, and understanding make being a pastor a wonderful experience. I find such a peace of mind in my priesthood that I don't think I could find anywhere else. I am able to touch my people at the beginning of their lives, at the end, and at the high moments in between. A priest becomes part of the fabric of their lives. It seems that I was made for the priesthood. I love giving my life to people. I see many turns in my life, even some dark moments. But mostly they have been wonderful moments.

When united, the people can do almost anything. During my first assignment the Church took a position against an ordinance about to be passed by the city, allowing the sale of alcoholic beverages. For obvious reasons, that would have been a disaster for the Pima community. Our parishioners fought against it, and the ordinance failed. That tells me the Church has an active, positive role in society. Here in Corpus Christi, a city of 400,000, we actually closed down an abortion clinic because of the constant pressure of the pro-life movement. We shut the clinic up tight. The building is now for sale.

Preaching is crucially important in parish ministry. I spend hours on each homily. I pray, I sweat, I am nervous. I tape my homilies and have them transcribed. I don't like to look down when preaching. I want to look in the faces of the people. I ask God, "Please don't block out what you want me to tell them." Sometimes the homilies are awful, but sometimes, the people tell me they are good.

I am generally uplifted by fellow priests and love to work with them. Not long ago one of my closest friends in the priesthood came to me about a problem he had involving a woman. We were like brothers, and we talked about it at length. He was falling apart because of the relationship, and he was miserable. There was no way I was going to tell him that it was all right. I wasn't going to say, "I understand, we poor celibates need a break once in a while." I was firm, but not harsh with him. I told him it was time to bury it and begin again. Then I asked him if he wanted to go to confession. He did. He broke down and sobbed. He went home, started all over, and today he is a great priest, doing a marvelous job. That would not have happened if I had told him not to worry, that we all have problems like that. He was looking for compassion, and I gave that to him. But he was also looking for reality, and I faced him with that, too.

Celibacy is both a charism and a motive toward pastoral charity. I would be lying if I didn't admit that I would enjoy having a warm, intimate relationship. But that's a no-win situation, so I have tried to focus and funnel my energies toward my parishioners, and that is why I am able to do so many things.

My spiritual director and confessor has a book on his desk which asks the question, "What is the best day of the year?" It goes on to ask if it is your birthday or Christmas, or some other special day. Then it says, "The answer is today. Yesterday is gone, tomorrow may not come. Only today has value." Is this a good time to be a priest? My answer is yes, because it is today; I can't live in the past nor in the future. This is the time God has given me. It is a good time to be alive, and it is a very good time to be a priest.

After being a pastor for ten years, I have reached two conclusions. The first is that God loves the people. Despite my unworthiness, my weakness, and my failures, God still touches them through me. If God loves them that much, then how much must God love me? The second is that to be a good priest, the most necessary thing is to fall in love and stay in love with God and with God's people incarnate. If I do that, I can't ever go wrong. Christianity is a form of sanity, and love keeps us sane.

Thomas M. Anglim
Fort Myers, Florida

Born November 15, 1928, in County Clare, Ireland, Father Tom Anglim was ordained in 1954 for the Diocese of Saint Augustine, Florida. He has always had a special devotion to Saint Francis Xavier. Wouldn't you know, he ended up as pastor of a parish named after his favorite saint.

Father Anglim is a delightful person, deeply religious, competent, practical, and knowledgeable about the changes of Vatican II. He is committed to regular daily prayer. He recently installed a chapel on the top floor of the rectory where he spends an hour daily being renewed for the tasks of his busy parish.

We say we can tell the character of a person by the company he keeps. Father Anglim keeps company with families, young people, the elderly, unwed mothers, ethnic groups, brother priests, and with the Lord in chapel. Father Anglim's story is the story of today's pastor. It is convincing testimony that there is no better time to be a priest than now.

I grew up in the little village of Feakle in Ireland. My parents were quite poor. My father worked for the government. My mother was the ultimate homemaker. She was deeply religious and trained all the kids in the basics of our faith. The life of the entire village centered around the Church. On Sunday no one worked. Everyone wore his best clothes, not just to Mass but all day long.

When I was about fifteen, I began to think about the future. To be a priest at that time in Ireland was considered a great gift from God. I spent seven years at Mungret, a minor seminary in County Limerick, run by the Jesuits. Recruiters came to visit the seminary from all over the world—Australia, England, the United States. When Monsignor O'Donovan, from the Diocese of Saint Augustine, came to talk to us at

Mungret, he convinced me and another classmate to sign up for his diocese, a choice I have never regretted.

During my second year in the major seminary, I began to have doubts about my vocation. I was shy by nature, and the thought of getting up in a pulpit to preach terrified me. I told the spiritual director I was thinking of leaving. When I told him why, he said, "Your reasons are not good enough." I had been trained to be obedient. I listened to him and decided there would be no turning back. Since that moment I have never questioned my vocation. And, I would make the same choice again because I love the priesthood.

In 1958 the Diocese of Saint Augustine was divided and Miami became the new diocese. The Miami bishop, Colman Carroll, was looking for priests to establish new parishes. He appointed me pastor of the first parish created in the fledgling diocese, Our Lady of the Holy Rosary in Perrine. Later that turned out to be a hot spot. During the Cuban missile crisis, hundreds of military vehicles came pouring down the highway, close to our church. Everyone feared a nuclear attack. That weekend I began confessions at 7:00 p.m. and finished at midnight.

In 1966 the pastor of Saint Francis Xavier's in Ft. Myers and the dean of the deanery fell from a mountain in Colorado and was killed. The bishop asked me to take over the parish and to be dean. I hated to leave the east coast, but I did accept, and have been here almost thirty years. In 1983 the new Diocese of Venice, Florida was established, with John J. Nevins as its bishop. Saint Francis Xavier's was a part of the diocese. The bishop asked me to become Vicar General, and I have had the job for over ten years.

Saint Francis was not a large parish when I came, but it has grown tremendously. About 3,600 families are registered; another 1,000 are not. The tiny school has developed into the largest elementary school in the diocese, with 640 enrolled. The many elderly in the parish need both spiritual and material help. For them we constructed our own sixty-unit apartment housing project, Villa Francisco. Since we used no HUD money, the apartments are totally independent of government control. Today the project is debt-free. And what a boon it has been for our elderly parishioners! The rent is affordable—very important for those with fixed incomes. The complex has its own chapel and the residents can walk to morning Mass at the parish. Three retired priests live there and two or three sisters. As elderly parishioners reach the twilight of their lives, it is so important for them to live in a religious environment.

About fifteen years ago we established a home for unwed mothers. It is staffed by a salaried house mother and a secretary; the rest are volunteers. The mothers who have stayed in that house have given birth to more than five hundred children.

There are quite a few people in the area from Haiti. The bishop thought it would be good for them to have a church of their own and a center where they could establish their own identity before getting into the mainstream, so we purchased a vacant Protestant church a few blocks away and began a Haitian mission there. One of our four priests, a recently ordained Haitian, lives at the parish house and administers to his people.

In my judgment, the first and most basic duty of a priest is to proclaim the word of God; in order to do that well he must be a spiritual person. Preaching is a key part of my ministry. I prepare well for each homily. Evidently my people enjoy them; at least they tell me so. An important part of the homily, often forgotten, is that a priest has to live what he preaches. If the people see a contradiction between what a priest says in the pulpit and what he does in the rectory, the most eloquent preacher loses all his effectiveness. He needs to preach the gospel, then show the people that he is living that message. People have a sixth sense about spirituality. They can pick out a holy priest right away. I think that as a priest I need to be with people. That is what I was ordained for. My job is to help them grow in holiness. I can't do that unless I am growing in holiness, and the only way to do that is to spend a lot of time in prayer.

Families with young children have a special need. One fourth of the 640 kids in our school live with single parents. We have an almost full-time youth minister who works with youth and families. It is mandated that parents come to the class when their children are preparing to receive first reconciliation, and two nights ago we had a hundred parents in the hall.

Is today a difficult time to be a priest? I don't believe it is as difficult as it was for the first twelve apostles, nor for Jesus. None of us is asked to go through what Christ did. If these are tough times, fine. They are a perfect time to be identified with the suffering Christ. Our society is saturated with sex. Television, radio, magazines, and the sexual revolution call on the priest to have a good spiritual life or he is a goner.

A very sad event in my life as a priest happened when I was pastor at Sacred Heart Church in Lake Worth. A young man shot and killed his mother and his wife, then climbed to the top of a tower at the University of Texas and began to shoot at students indiscriminately. He killed, I believe, sixteen people in all. His family belonged to the parish, and his brother was a religious education teacher. The family requested a funeral Mass for the mother and son in our church. The media reported every detail of the tragedy, including the possibility that they would be buried from the parish church. While the bishop and I were considering the request and the implications of our decision, an autopsy revealed that the young man had a tumor on his brain. The medical opinion was that the tumor could have affected the last actions of his life. We decided to have the funeral Mass at the parish. I was deluged with phone calls, many from members of the media, asking how we could give Christian burial to a murderer. Some two hundred media representatives gathered around the church during the Mass. We didn't permit them to enter, but issued a written statement explaining why we gave the young man Christian burial. I received about a hundred letters, many of them criticizing our decision. How do you make the media and the public understand that compassion is essential to Christian burial and that God is the ultimate judge? I have never quite gotten over the sadness of that incident, but I never regretted a decision which gave comfort and consolation to the members of a grief-stricken family.

What a great joy it was simply being ordained. That day was made doubly happy by the fact that the ceremony took place in such an historic spot, Our Lady of Leche Shrine in St. Augustine, Florida, where the first Mass was offered in the United States in 1565. For an Irishman, going back to my home in Ireland and offering a first Mass with my family was a very special joy that I will always remember.

Every marriage I perform, every time I baptize, every time I prepare someone for death, are occasions of joy not only for myself, but for the couples, the parents, and the families.

I do believe I have touched the lives of a lot of people, and have made a difference in this parish and this part of the United States. For example, together with several parishioners, I made a difference in the future of Saint Francis Xavier's during a conflict with the Department of Transportation. They wanted to put another span across the Caloosahatchee River that would have taken away 110 of our parking spaces and would have cut off access to our school. It would have literally choked the parish to death, and we would have had to move. Attorneys told us we would be wasting our time protesting because "the Department of Transportation never changes its mind." We did protest. We started a letter writing campaign, enlisted the support of the political people in our parish, went to see the governor, and prayed. The bottom line was that we won. The Department of Transportation came up with a new plan that did not involve taking any of our land.

I work hard to encourage vocations in my homilies and by talking to kids who seem to have all the qualifications. They face genuine difficulties today in accepting a call to the priesthood. Yet the Church has always thrived on adversity and persecution. Thirty years ago in Poland when the young people were forbidden to go to church, most of them went anyway.

Lately I have seen a rejuvenation of seminary training, and I am hopeful. I really think we are going through a purifying period in the Church and that in the next fifty to one hundred years we will see a new Church and new commitments, a priesthood the people of God can once again be proud of.

I have never seen a time when the opportunities for a priest were greater. Everyone today is looking for spiritual guidance. If we are seen as holy priests, they will knock down our doors asking for help. Today, often the shepherds are being sanctified by the sheep. That is not all bad, but it should be reciprocal.

Count me as being one of the happy priests. I wouldn't want to be anything else than a priest. I would have to say honestly that I often feel stressed, as pastor of a large parish with the biggest school in the diocese, operating a housing project for the elderly, supporting a home for unwed mothers, serving as Vicar General of the Diocese, and chairing our planning and development committees and our diocesan pension plan. However, when I go up to my chapel, do a few breathing exercises and a little meditation, I walk out of there with my heartbeat under seventy.

Let me offer a word to all the priests who may read this book:

> Thank God every moment of your life that you are a priest. If you are not happy in your vocation, you can be. All you have to do is make a few adjustments. If you are too busy to pray, you are too busy. If necessary, take your appointment book and write down an hour of prayer so you won't put someone else in that slot. That is your time to communicate with the Lord. That is the time to be fulfilled, and what a great blessing that fulfillment is to our people!

> Every problem we have can be solved on our knees. Read the letters of Saints Paul and Peter and James; they shared with their friends their relationship with the Lord. We have a great gift. We need to hang on to it, for our own sake, and for the people of the Church.

Richard W. Moyer
Carefree, Arizona

Monsignor Richard Moyer was born January 12, 1932, in Sandusky, Ohio. He was ordained for the Diocese of Tucson, Arizona, in 1964 and is now pastor of Our Lady of Joy parish.

Monsignor Moyer is a one-man army. He is pastor of a relatively new and expanding parish and holds several important diocesan jobs. His store of energy is unbelievable. He has served in the U.S. Navy, is a talented musician, a financial expert, and is deeply involved in one of the most successful youth programs in the country, Life Teen, a program that has spread to several dioceses. We might not expect the pastor of a large parish, a vicar general, and a financial expert to be deeply involved in teen ministry. But here is the story of one such priest.

My father was not a Catholic when my parents married. He came into the Church several years later. He was a tremendous example to me, a faithful, hard-working person who cared for our every need in the midst of the Great Depression. He died in 1960 of a heart attack at the age of 54, just before I entered the seminary. My mother remarried a man whose wife had died, and I witnessed that ceremony. Her husband had a son in the seminary, and five years after their marriage, I preached at my stepbrother's first Mass.

I attended Saint Joseph's grade and high schools in Sandusky, graduating in 1950. Unsure of what to do with myself, I dabbled in music for a while, substituting as an organist in the local parish church and working as a checkout clerk in the A&P store. I didn't have the finances to go to college. The Korean War had started and I decided to do two things: see some of the country and choose my own branch of the service rather than be drafted. In February of 1951 I took a trip to Arizona with two friends and visited my brother who was working in the Yuma area. I fell in love with Arizona and knew that some day I wanted to live in this state. When I got back to Ohio, I enlisted in the Navy and was sent to Great Lakes for boot camp. I was there for two years, working in the chaplain's office as a clerk and musician. At that time I began to think seriously of the priesthood because of a sort of conversion experience.

In the Navy, I saw two basic kinds of people: those who lived life recklessly and threw morals to the winds, and a group of very good people who were close to the Lord. I admired the second group. There wasn't much of a middle road. They either took the high ground or they went with the rest of the pack and engaged in a lot of drinking, sex, and gambling. I tried to face up to the type of life I was leading and made a conscious decision to take the high ground. When I shared with the chaplains my thought of becoming a priest, they gave me a lot of encouragement. I told my parents of my plans and both were very supportive. There was a girlfriend back home whom I considered marrying. I went to see her and told her I was thinking of other options. She said she understood and realized sailors have a girl in every port. I told her she was not reading me right and revealed my plans for the priesthood. She was shocked, but in a way I think she was pleased.

In 1953, after Great Lakes, I was assigned to an aircraft carrier, the *U.S.S. Coral Sea*, which was operating in the Atlantic, the Mediterranean, and the Caribbean. I did two tours of duty in Europe with the Sixth Fleet which was part of the occupational forces after World War II. There were opportunities to travel and see many of the biblical sites, including Rome, Greece, and some of the cities visited by Saint Paul on his missionary journeys. One of the strongest influences on my vocation was a wonderful chaplain of the *Coral Sea*, Monsignor Richard Holmes.

During my last year of formation in the seminary, the concepts of Edward Schillebeecx, a Dominican theologian, were introduced. The sacraments suddenly became relational, dynamic, and personal. This understanding—a movement away from the vending machine approach—changed my life.

My first appointment, to Saint Francis of Assisi in Yuma, was a great blessing. The pastor was Father Henry Miller. He was the type of person who discussed with you your strengths, gave you assignments based on them, and let you do your work. In 1967 the bishop sent me to Saints Peter and Paul's in Tucson and later to Phoenix, to be assistant director of charities. When the Diocese of Phoenix was established, I became director of Catholic Charities there. In 1982 Bishop O'Brien assigned me to Saint Jerome's. Saint Jerome's was the joy of my life. Shortly afterward the bishop made me vicar general of the diocese.

In 1984 the bishop sent me to northern Arizona to be vicar of that section of the diocese. Two years later, while I continued that job, I was appointed pastor of Saint John Vianney's in Sedona. I enjoyed administration but would have preferred to be only in parish work. In 1988 I came to the cathedral as rector.

Shortly after I arrived at the cathedral, the bishop asked me to become the vicar for finance. In 1993 the bishop offered me the opportunity to be the administrator at Our Lady of Joy, if I could handle that as well as the diocesan finances. Later he appointed me pastor. I now have three tough jobs: pastor of this parish, vicar general, and financial officer for the diocese. Using a computer hookup I can do much of the latter two jobs from the parish office.

For thirty-two years I have been trying to communicate to people that Jesus is real, that each of us can build a relationship with him just as we can with any other person. That concept energized me in the early days of my priesthood.

I celebrated my first home Mass with sixth graders after they had six weeks of instruction on the eucharist. I asked them to draw on posters what they had learned. I later used the posters as a backdrop for the Mass. What they expressed artistically was mind-blowing. I used those grade school kids to teach a group of religious educators at the diocesan assembly a year later. It was amazing what they accomplished, just like Jesus teaching the people when he was twelve years old in the Temple.

We studied each sacrament with the goal of finishing with a communal celebration. For example, when we studied baptism, one of the mothers of a child in the class was pregnant. That was our baby all the way through. The children made the birth announcements and the baptism dress. The child-to-be became their child, the family became their family. They learned by experience, better than any classroom instruction, how to welcome someone into the family of God.

My sense of the needs of the people is that those who are between 24- and 45-years-old require the most care of the priest. They went through a time when there were great upheavals—the Vietnam War, the so-called sexual revolution, the deterioration of values. They are the group that had the first large number of working mothers. They missed a lot, and their faith-life is at risk. We need to find ways to entice them into adult education programs, to enrich their faith. Many parents today have little faith to pass on to their children. Mass attendance is not important for them. We have a lot of drop-in Catholics, those who come when they need something for themselves or their children.

Teenagers also need help. They face a far greater challenge than we did at that age. My ongoing work with youngsters tells me that if we give them something solid, if we open up to them what faith is all about, they respond very well.

In 1978 Father Dale Fushek was assigned to Saint Jerome's right after his ordination. He has an unusual talent with youth and founded Active Christian Teens. He and I worked youth retreats together. In 1985 he became pastor of Saint Timothy's in Mesa and there founded the Life Teen program that has now spread to 350 parishes throughout the country. I became involved in that program and still teach in the training sessions during the summer months. In the last five or six years we have trained over 800 youth ministers and priests. We have a small branch of Life Teen at this parish.

That program centers around the eucharist and the Life Teen Mass. Between 1,500 and 1,700 attend the teen Mass at

Saint Timothy's. Not all of them are teens. Some are parents and younger siblings. The music and the homily are geared to teenagers: teenagers serve the Mass, they lector, they bring up the gifts, they sing. Much of the program is based on peer ministry and aided by a core group of youngsters experienced in Life Teen. A single program will have as many as thirty core group members. Right after the Mass, the Life Night is presented. Some nights are social, some educational, some are issue-oriented, dealing with problems teens face, such as morality, abortion, and peer pressure. We try to take advantage of what is happening in the local area. Timely crises can quickly change the direction of the Life Night. The Mass lasts about an hour and a half. The teens are together for another hour and a half after that. They meet every Sunday of the year. Many vocations have come out of our Life Teen program. Last year about thirty teens joined the church at Saint Timothy's. They were brought to the parish by other teenagers and joined with their parents' permission.

What parishes participate? All that have the Life Teen programs. Some don't have the capacity to put on the program each Sunday and may do it only once a month. In my parish we have few teenagers, so we don't have a Life Teen Mass yet. Instead, we integrate the young people into the regular liturgy. We have them lector, sing, and work in different ministries in the parish. Much of the work is done on retreats. We try to have two closed teen retreats during the year. We take the teens up into the mountains, to a camp in the middle of a national forest. There are no distractions. We bed down 192 kids each time. Many transformational experiences take place there. Father Dale is the founding father of Life Teen. I have been a silent partner and still do some of the three-day retreats. You don't even have to talk the kids into going; there is always a waiting list.

I also work hard on the sacrament of reconciliation, especially with young people. I see much greater honesty in adolescents than I found in my companions when I was a kid. Young people today are willing to share their lives with you. They are open to suggestions and ready for change. It is enriching for me to listen to them, encourage them, challenge them, accept them.

Even though a lot of my friends left the priesthood, I have never thought of doing the same. First, I made a commitment, and I don't take commitments lightly. Second, it has been such a rewarding and enriching life. It is so wonderful to become an important part of the lives of a lot of people, not just one. The priesthood has kept my faith alive. I have seen people go through crises and tragedies, and their faith was the one sustaining thing in their lives. When we reach out to people who are suffering, we make a great difference in their lives.

The relationships we form as priests are really beautiful. When we construct a building, after it is finished we can see the results of our work. When we work with people, we never see the total result unless they come and tell us. But we do form relationships that are sustaining and helpful. When I was a social worker, I would take people to a certain point in counseling, then turn them over to a priest. I went to the seminary because I wanted to be that person who did not have to stop at the sacramental door and turn them over to someone else. I wanted to take the process full circle.

Arnold Weber, O.S.B.
Medina, Minnesota

Holy Name of Jesus in Medina, Minnesota, began as a tiny German national parish around 1865. Today it has 8,000 members. The pastor, Father Arnold Weber, is known throughout the Midwest as a competent leader, a fine homilist, and an excellent liturgist. The parishioners videotape his Masses and send copies to shut-ins. At each Mass, as part of the offertory procession, children bring food to the altar for the poor. In 1995 the value of the food distributed to needy families was $40,000. Those programs and others have given Holy Name of Jesus a reputation as an alive, participatory, faith community.

Apparently what each parish priest does defines him as a priest and adds to the definition of the priesthood. In Father Weber's story, we discover a priest who energizes his own parish by helping to meet their needs, and then encourages them to reach out to others who are in need of help.

Father Arnold was born in 1925 in a German-speaking family and grew up on a farm. Half of the twelve Weber children joined a religious community. Four of his sisters became Benedictine nuns; he and one brother became Benedictine priests. Father Arnold was ordained in 1952.

My priesthood has always been a joy to me. I see our principal job as priests as service to our parishioners. The laity don't look to us for great learning, but for holiness. They want us to have faith and love and respect for them.

Our farm was near St. Martin's, a tiny town that was 100 percent Catholic. Vocations to the priesthood and the convent were plentiful. From that town with only two hundred families, there were about seventy-five religious sisters and twenty-five priests.

When I came of high school age, my father sent me to Saint John's Benedictine Abbey. Thirteen of my class of thirty-five became priests. Right after ordination I was assigned to teach in the college preparatory school at Saint John's. Soon I was appointed the first vocation director for the abbey. In 1970 Benilde High School in Minneapolis nearly closed for lack of brothers to staff it. The bishop asked Saint John's to take it over. We did and I taught there for three years.

I served in a parish in Detroit Lakes for four years, then returned to Benilde. At that time problems were developing at Holy Name parish in Medina, and I was asked to come here. I had a lot of energy in those days and said I could take care of both Holy Name and Benilde High. I did that until I became full-time in the parish in 1980. On my first day in this badly divided parish, I received twenty letters from people wanting an appointment to talk about the problems which divided them. I agreed to meet all of the letter-writers. By the next weekend, though, I changed my mind. In my homily I said I would honor those appointments under two conditions. One was that anyone who came to see me would not be critical of any group in the parish. The second condition was that each person would tell me what their own problem was. No one showed up.

When I was in vocation work I became acquainted with Father Andrew Greeley, the author and sociologist. He often wrote for the Benedictine magazine, *Orate Fratres*. He gave the best definition of a priest I ever heard. "A priest is somebody to turn to." Being the one to whom people turn is both an overlooked and a humbling service. If we aren't available, they won't turn to us. If we live away from the parish, we are not accessible. We have no need to copy the corporate world with office hours. I would find it hard to get my work done in a forty-hour week. I read a lot about overworked priests, but I don't see that as a problem for me. We have to be hard working priests. By the same token, we do need our privacy. Of course, I am a religious order priest and don't expect diocesan priests to follow my schedule.

Young people ask me what it takes to be a priest. I tell them,

> You need two things: a funny bone and a backbone. If
> you don't have those two, you won't make it because our
> culture is so different from what priests stand for. If you

don't have a sense of humor, if you get depressed by the
problems, you won't be able to preach the good news.
You also need a backbone; if you don't, you will soon fall
in line with the surrounding culture.

We clergy need more backbone. Seldom do we attack the
serious problems of our world in our homilies or the Sunday
bulletin. We avoid speaking about divorce, perhaps because
we fear offending the many divorcees in the parish. But
divorcees only want us to be more compassionate. We priests
need both high ideals and compassion. Years ago we had all
the ideals but were not very compassionate. Now we have
cashed in our ideals and gone over completely to compassion.
We need both. We shouldn't let compassion destroy our ideals.
That is what is going on with the problems of abortion,
divorce, and cohabitation—a loss of ideals. If we merely
appeal to compassion we are missing the teaching of the message of Christ. On the other hand, if we preach that gospel
message without knowing to whom we are speaking, we are
going to come across as being heartless. So we have to give the
message with compassion without being condemnatory. I personally find implementing that combination a challenge. I
have learned a lot from the parables: let the wheat and the
weeds grow side by side; some sown grain falls on good soil,
some on poor soil. Our job is not to be successful, but to be
faithful.

One of the things that makes it easier for me to be a priest
is that I understand now what it means to empower lay people, to really believe in the sacrament of baptism. Any community that wishes to be strong in liturgy and social action
needs to understand how the sacrament of baptism gives
power to the laity. Some priests don't empower, but over-
power. There was a time when I thought I had to be a part of
every decision. My strong German background made me that
way. But now I can not only delegate but trust that the laity
will do the job as well as I would, if not better. To be dictato-
rial today misses what Vatican II was all about.

My most important work as a priest centers around the
eucharist. My most important work catechetically is giving

homilies. I spend from seven to ten hours preparing each weekend homily. The growth of our parish is partly due to preaching. Our parishioners come from about seventy-five different zip codes. They come to Holy Name because of the liturgy and the preaching. When I began here sixteen years ago there were 250 families; now we have 2,500 families and 8,000 people. Parishioners today just don't respond unless the liturgy, the music, and the preaching are good. For example, I'm not going to talk about war or birth control every Sunday, important as those topics are. That is not feeding the people. The Sunday liturgy calls for preaching the gospel. For the president of a Serra Club I did a study asking what the Serrans expected in a priest. They said what they looked for most was solid piety and good theology.

People are hungry for spiritual things. One of my favorite beatitudes is, "Happy are those who hunger and thirst for uprightness, they shall have their fill." If that is true, those who do not hunger are the emptiest of all. In my counseling I find a great deal of emptiness. A good deal of emphasis must be placed in the area of social action. I can spend a lot of time working on a personal commitment to Jesus and salvation by faith alone and forget about Matthew 25:

> For I was hungry and you gave me food,
> I was thirsty and you gave me drink,
> I was a stranger and you made me welcome,
> lacking clothes and you clothed me,
> sick and you visited me,
> in prison and you came to see me (35-36).

Our parish takes Matthew 25 seriously. We just finished a drive in which we raised $600,000 for a parish in the inner city. We will give them $60,000 a year for ten years to run their school. When disaster struck in Oklahoma City, our archdiocese sent money for relief. Fourteen percent of the total came from this parish. We have a cookie cart program; we take people off the street, let them bake and sell cookies. We raised $75,000 through that program this year. Our parish income is almost $3,000,000, and we give 24 percent to charity. We have 360 children in the parish school. We help youngsters going to Benilde High School with a $1,200 scholarship. We don't keep a dime from our many projects. Our festival is coming up. It will clear $35,000, and we will give it all to charity. There are about five hundred people in the parish who need someone to shop for them. We started a scrip program selling gift certificates to local businesses and told the lady who ran it to use all the income for the parish social programs. Our second collection goes to charity. We have about ten social projects in all.

People today aren't spiritually strong. They need healing. When I was first ordained and someone died, we didn't have a healing Mass for the family. Now even before the burial we begin to arrange help for the survivors. The other extreme, of course, is to say that it is all God's will. Genuine compassion is needed, of course. My degree is in marriage counseling, and I average twenty hours a week in that work. I appeal to people's faith and to their will power. I am always astounded at how many people are capable of solving their own problems, if they only lean on two things—their faith and their own judgment.

In my opinion, a parish needs a variety of spiritual exercises. I don't push private devotions, but I don't kill them. We have adoration of the Blessed Sacrament during the week from 7 a.m. to 9 p.m. , five days a week. Our parishioners say the rosary after the daily Mass. Some of our Medjugorje people may tend to go to extremes, yet those pilgrimages produce good results. I took a group of forty youngsters there and gave them a retreat. After we returned, three of them went to the Peace Corps, one went to the seminary. People ask if I believe in Medjugorje. My answer is that it is not my job to give an opinion on the apparitions. All I know is that I took some people there who didn't pray much and they are now prayerful. I sent a schizophrenic girl over there; she is now married, has four children, and hasn't seen a doctor since. So the issue for me is not "did Mary appear?" The issue is "does Medjugorje turn people to prayer?" The pope gave a talk on the subject and said the phenomenon can't be bad if the results are so good.

One of the joys in the priesthood is to see the return of people to the Church before their deaths. In Detroit Lakes I knew a family with seven children who had an alcoholic father. Neither the kids nor the wife would talk to the man. When I visited him in the hospital, he was near death. I said, "They tell me you don't have much time left. It would be nice if you made your peace with your family." "Yes," he answered, "but they won't come." I called the wife; she agreed to come. That night the entire family came to the hospital. I left the room and returned in an hour. The wife and kids were hugging him, all apologizing. He died a happy man.

In all my years of priesthood, the last five have been the hardest, yet also the most rewarding and enjoyable. I am the only priest in the parish. I take all the Masses. On the weekends there are five Masses, and sometimes seven if I have two weddings. I average eighty weddings a year and 250 baptisms. When those I have married have their first child, they want me to baptize it. I finally had to call a halt to that practice and turned the baptisms over to deacons. Even though I have to take care of 8,000 people, I don't feel stressed. I don't take a day off. I regularly work seven days a week. Once a year I take a trip. And I do space my time. I don't recommend my schedule for others and don't feel virtuous about it. But I can do it, so I do because that is what I think my people need.

I would say to any young fellow thinking of the priesthood, that he is making his choice at the best possible time. Never in my life time have we had more challenges than right now. Is this a good time to go into the computer world? The uncertainties there are huge. Yet people go into it and find it is a wonderful challenge. To be a priest today is a greater challenge because we live in a society that needs a lot of converting. Getting people to make a commitment to Jesus involves more than an altar call; it requires the transformation of a value system. I don't know anyone who can do more in that area than a priest.

William Trienekens
Calgary, Alberta, Canada

Father Bill Trienekens was born in the Netherlands in 1932 and was ordained in 1961 for the Canadian Diocese of Calgary. He is pastor at Saint Luke's parish in Calgary, Alberta, Canada.

During his childhood in the Netherlands, Father Trienekens and his family experienced something unknown to those raised in the United States—foreign occupation. The Nazis had taken over his country. Jobs, food and schools were scarce commodities. After a lengthy struggle to support his family following the death of his father and a further struggle to obtain the bare essentials of an education, Trienekens emigrated to Canada and studied for the priesthood.

Though his early experiences made a man out of Father Trienekens, in his modesty he credits that growth to the priesthood which he loves.

I was born in a small farming town in the Netherlands. Near the end of World War II, when I was thirteen, my father died. After his death we moved to a little farmhouse on the outskirts of town, and our style of living changed considerably. We lived near a military airport which was occupied by the Germans. They took over all the school buildings. We had little formal education during the war years. When on rare occasions the Germans would allow us to go to class, we had to use the local pub, the carpentry shop, or a barn. Some of the teachers were involved in underground work, and there would be days when they wouldn't show up for classes. As a result, when the war ended some of us could barely read or write.

After the war I went to a boarding school for one year. The minute I got there, I found out how dumb I was, far behind the other students. But a very fine man took me under his wing and helped me with my rhetoric and math. Next I attended a day school, followed by four years of grammar school and high school, where I finally began to succeed in my studies.

The idea of becoming a priest was with me from the earliest years of my childhood. Looking back, I recognize that my parents must have had a lot to do with it because of their love for the Church and the priesthood. Our parish priest also had an impact. He was a good man, devout and prayerful, positive and warmhearted. He influenced not only me but a number of young men and women to enter the priesthood and the religious life. Tiny as our town was, he had a broad world vision and invested much of his personal income in the education of the children, especially those who went to the seminary. He helped people both spiritually and financially. He inspired us to follow our goals, not to sit back and let things happen, but to make decisions that would cause things to happen. When he died, people from all over the world came for his funeral.

Encouraged by these surroundings, I decided to enter the novitiate. It was the most backward place I had ever seen, and I stayed only two months. My father's death near that time had left a large family, the youngest only three months old, and we had very little income. Two of the older sisters, a brother, and I took turns working to support the family while the others went to school. At the age of 22, I was going steady with a girl, but kept putting off the thought of marriage because I was needed to help the family. The three youngest boys looked to me as a father and followed me everywhere I went. Finally my girlfriend told me, "You better make up your mind whether you want to be my husband or keep on being a father to your brothers and sisters."

With these two pressures on my mind, a third one came along: a renewed desire to study for the priesthood. My pastor said to me, "If you really want to be a priest, don't stick around here. As long as you are in your hometown you will be called on to be the father of your family." So I emigrated to Canada and spent six years at Saint Joseph Seminary in Edmonton.

My perspective of my role as parish priest is that I should be primarily the unifier, the one who brings people together and keeps them together. I must be careful never to set up conflicts; rather, I am the one who works to resolve the conflicts that inevitably spring up wherever there are groups with different goals. I need to keep people together so that when they come to celebrate the eucharist, they are of one group, of one mind, and of one heart. When I see the world of the priest today as being so different from the time of my childhood, I might think the role of the priest has changed. It has not. That venerable pastor in my hometown and I share the same roles; we are the unifiers of our parishioners.

Each priest seems to have a special apostolate that corresponds to his talents. I like city parish work. I like to work with young people, and I enjoy preaching.

I do well bringing groups together. Youth and young families are so caught up in what society tells them they should do, what they should buy, what they should own, that their relationships don't receive enough attention. The bond between couples is weak; it doesn't grow as it should. So many high school students are from broken families. There is a lot of drifting. And so our dedication and our attention needs to be focused on the young. If we have the youth, we will have the future.

Preaching affords a wonderful opportunity to unite people. In my parish there are 2,400 families; about 3,000 members attend the weekend liturgies. Who else has the ear of 3,000 people on a regular basis? When I speak to them, I had better have something worthwhile to say. Those few moments are going to be the peak moments of my whole week. There will never be another time when I can influence so many with so few words.

But as a preacher, I must have compassion and understanding of the problems faced by my parishioners. Recently a young fellow came to visit me. His pastor had preached a fire and brimstone homily against divorce. The young man said to me, "I have been married seven years and have three children. My wife is mentally ill. She walked out and took

the children with her. I needed some hope that I could somehow work out my problem. Then I heard this diatribe
against divorce without any compassion or understanding
of my situation."

Those with marriage problems or difficulties with their
job or their health very much need someone to give them
hope. When we have hope, there is peace.

Nothing seems to be stable any longer in our society. It must
be especially difficult for our young people to try to make a
permanent commitment. When we assume an obligation, we
necessarily put aside a number of things for a single goal. But
today we want to have a finger in everything. We want the
good things, the comfortable things, and society today doesn't
encourage us to give up anything. That kind of milieu doesn't
inspire a man to make a lifelong contract to the priesthood.
When a man makes a decision to marry a woman, there are
10,000 more women out there whom he does not marry. So
when we make a decision to do anything, we have to set aside
a host of other possible actions. When I say I am going to live
a celibate life, that means I have to put aside many things,
including of course a particular friendship with one woman
and the children that we might have. Any commitment
involves a struggle. I have to constantly remind myself that I
am a celibate and that I want to follow that resolve for the rest
of my life.

When I was ordained I accepted the fact that it was to be
for life, but the struggle is always there. Maybe it is a good
thing to have that struggle. A commitment that is easy is really not a commitment at all. The joy comes from staying the
course when the winds are howling everywhere. How sad it
would be to look back at the end of my life and see that the
worst mistake I ever made was to leave the priesthood. I
would say to myself, "I worked so hard for so many years,
then I was finally ordained, and I let it all go down the drain."
Too often we forget that any commitment calls for a sacrifice,
a total dedication of self. It is not a one-time commitment. We
have to make the commitment every morning.

There were times when I thought of packing my bags and leaving. Most of my classmates left. Some of them write and say they are not happy. It is sad to see how they are floundering. One of the problems I see in bringing married priests back into active service is this: so many of those who left are elderly. The youngsters of a parish need a younger priest with whom they can relate.

The joy I experience daily comes from knowing that the service I am giving is appreciated. It is wonderful to hear people say, "I am so glad that you are here," or, "I am glad you are back from your retreat." At a recent marriage rehearsal, one of the bridesmaids asked to talk to me. She said, "I went to confession to you just about a year ago. My life had been a mess, and you really helped me. I did exactly what you asked me to do, to accept the values that Christ has laid before us. I have completely changed my life, and now I am so happy. I stand here today free of drugs and all the habits that were hurting me." A small but rewarding incident.

Why do I stay? I believe I have a solid faith in God. I thank God daily for it. Another thing that affirms me daily and makes it easy to stay is the wealth of love that people have for the priest. A warm relationship with my parishioners is an invaluable gift. A priest who comes to a parish is much like a ship. He unloads and unloads through his service and his homilies. But he also loads. He receives so many things from his people, and when he leaves the harbor, his cargo is full again.

Where would people go with their troubles if there were no priests? So often people come back to me long after I have counseled them and say, "I don't know what would have happened to me if I hadn't talked to you." One or two people like that outweigh all the sacrifices we are called on to make. The priesthood has an enormous value in society even though we have received a bad press today.

The priesthood has kicked me around, but it has also made a man out of me, and it has brought me joy. We now have a totally different priesthood than when I was a boy. It is no longer that romantic calling of past years; it is a far more real-istic vocation. We are like the prophets of the Old Testament. Many of them were persecuted; many lost their lives. We are God's instruments to bring the truth to people as clearly and as convincingly as we can. If anyone is looking for a picnic, let him take his basket and go down to the river. He won't find it in the priesthood. But he will find the priesthood to be a won-derful life, a joy-filled life. He will discover that he can be a good influence for hundreds and thousands of people.

William J. Bausch
Point Pleasant, New Jersey

Father William Bausch is a talented and ingenious pastor, a writer, a master story teller, and a preacher whose homilies were so intriguing that his parishioners taped them and insisted that he publish them. His ongoing youthfulness is partly accounted for by the fact that he took early retirement in 1996, at the age of 67. He was once described by the National Catholic Reporter as having "the energy of a five-year-old on a chocolate binge" and the parish from where he retired, Saint Mary's, in Colts Neck, New Jersey, as a "model of collaborative, post-Vatican II worship and ministry."

Any priest who leads the development of a model parish in the spirit of Vatican II is a pastor not only of the present but also for the future. That is Father Bausch. Born March 3, 1929, in Janesburg, New Jersey, Father Bausch was ordained in 1955 for the Diocese of Trenton.

I was a recalcitrant, even in third grade. In order to keep me in line, Sister Frances Carmel moved my desk next to hers. Such close proximity resulted in frequent conversations, and she got me interested in becoming a missionary, specifically a missionary to China. That country fascinated me for the simple reason that it was at the other end of the world.

After two years in high school, I decided to go to the seminary. I was accepted at Saint Charles College in Catonsville, Maryland, at that time an eight or nine hour trip from home. One week later I was back on my parents' doorstep in New Brunswick. The rector, Father Gleason, found that I knew no Latin. On my preliminary tests I got a total score of sixteen including the ten points they gave me for spelling my name right. So they shipped me back home. My poor mother nearly had a heart attack when I rang the bell. But the family rallied behind me.

After I picked up a third year of high school, I re-applied to Catonsville. They would accept me, but only as a freshman. So here I was, a seventeen-year-old hotshot, spending a year with the thirteen-year-olds in order to learn Latin. The next year I was put in what was popularly known as the class for dunces. I had a lot of time on my hands, and it turned out to be a bonanza. I discovered a library on the top floor of the seminary and began to read intensely. That started a process of self-education. What had begun as a disaster in my life, being left behind in school, turned out to be a gift.

We priests, being ecclesial persons, offer people a connectedness in a very unconnected world, where relations are so easily broken. We are connecting them to something larger than themselves—to the diocese, to the universal church, to the great communion of saints, and to a community that is both horizontal and vertical, both natural and supernatural. We offer people a sacramental sign that there is always something bigger than what they can see.

A recent survey shows that 75 percent of Catholics love their faith; they have no notion of ever leaving the Church. I think part of that commitment is due to the fact that priests are there to connect them, to join them, to let them know they are related. That is one thing priests can do. Another is that we can speak freely about spiritual realities. People are hungry for God. Look at the books on angels and after-death themes. The bookstore shelves are full of them, as well as writings on scripture and the spiritual life. And people are buying. Priests are here to point people toward the authentic gospel, to celebrate with them the key sacramental times in their lives that are so meaningful even to indifferent Catholics. The media offer them a flat dimension, a secular dimension for their lives. The priest offers another.

One group that most needs priests today is young adults. Many of them have no notion of Vatican II and they don't have the vocabulary that older Catholics take for granted. For example, they have no experience of novenas or rosaries.

They see themselves as Christian rather than Catholic, and so Catholic identity is a big question for them. Many of them don't even go to church. Yet they have a wonderful honesty and authenticity. Think of this: hundreds and thousands of kids in their thirties will traipse to Taizé and to Weston Priory. Catholics in this age group are also the ones who are buying the books filled with shallow theology. They are hungry for something and too easily they follow the Pied Piper. They are both in need of ministry and ripe for it because of their natural qualities.

For some reason I have not encouraged vocations as much in the past few years as I did when I was first ordained. I'm not sure why. Perhaps some of the spirit was punched out of me by friends who left. Or, perhaps I just feel so bad about the clergy scandals. I have tried to promote vocations more by my writing than by personal invitation. And while I'm not sure if any went to the seminary because of my books, I do know several priests who have stayed in the trenches after they read them, especially *Take Heart, Father*.

The commitment of priests has a strong witness value for society. In this culture, our relationships are so fragile—there is a forty percent divorce rate, one-fourth of our kids live in homes without fathers; people don't keep their word; downsizing has ruined company loyalty. Happy priests who stay with it say to people that commitment is not only possible, it is rewarding. But the same is true for couples who are married fifty or sixty years. They too are a sacramental sign to society. Notice how people stand and applaud when an announcement is made that a couple has just celebrated their silver or golden anniversary. They sense an authenticity that is appealing even though they themselves may not have been able to make such a commitment.

I have found the priesthood to be such an enormously fulfilling and happy life that I couldn't imagine any alternative for me. So I can't really take any credit for being committed to my life; it has been such a wonderful experience not only to be creative but to have the opportunity to carry out my ideas.

I think commitment becomes difficult when there are down times in life. But I have had so much support, so much affirmation from the people I served, that the down times are few.

Interestingly, there is one thing that prevents or at least restricts doctors, lawyers, journalists, and others from pointing to the spiritual life, namely the fact that they are looked upon as being scientific persons. It is assumed they are going beyond the bounds of their discipline if they mention spiritual realities. But they expect a priest to talk about the supernatural and, if he is competent, they respect his expertise in that field.

I have had incredible joys during my priesthood including implementing the teachings of the Council and seeing parishes come alive, especially at Saint Mary's in Colts Neck. Even today when I go to Saint Mary's, I find the parish vibrant. People come from all over to drink in the exuberance of that place. To have been an instrument in bringing Saint Mary's physically and spiritually to life is my greatest joy. And only a priest can do that. When I renewed my vows on Holy Thursday, I was wonderfully reminded that I was father of no one, yet father to everyone; spouse of no one, yet spouse to everyone. The reward is intimacy, knowing the secrets of people, knowing they trust you never to reveal those secrets, knowing that you are an unspoken family member.

I really believe—I *know*—that people trust priests in things they will reveal to no one else. They do, of course, if the priests are authentic. All of us carry a million secrets of people. One of our great joys is to celebrate the liturgy with people we know. We sit in the presider's chair and look out over the people. We know one is a lesbian, one has a son that committed suicide, one is dying of cancer, one is having marital problems. But there they are, with all their crosses: singing, praying, and being more than the sum of their individual selves. Often I look out from the sanctuary and have this very powerful experience of sensing an extraordinary presence of Christ. When they come to communion, I can see Christ there, in spite of things that I know. That is a great reward for me. I share their secrets. I am their family. Once in a while I even have the great experience of seeing more than what is present and deeper than what is there. Those are beautiful moments, and I cherish them. Those are moments only a priest can experience.

Of course the priesthood has its down side. I guess one of the most difficult things I have had to bear was the lack of affirmation from my superiors. A few years after ordination, I was assigned to Our Lady of Perpetual Help in Maple Shade, New Jersey. That move was supposed to be an exile after I had written something in the *Ave Maria* magazine about the slow pace of changes after the Council. The diocese didn't like that. They wanted to excardinate me, but the pastor of my first assignment, Monsignor Robert Bulman, spoke up for me. So, the chancery did the next best thing: they sent me to the very edge of the diocese. I guess I have always been happy as a priest, even when I was being battered about by superiors. That never got me down, because I saw so many wonderful contributions I could make to the world. We fought tooth and nail over many things. The bishop would call me up once a year and I would go to the chancery and be bawled out. He would tell me not to conduct certain workshops. I would go back to the parish and do what I felt best. The diocesan paper was forbidden to use my name. I resolved my problem by simply not consulting them any more. I'm not proud of that solution, but it happened. The beauty of my life has been the people of the parishes. They were co-workers. Commitment has not been a challenge for me, but a companion for a fulfilled life.

I have had other disappointments. When I was ordained, I was so idealistic. Then I had a few rude awakenings. An Italian lady was dying of cancer. I brought her communion daily. She was married out of the Church. Near death, she asked me if she could be buried in a Catholic cemetery. I wrote to the chancery for permission and permission was denied. For Italians, to be buried in a Catholic cemetery is tantamount to salvation and to be turned down is practically damnation. I could not accept the decision of the chancery. She now rests in a lovely plot in the parish cemetery.

Celibacy is a problem with just about every priest. Yet personally I would have to say it has been a good thing for me, from both a practical and a spiritual viewpoint. I tend to be an activist. I could not in justice have a wife and children and keep up this crazy schedule. From the spiritual side, celibacy enables a priest to become a part of people's lives. I become father, mother, brother, and sister to them. That dimension, that presence, and the fact that I am there without an agenda, creates a bond. It doesn't come, of course, without a struggle.

My own thought about the future of celibacy is that I would never want to do away with it completely. It is a good charism. Vowed celibacy has a lot to say in the crazy world. However, since it is a charism, it is difficult to legislate. Even our Lord said that, "Let him take it who can." Rome is set on the principle, but Rome has always been susceptible to pastoral needs. Rome gives us thirty thousand canons condemning a practice, but the last canon says that if we are sorry, forget it. What could happen is this: some bishop who is desperate is going to say, "Some of our people haven't had Mass for twelve years. Holy Father, can I just make an exception? I have a deacon who is seventy-five. His wife is still living and he has no children. Can I ordain him?" Rome will say, "Of course," and that will open the door.

Let me tell you about a pivotal point in my life. Call it a surprise or an awakening if you will. About six years after I was ordained, the Crowleys came out with the Christian Family Movement. In our area it was called Christian Family Action. Couples and families met in their homes with workbooks and scripture. The priest could attend, but could say nothing until the final five minutes. Sitting there listening to those couples grapple with problems like the 2:00 a.m. bottle, the kid on drugs, the guy worried about losing his job, made me realize what a sheltered life I had. I learned to respect the laity and honor their charisms, gifts, and spirituality. To this day I am still awed by those people. CFA lifted a scale from my eyes and enabled me to see the power, beauty, and strength of the laity in the midst of huge problems. From that point on I knew I would never teach them. They would teach me. That is why I emphasize a shared and collaborative ministry.

We can also have great moving moments with other priests. I just had a letter from a monsignor in England. He had read my book, *Take Heart, Father*. He said he was thinking of leaving the priesthood. After reading the book, he decided to stay. Another priest at Nashville told me the same thing. I wrote a book called *Confession, It Is the Lord*. I received a powerful letter from a nun who said it had brought her back on an even keel.

I have been ordained for more than forty years, and I believe I have seen a radical change in the role of the priest. In my early years, the priest was basically in the business of helping. Now he is in the business of training. The priest of 1955 was a nurturing person. He dispensed the sacraments, visited the sick, comforted the dying. With the shortage of vocations and the shift in focus brought on by Vatican II, especially the Decree on the Laity, we now nurture the nurturers and minister to the ministers. It is a different ball game.

The future of the Church? I have a lot to say on that. I have material for another book: *The Parish for the Next Millennium*. Based on what we are already seeing, I predict:

- that the Church of the future will be lay-oriented, one of shared and collaborative ministry. Communication from the top on down will disappear;
- that the Church will be far more grounded in baptism and charism rather than ordination and office. Charism, not office, will get the job done;
- that the Church will be relationally rather than numerically or institutionally defined. We will have more of a covenantal, intentional community. We called for obedience in the past. In the future we will call for commitment;
- that in a very pluralistic, multicultural society, the Church of the next millennium will speak from weakness

rather than from power. The fundamental truth we have to live by is that Christianity is increasingly an optional religion;

➤ that the parish of the next millennium will emphasize the wisdom tradition rather than the intellectual tradition;

➤ that the parish of next millennium will be less program-oriented and more spiritually-oriented, uncovering God in marriage, neighborhood, place of work, etc.;

➤ that the parish will focus on intergenerational education rather than on the education of just children. We won't put all our eggs in one basket;

➤ that the parish will remain, as it must, true to our ecclesial tradition. We will continue to be an ecclesial community, as opposed to being congregational, autonomous, separate units. And I think that is where the priesthood will find its strongest emphasis. The priest will be the sacramental sign of the larger diocese, the universal church, connecting us as a sign so that we don't become a congregational church.

Is this a good time to become a priest? Yes and no.

No, because of the adverse publicity, the pedophile scandals, and the anti-Catholicity of the media. Yes, and this is the real answer, because people are beginning to put those problems in perspective.

Yes, because of the recent Gallup poll that showed a ten percent increase in people's regard for organized religion and for priests. Yes, too, because it is such a challenging time, a time of transition. We are rekindling the spirit of the early Church, back to the era of discipleship, where the Church worked from weakness.

And, finally, yes, because we are aborning. We are mid-wifing a new Church. We are asked to serve as disciples, and that is precisely the joy of being a priest today. We are starting again to wash feet. We are facing challenges that did not exist before except in the first fifty years of the Church.

Let this be my message to those who might consider the priesthood: "Hop aboard! This is an exciting time; you will have many hardships, you will face persecution, but the victories will be great."

IV. Look After My Sheep

Priests Who Became Bishops

WHEN THEY HAD EATEN, JESUS SAID TO SIMON PETER, "SIMON SON OF JOHN, DO YOU LOVE ME MORE THAN THESE OTHERS DO?" HE ANSWERED, "YES, LORD, YOU KNOW I LOVE YOU." JESUS SAID TO HIM, "FEED MY LAMBS." A SECOND TIME HE SAID TO HIM, "SIMON SON OF JOHN, DO YOU LOVE ME?" HE REPLIED, "YES, LORD, YOU KNOW I LOVE YOU." JESUS SAID TO HIM, "LOOK AFTER MY SHEEP."

—JOHN 21:15-16

In this section, three bishops refute a formerly popular assumption that ambition is the path to the episcopacy. They tell how they felt fulfilled and happy as priests long before the miter was offered them. Two of the stories tell of men who were astonished at the call to become a bishop and were reluctant to accept. The third traveled an unusual route to the episcopal chair and was called to become a bishop after the interview for this book. Like Peter, all three agreed to take on new and greater responsibilities because the Church asked it of them. Their ministries as bishops speak of another aspect of the priesthood.

Leonard J. Olivier, S.V.D.
Washington, D.C.

The Most Reverend Len Olivier is a quiet, gentle, talented, compassionate man who began his priesthood as a member of the mission Society of the Divine Word. Desirous of one thing only after ordination, to become a pastor, he was promoted against his wishes from one position to another, finally being named Auxiliary Bishop of the Archdiocese of Washington. Bishop Olivier is typical of a new wave of shepherds like the late Cardinal Bernardin of Chicago who lead through humble service.

Bishop Olivier was born in 1923 in Lake Charles, Louisiana, studied for the Society of the Divine Word and was ordained in 1951.

The town in which I was born, Lake Charles, Louisiana, is in the southwestern part of the state, near Texas. I can't give you a street address because we didn't live on a street. Our home was in an alley in the mostly black section of the city. My home life brings back good memories. Both of my parents were very religious people. Dad was an usher, a Knight of Peter Claver, and a member of the Holy Name Society. He lived for the Church and for his family, and we had a strong family prayer life. Mother didn't belong to any organizations, but she was a workaholic. She was an excellent cook. It was because of her care for the family and her hard work that it was possible for my dad, during hard times, to leave home, find work, then return to help care for us eight children. Dad loved all the children, and enjoyed playing with us when he got off work. He was employed as a laborer for Gulf State Utilities, which supplied electricity and water to the town, even though we had no electricity at home. By training he was a carpenter and used to do side jobs for extra income. It was depression time, and although people were not actually fired, they would work two weeks, then be laid off for the next two. Unable to support his family on that modest income, during the two weeks that he wasn't working, Dad would hop a freight train, go to Texas, find work for a fortnight, then return home.

All of us went to the Sacred Heart of Jesus Elementary School. It was staffed by the Sisters of the Blessed Sacrament who worked with Native Americans and blacks, and by the Holy Ghost Fathers whose special mission in this country was with blacks.

My jobs at home were to slop the hogs, feed the chickens, cut and stack wood. And since I was the fifth from the top I took care of the younger ones. I was an altar boy and saw with admiration the work that the priests would do around the parish. The pastor was great with kids. He taught both boys and girls how to play basketball. He was also a fine golfer, but he gave up his time on the links and devoted himself to working with the poor, especially during the Depression. The Mass and the sacraments attracted me to the priesthood, but perhaps more than anything else it was the sense of service our pastor had. I began to think about and talk about the priesthood during my last year in grammar school. When I asked to go to the seminary during eighth grade (which was considered the first year of high school), Mother told me to wait a year, because we were planning to move and finally get a home. After that year she had no more excuses. She was not anxious for me to go, not because of a lack of affection for the priesthood, but because of her love for all her children. Two nieces used to ask Mother if she wouldn't give them one of the children to raise. Mother's answer was: "They are my children. Go get your own."

And so home life was beautiful. We had little, but didn't realize our poverty because there was so much love. Both parents taught us our prayers, mostly Dad because my mother was brought up speaking French, and it was difficult for her to master the English prayers. After my first year of high school, I went to the Divine Word Saint Augustine Seminary in Bay Saint Louis, Mississippi. The rector, knowing the finances of our family, said that tuition would be supplied. I have always looked at the work I have done since ordination as payback for the training I got without putting a burden on the family.

As is the custom with several religious congregations, we were ordained at the end of our third year of theology. During our fourth year we were called scholastic priests. We could say Mass and do a limited amount of ministry, but were still in studies. My parents hoped that I would be assigned near home, but to our surprise I was kept at the seminary to be an assistant dean in the seminary high school. I had no special skill in sports, but they must have wanted me for other gifts. So, for the next four years I did some teaching and worked with the seminarians in the dining room, study hall, and classrooms. Then another surprise: I was appointed dean. A dean is supposed to be an aggressive person, who can come down with his fists if need be. Again it seemed they were not looking for that in me. I held the position for eleven years, keeping up my prayer life and hoping I would soon get into parish work. Once again I was derailed; I was appointed director of my religious community. I stayed in that job for another six years until 1973. By that time I was ordained twenty-two years, and in our society we have the privilege of taking a break after a period of steady work. I went to our House of Spirituality outside of Castel Gandolfo, Italy, in the town of Neri, for five months. It was a marvelous time for study, prayer, and travel. I visited the shrines in Rome, took several tours, and relaxed from my many years in administration.

After that, I thought surely I would finally get into parish work, the dream of every ordained priest. But I was appointed Secretary for Studies for all the Society of Divine Word seminaries in the country, about fifteen at the time. My headquarters were in Epworth, Iowa, from 1974 to 1982. During that time I was also elected director of the Epworth Seminary. It was a novel experience for me because there were so few blacks in the area—only those in the seminary and some who came from the large cities to attend Loras and Clarke Colleges in nearby Dubuque.

While at Epworth I became acquainted with Marriage Encounter. A professor simply handed me an application form, told me to fill it out and send it with $10 to a couple living in Cedar Rapids, Dick and Carol Lensing. They were on the team for the weekend, and those three days became a turning point in my life. I used to be afraid of married couples. That may sound strange—coming as I did from a loving family—but I figured there was such a gap between married life and the priesthood that I always had to be on guard. That weekend with the Lensings, two other couples, and a priest showed me how common human nature is in all walks of life and how I could be loving and receive love from others without hesitation. I was asked to help give the Marriage Encounter weekends. To prepare I had to write fifteen talks. Those talks brought a lot out of me, and the couples challenged me in a way far deeper than did my seminary training. I learned how to form appropriate intimate relationships with them.

A black parish, Holy Ghost, in Opelousas, Louisiana, became vacant and the bishop asked me to take over as administrator until a pastor could be found. It was the largest black parish in the state, with about 10,000 members. Four months later I had a call from the Apostolic Nuncio, Archbishop Pio Laghi, telling me the Holy Father had appointed me Auxiliary Bishop of Washington, D.C. It was a confusing conversation. Holy Ghost parish was split into two factions, only one of which had accepted me. The people had actually gone to the bishop several times asking to have their former pastor back. And so when the Nuncio called, I thought the parish council had gotten no satisfaction from the bishop and had gone a step higher. So I said, "Archbishop, I don't know whether you realize it or not, but there is turmoil going on here." And he said, "Well, if you accept the Holy Father's offer you won't have to bother about that. Someone else will have to work it out."

It finally began to dawn on me that he actually wanted to make me a bishop. "You may have me confused with someone else, " I told him. "There is a priest twenty miles from here. His name is Oliver, spelled just like my name, except that I have two "i's" in my name." The Apostolic Nuncio said, "We know who you are. I don't have you confused with anyone else. I want an answer in a day or two. Please call Cardinal Hickey (ordinary of the Washington Archdiocese) and speak with him." Then I protested, "I am already sixty-five years old." And he answered, "What does that have to do with it? The cardinal wants someone near his age." Finally I said, "But I am not a good preacher nor am I aggressive." He replied, "We are not looking for those things; we are looking for someone with a pastoral mind. Please call back in a day and accept. And remember, Father, you don't refuse the Holy Father anything."

The Nuncio did say I could speak to my spiritual director, and I did. His advice was to accept, and so I came to our nation's capital. Like my predecessor, Archbishop Marino, I was given a special ministry to black Catholics in Washington, but not only to them. The whole archdiocese is part of my ministry. The people have accepted and supported me. I have been here seven years and have been very happy. I am over seventy now and hope to serve the archdiocese as long as the cardinal wants me. Then I will retire and return to my religious community.

I learned the value of commitment from my parents. They had an incredible dedication to each other and to their family. I came into the priesthood during difficult times, but it never occurred to me to back out of the priesthood or from the jobs I had in the seminary, even though I realized that I was training young men for the priesthood when others were leaving. I never doubted or thought of giving up the role I had undertaken. I guess I just followed the example of my parents.

Another moving force in my priesthood is the charismatic experience. I had gone to several charismatic prayer meetings in the Dubuque area, but they didn't grab me at the time. Later, when I was a pastor, the leader of a group asked me to look in on their Tuesday night meetings. I did, and also went through the Life in the Spirit Seminar. Still no fireworks. They invited me to attend the charismatic vigil of Pentecost Mass for the entire Archdiocese of Dubuque. At that Mass some people prayed over me. I simply went wild. I can't explain what happens in those prayer sessions, except that in some way the Holy Spirit seizes you and does something with you. I became active in the movement and received the gift of tongues, which I sometimes use in my own private prayer life. I think it important that I had those experiences so that I can encourage people in conversion experiences: Marriage Encounter, Cursillo and the charismatic movement. The Spirit has different gifts for different people, and an essential part of a priest's ministry is to develop in people the gifts that God blessed them with.

The greatest thing that a priest can do is to offer the message of Jesus Christ. His message is the answer to every human need. Combine that with the sacred liturgy and the other sacraments, as well as the frequent opportunities the priest has for counseling, and we have a life that is graced, influential, and satisfying.

I have no trouble at all with the vow of poverty. In fact I like to be free of material things. That may not be the best motivation for my vow, but it helps. It came as a surprise to me that when I was ordained a bishop I was no longer a religious and no longer had the vows of a religious. Basically I have become a diocesan priest. I have no economic connection with my congregation, only a fraternal relationship. Because of my home life as a child and my living in the seminary, my vow of obedience never caused me any problem. Yet memories of my home are precisely what makes celibacy a challenge for me. My mother and father showed signs of intimacy in the presence of the children, and that is something I long for. It was part of a valued family life. However, I can't really say I am lonesome. I have remained very close to my family, have a host of friends, and I see celibacy as a good thing. It frees me to be 100 percent devoted to the people whom I serve, to be less distracted than if I had a spouse.

I think being a priest is a wonderful life. I know there have been scandals and they have hurt. But in a way the scandals have done a service to the Church. They have reminded us that the Church is both divine and human. They show us that God can bring good out of evil and pain. This period has been a kind of purification, a renewal. It has been a way of learning to trust God more, of not being overly self-reliant. It has taught us that there are parts of our life that we can't control and that we have to rely on God's goodness.

John Mackey
Auckland, New Zealand

The Most Reverend John Mackey was born in Bray, County Wicklow, Ireland, in 1918. At an early age he migrated with his mother and an uncle to New Zealand. He studied there, was ordained in 1941, later was ordained a bishop, and retired several years ago. He is a wise and witty man and he narrates a delightfully droll discourse on his days as an associate and a fine analysis of the present condition of the Church. His story runs from his flight from Ireland to his growing up in New Zealand and beyond.

When I was only a year old, my father died from the black flu that swept through Europe from 1916 to 1918. A maternal uncle, Peter, took charge of my mother and me. We left Ireland because of the Troubles, meaning the period after the signing of the 1922 treaty. In 1916 the Irish people had risen up in rebellion against England. That was crushed. During the post-war years the Black and Tan, an armed British soldiery, was brought into Ireland. They were ruthless. In 1922 a treaty was signed between England and Ireland, and that is the cause of the present dispute. Twenty-six of the counties became independent and six remained part of England. Then the common Irish front broke into the Sinn Fein which accepted the settlement and the Irish Republican Army which did not. It is the IRA that started a civil war against the Sinn Fein, with brother killing brother. That conflict continued into the late 1920s.

To get away from that situation, we moved to New Zealand in 1924 to live with another maternal uncle, John, the pastor of Our Lady of the Sacred Heart parish in Epsom, a suburb of Auckland. My mother kept house for him, so a great deal of my early life was spent in a rectory. I used to tell my students in the seminary that I could never appeal for laicization claiming a misunderstanding about what the priestly life was all about because I had experienced it more closely than most anyone. But happily those experiences more than anything else led me to think that I had a vocation. I liked my uncle very much, was his altar boy, went with him on sick calls, and was active around the parish. I grew up in an atmosphere of family warmth, trust, and understanding, and from the point of view of outsiders, spoiled rotten. When I completed high school, I asked the bishop if I could be accepted for study and he asked why I wanted to be a priest, and I told him because I wanted to save my soul. He said that was a good enough motive.

One night I was sitting down on the beach, looking at the sea and watching the moon rise. I had a sense of the presence of God. I thought, "He is omnipotent, yet so close. He has me in his hand." I have tried always to live with that sense of a divine presence.

My first assignment after ordination was to a lovely parish in the city of Auckland, called Remuera. The pastor was an unhappy man, what the Irish call a "Black Irishman." He came from the North and had a great contempt for Protestants and everything that was not Irish. He wouldn't let me or the other associate preach. Our only job was to visit the parish families, on foot. We had no car, and during the war years could not afford a bike. Rationing was on, and the housekeeper raided our stamps to provide some good meals for the pastor. Still, they were happy days for me. In 1942 the Americans built a naval hospital in the middle of the parish, and the diocese was asked to supply a chaplain to take care of the wounded coming from the Solomon Islands. The pastor looked over the two of us, decided I was the more useless and assigned me. So for fourteen months I took care of sick and wounded Americans. The hospital began with eight hundred patients and finished with about two thousand.

I would go to the hospital at 4:00 a.m. and spend most of the day visiting, then return to the parish at night. When I saw those lads shell-shocked, burned, riddled with machine gun bullets, bitten by sharks, run through with sabers and blown up by mines, I just couldn't stay away from them. They needed someone so badly. That first association with Americans would later turn my thoughts to their country. I kept up my friendship with the men on the hospital staff and the corpsmen in the years that followed, hearing about their marriages and the births of their children.

About a year later, I was sent to a country parish in Thames as a form of punishment. The bishop said I had been neglecting tasks I should have been doing when I was in Remuera.

The move to Thames was providential. In addition to ripping me for neglecting my duties, the bishop told me to organize the pastor's silver jubilee and to give talks to the Catholic Women's League. Father Lyons was the pastor, one of the loveliest, most enigmatic men I have ever met. He had constant arguments with the bishop and so spent his life riding the boundaries of the diocese, never in a comfortable parish. But while doing that, he acquired a master's degree in history, diplomas in journalism and social science, and won an award for journalism at the university. When I told him the jobs the bishop had given me, he said, "I will organize my own jubilee, and the Catholic Women's league has much more to do than listen to your talks." That suited me fine. He asked if I liked to study, and when I said I did, he arranged for me to study for a master's degree in history. After I had a degree, the bishop asked me to take over the school system in the diocese.

When I got back to the city, I earned a diploma in education. One of the professors suggested that I continue my studies and that I ask for a Fulbright Scholarship. I did, and received a grant to study at Notre Dame. I was delighted to go to the States and be able to renew my friendships with all the military I met during the war years.

The bishop had allowed me only a year. I knew I couldn't get a doctorate in that time, so I took as many classes as I could. My grades were good and the department wrote to the bishop telling him I was doctoral material and asking for an extension. With two years and two summers available at Notre Dame, I applied for candidacy. That still wasn't enough time. Finally I had to return to New Zealand with my work unfinished. Six years later I completed my studies and went back to Notre Dame for my orals and defense.

Back in New Zealand, the government had passed the Integration Act in which the state system was changed to a national system. Under the act, privately owned schools could apply for integration and be approved if they had land suitable for a school and if the buildings fulfilled state requirements. It was a boon for Catholic schools since they could retain their Catholic identity and still apply for integration. If approved, the government would provide teachers' salaries, books, and all the other benefits of state schools. The Act of Integration was slanted to integrating individual schools rather than school systems, so a whole program had to be set up in which each school was examined.

About 1970 the bishop asked me to go to the seminary and teach ecclesiastical history and education. It was a wonderful two and a half years. I wrote a short history of the Church and was planning to write on Vatican II when, in 1973, I was consecrated Bishop of Auckland by Pope Paul VI. At that time New Zealand was divided into four dioceses. One of my main tasks was to help create two new dioceses. I worked in the diocese for ten years, then began to have severe headaches. It appears that I had some residual head injuries from three motor car accidents. The doctors said that I would be in agony if I continued on the job, so Rome permitted me to retire.

When I became a priest I never thought of it in terms of commitment. I just grew up with the idea that the priesthood was a gift and I was lucky to be accepted. Whenever I came home from the seminary at vacation time, non-Catholics used to ask me why I would ever go back. They thought that somehow we were forced into staying and that being at home provided a good time to run away. Getting kicked out was not the problem, staying in was the problem! The priests at the seminary didn't try to hold us there. They thought up every conceivable excuse to throw us out, at least that is what we thought as students. But I decided to make up my mind about what I wanted to be. Under providence, if my choice were a good one, it would grow and become more enriching and satisfying over the years. Something like minerals coalescing around a core.

That reminds me of a story. An architect friend of mine asked me when I made the decision to become a priest. I told him,

> This morning. It is not something I do twenty or thirty years ahead. It is something I decide with twenty-four hours in front of me. What I committed to is that twenty-four hours. And if what I am doing is valuable to me and to society and the Church, I keep on doing it.

A big disappointment for me was when I was made a bishop. I thought they had ruined my life. But on retiring I told my priests,

> I never wanted to be a bishop, yet I count these last ten years as one of the great blessings of my life. You are never able to conceive of the mystery of the Church, the reality of Christ, the wonder of faith, until you run a diocese. Even running a parish is not enough. When you run a diocese you see the human qualities of courage, commitment, fidelity, and generosity, exercised by all the people who do a multitude of jobs that go to building up the Church.

Some people think the opposite would be true, that all the problems laid on the desk of a bishop, many of them unknown to the clergy and the laity, would discourage him. Let me tell you how I face that. When I give a homily or a talk, if I don't say "This is a sad and sinful world" at some point people are disappointed, because I have been saying that for years. They will probably put that sentence on my tombstone. But I say to idealistic priests,

> Be sure to start out with that as a proposition. Then realize that Christ had to die to save this messy human condition, and you will grow to a sense of the wonder of all the things that are not sad and sinful.

The role of the priest today is exactly as it was at the beginning of Christianity. The Church has changed, perceptions have changed, but not the priest's central job. Vatican II said that the Church is the sacrament of the wonder of God's love, revealed to us in Christ. And the priest is the one who is called by God and committed to making that a reality in the lives of those in his parish. We priests are called to the specific task of preserving the wonder of the presence of the transcendental God in the midst of human history.

I can't think of a more rewarding vocation than being a priest. Take the most successful person in the world, someone who has achieved the highest possible goals: the life of that person is going to be enhanced and enriched by faith. And that is precisely what the priest is doing, encouraging and creating and developing faith. There is nothing a priest cannot turn into gold.

Psychologically there are two pivotal points in the life of every person: late adolescence and the forties. It is at those stages that people most need the help of a priest. In late adolescence people make choices which by and large will determine the way in which they will live for the next thirty years. Then, in the forties, they suddenly realize what they have made of their lives; they are either going to try to fine tune it and be happy, or they will try the impossible, repudiate the entire past, and start off on a new life. A priest is especially needed by young married couples today because the family today is under attack.

One of the worst things I have had to deal with in the priesthood is expounding on sexual morality as taught by the Church when we are in the process of change. The only way I could reconcile myself to that was by remembering that the martyrs of the Church died for things that the Church gave up years later. Saint Thomas á Becket, the Archbishop of Canterbury, found himself in a conflict between the pope and the kings. The temporal rights of the Church were monetary and land-based. Henry II attacked those rights; today we would say he was only doing what a good king should do. But in the process Thomas had to defend the position of the Church, and he was martyred. What he died for is long since gone. On the other hand, had he not died for it at the time, the Church in the Middle Ages could have been in a sense emasculated. So we never know the direction that providence is working. I think there will be changes in the teaching of sexual morality. At the same time I agree with the Holy Father that we have to hold to the center until there can be a genuine consensus on change. I do feel the sexual morality teaching of the Church has been somewhat inhuman and hasn't taken into account the fact that this is a sad and sinful world.

Two claims are being made about the requirement for celibacy today by the media: first, that it is a primary reason for the shortage of priests and, second, that it is a hindrance and a shackle for the ordained priest. The first may be true. The second is not, at least in my case. I can't really speak for others. When I was at Notre Dame I used to say facetiously that I had no problem with celibacy. The problem is with chastity, which is a different proposition.

I don't have a specific solution to the shortage of priests, but I do have a few reflections on some general things that need to be done.

First of all, we have to try to get our Catholic people to again have a sense of the wonder of a vocation, a sense of sacredness in what it means to be a priest. To a large degree we have lost the distinction between the sacred and the secular. Maybe in the past we were too religiously oriented, but we have gone too far the other way. In our desire to build fellowship, we also build familiarity. Familiarity brings contempt. There is a kind of contempt today for the sacredness of what we do. Second, there is a loss of morale among priests themselves. We have to restore the wonder of our calling. If we don't see the wonder, no one else will.

In spite of the fact that we are living in tumultuous times, the future of the Church looks bright to me. We used to say that the Church is like a beleaguered city under threat and surrounded by hostile forces. We do live in times of enormous change. One of the gains of Vatican II was that we relinquished the concept of Christendom. We had lived with the certainty that God would some day bring all the nations of the world into the Christian fold. That hope is gone. We will remain like yeast within the loaf: permeating it, moving through it, affecting it, but not dominating it. So I guess I would say that we are neither in a bad way nor a good way at the present. We are in the way in which the Church has always been and will be until the end of time. We are the presence of the incarnate God in his people.

Tell those who read this book to take seriously the words of Socrates: a life unexamined is a life not worth living. Tell them that if they want their lives to be worthwhile, they must examine them in the light of faith, keeping eternity in mind. Eternity is already within their grasp. They are molding it, holding it, shaping it. Until they begin to examine their lives, they will be like the flotsam and jetsam on the waves and may be cast up on the beach with nothing to show for their having been here.

It is a sad and sinful world.

Michael W. Warfel
Juneau, Alaska

Born September 16, 1948, in Elkhart, Indiana, Father Warfel was ordained in 1980 for the Archdiocese of Anchorage. He could hardly have imagined what a proposal of marriage would lead to, or how a vacation with his sister's family would change his life, or where a visit to a unfamiliar group of people standing outside his church would take him.

This talented priest spent months in Central America and the Philippines learning the languages of the peoples there so that he might better minister to Alaskan residents from those lands.

At the time of this interview, the energetic and enthusiastic Father Warfel was pastor of Our Lady of Guadalupe parish in Anchorage. Today, he is the bishop of Juneau.

My family is a curious mixture of religious beliefs. My mother was a non-practicing Catholic whose parents immigrated from Lithuania in the early 1900s. My father, whose family grew up in the Pennsylvania Dutch country, was even less religious. His mother was Methodist. He himself professed to be a Baptist, but didn't go to church with any regularity. When my parents went to a Catholic church to arrange for their marriage, they were told they couldn't marry in the Church. Mom, a feisty person, walked out of the rectory and married my father in a Methodist church. Though Mom always considered herself a Catholic, she discontinued going to Mass. My older sister was a nondenominational Pentecostal and a very charismatic individual. She died a year and a half ago. Another sister, searching for some kind of faith as a teenager, joined the Lutheran church, but is presently not practicing. An elder brother is not baptized. My twin brother is a Jehovah's Witness.

When I was about ten years old, I began to think about God. One day, after reflecting that there surely must be a God, I came home and announced to Mom that I was going to start attending the Lutheran church being built down the street. Something still remained of her native faith, and what I said must have pushed a button with Mom, especially after my sister had already been baptized a Lutheran. Within a week I was enrolled, together with my twin brother, in catechism classes at Saint Vincent de Paul's. We studied the *Baltimore Catechism* for a year and were received into the Church. We followed up with religious education classes and first communion, and a year later, confirmation. As a result of our instructions, my mother began to attend Mass regularly.

I did all the things that a typical teenager does and was actually a little on the wild side. After my junior year in high school, I became very rebellious toward this newfound faith of mine, resentful of the need to go to Mass every week. My party life was at a peak, and somehow my sense of honesty wouldn't permit me to carry on my lifestyle and still go to Mass, so after I entered college I stopped going altogether. I enrolled at Indiana University in Bloomington and studied music. I was very successful at partying, not in my studies, and definitely not with grades. After a year, I transferred to the university campus in South Bend. It was a time of turmoil in my personal life. After half a semester in which my grade point was zero, I decided to join the military. I didn't care which branch. I walked down the street, saw an Army recruiting station, and signed up for the Army. That was in 1967, a bad time to join, because there was a lot of buildup in Vietnam.

What a rude awakening basic training was. I was compelled to follow regulations and endure difficulties that I never faced before. After one week I considered going AWOL. But then after a few weeks, I began to actually enjoy the discipline and the structure. When I completed my enlistment, I was faced with what to do with the rest of my life. I was free as a bird, but once out I had no money, no job, and still no plans. I went to an employment agency, and they signed me up to do time-study in the production control department of a pump company. It was a dull, colorless job, collating information on how long it took to machine tool certain parts. And my life was dull: going to work, out to clubs in the evenings, spending all my money. Somewhere along the line it was as if I hit a wall. I was depressed; there was nothing to my life. Life had no meaning. On my way home from work I would pass the parish church. One afternoon after work, I saw that Mass was starting, so I went in. I came back to that church day after day. I would sit in the back like the publican in the gospel. Gradually I worked my way toward the front, and one day I met the pastor, Father Fred Cardannali, a very kind Italian priest. I told him my story. He just listened, nodded, and smiled. He guided me through difficult times, both then and later.

After a while I began to see the importance of going to Mass. I would leave home through the back door so no one would see me go. I started to look into the religious life and read everything I could find about it. The life of a religious brother was very attractive to me. I gave no thought to the priesthood. I had serious doubts about my ability to handle the studies required of a priest, and also I was too much of a sinner. Perhaps I was a little on the scrupulous side since the smallest things would send me off to the confessional.

Somewhere along the line, about Christmas, I met a young lady and fell in love. We began to date. Party life returned, and her style included lots of drinking. She was not Catholic. She shared none of my values in the area of religion, and I found myself being drawn away from my newly regained faith expression. Still, I was in love, and I asked her to marry me. After a while some of the things in our relationship became negative and we broke up. That was a blessing for me, because our marriage would have been a disaster. Once again my life began to turn toward the Church. I became acquainted with a seminarian from the Diocese of FortWayne-South Bend and another seminarian who was assigned to my parish. We became good friends. At one point, one of them asked me what I thought about entering the seminary. I talked to Father

Cardannali about it, and he said, "Why not give it a try?" I told
him that I didn't think I was capable of being a priest. "How
will you know for sure unless you try?" Father Cardannali
asked. His questions made sense. Father Cardannali put me in
touch with the vocation director. I began the screening
process, took the tests, and was approved to enter the seminary. It would be several months before classes began, so I
continued to work. But the patterns of my life were changing.

My family was in the plumbing business. My father was
a plumber and had arranged for me to enter into a plumbing
apprenticeship. One day in the kitchen I told him that I was
going to the seminary and wanted to be a priest. He was dis-
traught. He said I was making a big mistake. "That's not
right. You are meant to be a plumber." Eventually, after a period of years, he came to be very proud of what I was doing. A
sad note, though: six months before I was ordained, he died.
I recently spent some time with my older sister (the
Pentecostal) when she was dying of cancer. She was supportive of what I was doing. She cried at my ordination, and
thought it was a powerful, beautiful thing. During her last
days she was strongly attracted to the Church. She attended
Mass often and she loved the liturgy. Had she lived, I think
she would have become a Catholic.

How did I wind up in Alaska? One of my sisters and her
husband lived in Anchorage. They asked me to visit them at
Christmas during my second year in college seminary. The
next summer I drove to Anchorage and worked in a printing
shop. I did that again two summers later. Alaska became
more familiar and more attractive to me than Indiana. When
I returned to theology, I told my vocation director I would like
to be ordained for the Archdiocese of Anchorage. He discussed the matter with Bishop McManus, who directed me to
contact Archbishop Hurley in Anchorage. The two bishops
agreed that the change could be made. I professed candidacy
for the Archdiocese of Anchorage. There was personal tension
in my decision. What do you do when you have two excellent
bishops? Archbishop Hurley invited me to fly up to Alaska so
I could look at parishes, and he could take a look at me. I

came for the summer and resided at Elizabeth Ann Seton's, working for Catholic Social Services. It was a wonderful experience. We worked out the details and I was accepted into the archdiocese.

Returning to Cincinnati, I continued my studies and was ordained to the priesthood. A week later I left for Alaska, where I was appointed to Saint Benedict's in Anchorage. I was there for five years, my only assignment as associate pastor. Then came three pastorates followed by my current parish, Our Lady of Guadalupe.

When I was at one of those parishes, Saint Mary's on Kodiak Island, I noticed a number of people standing outside the church by themselves, not visiting with the parishioners. I went over to talk with them and discovered they were from Mexico. Two of them spoke only fair English. I got to know them and became aware that there was a definite Hispanic presence in Kodiak. One Hispanic couple asked to have their child baptized. They spoke no English, and I spoke no Spanish, so I worked out the wording for the ceremony with a bilingual couple. I rehearsed the Spanish words so I could at least make the parents feel comfortable at the ceremony. That Sunday I baptized my first baby in Spanish.

During the ceremony I was struck by the fact that this is a highly significant moment in the life of a family, and they weren't able to understand what was going on in liturgies except through symbolism. That got me thinking. I began to notice more and more Hispanics in the parish. They asked if I would consider offering a Mass in Spanish. I suggested that first I should be tutored in the language. I purchased a Spanish missalette and learned to pronounce the words. Then I scheduled a Mass in Spanish. A priest fluent in the language was supposed to come from Anchorage to celebrate the Mass, but he had to cancel and I was on. I sweated bullets, but somehow got through it. I played a tape in Spanish for the homily and managed to finish the ceremony without butchering too many words. About two hundred Hispanics whom I had never seen before showed up for the Mass. I saw these people living on the fringe of the Church, desperately wanting someone to recognize their language and their culture, and I was anxious to make them a part of the parish. The following year I took my vacation in Guatemala, signing up for a three-week intensive language school. I was a little more familiar with the language when I returned home. These events led to my application for a sabbatical to study Spanish in the Dominican Republic for sixteen weeks, then to El Salvador. From there I went to Mexico City, where I lived in the major seminary and studied at the university. When I returned to Kodiak, I began weekly liturgies in Spanish. That experience became a very significant part of my priesthood.

I was on Kodiak six years and missed regular contact with my fellow priests. I had belonged to a *Jesus Caritas* group which met monthly and had an annual retreat, but it was difficult to get to the meetings from Kodiak. For that reason I asked to be transferred to Anchorage. I was assigned to Our Lady of Guadalupe where I have been able to offer a weekly Mass in Spanish.

In addition to working with Hispanics, I have done some outreach among the Filipinos. One year I traveled through the Philippines learning about the social, economic, and political problems there. I also studied how to celebrate Mass in Tagalog, the Philippine national language. There is a Filipino heritage week in Kodiak every year, and I was invited to have the Mass. I celebrated it in Tagalog, and the Filipinos were overjoyed. The population base in Kodiak was about 3,000 or 4,000 Filipinos and 1,000 Hispanics, out of a population of about 11,000. Most of the Filipinos were Catholic. By the time I left Kodiak, the parish reflected the community.

One of the most rewarding experiences in my life, and I am sure it is true for most priests, is when someone has a profound healing through reconciliation, that is, someone has been alienated from the Church, then returns. Those incidents give me a sense of worth, a feeling that somehow I have accomplished something very meaningful—rather, that God has accomplished it through me and that God needed me for that moment of grace. What a marvelous thing to be an instrument of bringing peace and healing to a wounded person!

Commitment is an important concept for me. I don't take commitments lightly. When I make one, I need to follow through. In the early days, I didn't do that, but in the military I had no options: I simply had to follow through. It was a learning that I prized, and I always felt better when the military forced me to keep a commitment. I came to realize that the more I completed something I started, the better I felt about myself. Commitment in the priesthood and in matrimony is vital. There needs to be stability in every state of life.

Celibacy is a problem for quite a few priests. I see much value in it for myself. It is a sign of contradiction, a sign of the kingdom, and a source of evangelization. When someone lives a life that is contrary to the values of secular society, people are bound to ask themselves, "Why are they doing it?" If the discipline were changed tomorrow, I wouldn't go rushing out to find a bride. Obviously there are some benefits in terms of freedom and the opportunity to be present to more people. I see it as a gift to me, but not a gift to everyone. Many have left the priesthood, yet I stay. The bottom line is that I believe God called me to be a priest. That may sound simplistic, but I am convinced that the priesthood was not my choice: it was God's choice. This is the gift that God gave me for my life. I also realize that no matter what call God may give a person— whether marriage, or the priesthood, or the single life—it is never going to be easy.

Frankly I would like for us to explore optional celibacy. In this archdiocese we will soon ordain a married man, Scott Medlock, a Methodist minister, whose wife and children are Catholic. He was interested in Catholicism but also wanted to be a minister. Given the new directions after Vatican II, he investigated the possibility of being ordained. He found a supportive bishop, came to Alaska, and converted. [*Pope John Paul II gave the permission, and Medlock was ordained to the priesthood for the Archdiocese of Anchorage on July 26, 1996. His sons served the ordination Mass, and at his first Mass, Father Theodore Hesburgh, the former president of Notre Dame and the priest who married him, gave the homily. Archbishop Francis*

Hurley referred to Medlock's ordination in "The Return to Ministry of Inactive Married Priests" (America, 28 February 1998, pp. 13-16).] The Rev. Medlock will give a dimension to the ministry through marriage and children that others cannot give. While there is a sign value to celibacy that shouldn't be lost, the gifts this man has are also important.

The heart and center of the priest's life is the eucharist. It is the primary thing for which the priest is indispensable—that and the sacrament of reconciliation. Basically the priest is vital to the sacramental life of the people of God. The priest is also vital to his brother priests. I often think of the experience of Father Michael Shields. He was ordained a year before me. He went through a difficult time of discord and searching. He seemed to be feeling a call to follow the Lord in a special way, one which would help renew the priesthood. Eventually he took some time off for reflection. He made a lengthy retreat, after which he believed he had received a call to go to Russia and also a call to radical poverty. He gave away all his possessions and donned a habit. He met weekly and prayed with the archbishop for an entire year to discern his call. I was touched by his spirit, enthusiasm, integrity, honesty, openness, and surrender. I was also touched by the priest-to-priest relationship between Michael and the archbishop. Father Michael is doing fine work as pastor of the parish in Magadan, Russia. Magadan is the city that seven million prisoners passed through to go to their deaths—the area of the worst of the gulags. It was the place that Solzhenitsyn called the "cold pole of the gulag."

Priests can do much toward encouraging vocations. We need to demonstrate that our life is happy and full, that there is fulfillment and contentment in what we are doing. Am I a happy priest? Yes, I am. Some days I don't feel happy, but there is always meaning and fulfillment in what I am doing.

We priests also need to invite men into the priesthood. A young man had talked to several pastors about a vocation. When I talked with him, he told me that I was the first person to ask him to become a priest. Yes, I do ask. I met a kid at a conference recently and told him he should think about the priesthood. He replied that he had been thinking about it for five years, but hadn't received any encouragement. He hopes to enter the seminary this fall.

I tell men of all ages that the priesthood is a challenge and adventure. I tell them that they won't find it a nice tidy package. Rather, they will find a ton of things to be done and they will have a lot of trying moments, but those are a part of any profession. I add that one thing they will definitely find is an enormous satisfaction, a deep happiness, and a sense of contentment and accomplishment every time they bring someone closer to God, every time they help someone find meaning in life, every time they find the lost sheep, put that sheep on their shoulders and bring him or her back to the fold.

V. Other Sheep I Have

Priests From Different
Faith Traditions

AND THERE ARE OTHER SHEEP I HAVE THAT
ARE NOT OF THIS FOLD, AND I MUST LEAD THESE
TOO.

—JOHN 10:16

John's gospel has a very explicit purpose. It was written so that all may believe that Jesus is the Christ, and that believing, they may have life in his name (20:31). The universal mission of Christ's Church is expressed clearly in the parable of the good shepherd: Anyone who enters the kingdom through Jesus Christ will be safe.

One of the delicate issues facing the Church and priesthood is the acceptance of a minister from another denomination (as referred to by Bishop Warfel).

In the two stories which follow, two men tell of their journey from their proud Episcopalian roots to the priesthood of the Roman Catholic Church. They tell of their abiding faith and the pain of many of their lifelong friends who did not reach the same destination. In both cases, the pearl of great price they were seeking was the priesthood.

Jack D. Barker
Palm Springs, California

Since Vatican II, about one hundred Episcopal priests have joined the Roman Catholic Church. In November 1976, the Episcopal Church approved the ordination of women. Was the attraction of former Episcopal priests to Catholicism a conservative reaction and a protest of that decision, or were there other reasons for their transitions? Father Jack Barker, pastor of Saint Francis of Assisi in Palm Springs, California, answers this question from a different perspective.

Father Barker is a scholarly, energetic, and courteous individual. His insights into the Catholic Church and knowledge of its history are extensive. Father Barker has received an appointment perhaps unusual for a former Episcopalian—he is in charge of vocations in the Palm Springs area of the Diocese of San Bernardino.

Father Barker was born in Sisseton, South Dakota, and raised in southern California. He was ordained to the Episcopal priesthood in 1970 and to the Catholic priesthood in 1992.

In college I met a dynamic Episcopal priest who had the first powerful impact on me in terms of a vocation. He forced me into some deep thinking about what I was going to do with my life. Up to that time, 1963, I had thought simply of making a living. Through his influence I was able to go to England and read theology. I attended the College of the Resurrection in northern England, which was run by the Community of the Resurrection. Their special apostolates are education, staffing seminaries, and working with the poor.

The College of the Resurrection was a new religious experience for me, a true training in high church. The daily schedule was almost identical with that of the Roman Catholic seminaries of the time. Grace at meals was in Latin. We had the great silence after compline. The liturgy was entirely in the Catholic framework and had all the signs and symbols of the Catholic monastic life. So my religious experience as a seminarian was catholic—with a small "c."

After my seminary training in England, I applied for acceptance with the Episcopal bishop in Los Angeles. First I had to earn some money, so I worked as an engineer for three years, then returned to the seminary for a final year. I was ordained in 1970.

After ordination, I worked for a year in one parish, then served as pastor from 1971 to 1986 at St. Mary's, a small but significant Anglo-Catholic parish in Los Angeles. During my first years there, I became involved with the American Church Union. The Union was a group of clergy and laity which promoted Catholic teaching within the Episcopal church in the areas of ministry, sacraments, and liturgy, and which worked toward corporate reunion between Roman Catholics and Anglicans. During the 1960s and 70s the achievement of that goal looked very possible. I was completely dedicated to the work. I believed that the lack of unity was an offense against God, a betrayal of the unity which Jesus prayed for in his high priestly prayer (John 17). But in the 70s it became increasingly clear that this unity was not going to happen soon because the Episcopal Church chose to take more progressive steps in the ministry. They began to ordain women despite the fact that Pope Paul VI warned that it would create a barrier for continued in-depth study toward corporate reunion. I came to the conclusion that such a reunion would not happen in my lifetime.

That is the moment I decided to begin a journey to the Roman Church. If I couldn't be a part of a reunion working from the Church of my forefathers, I wanted to do it myself. No, it was not a matter of being angry with the Episcopalians or opposed to the ordination of women. I simply saw that the direction taken by Episcopalians meant that, for the present and foreseeable future, the reunion of churches was not a viable possibility. The issue for me was reunion. So, my journey toward Roman Catholicism, while it began long ago, took a radical turn in 1977.

A Franciscan priest in Portland, Oregon, who was a friend of Cardinal Seper, former archbishop of Zagreb and Cardinal

Ratzinger's predecessor as head of the Sacred Congregation for the Doctrine of the Faith, told the cardinal about my interest and asked whom I should contact. The cardinal sent word through the Franciscan for me to come to Rome and visit him. I went there in November of 1977.

I met first with Father William Levada from Long Beach, California, who was the cardinal's secretary. He is now archbishop of San Francisco. Finally the cardinal entered. I was completely overwhelmed with his generosity and kindness. I told him about my involvement with the American Church Union and said that I represented several hundred priests who were interested in becoming Roman Catholic. I described my dilemma and concerns, and we made decisions how we were to proceed from that point on. We had a second meeting in which we worked out some details. He said, "Continue to minister to your people. Marry and bury and baptize them until you can come in together." From that time I felt bonded to the cardinal. I had now left behind moral obedience to the Episcopal church and was prepared to resign my parish unless the parish wanted to come with me. Actually, in the end, half of them did.

In 1978 things slowed for some time because two popes died within a month of one another. Then John Paul II was elected. In 1979 Cardinal Seper was reconfirmed as Prefect of the Congregation and asked me and other representatives to return to Rome. Further conversations took place. It was a time filled with anxiety and difficulty primarily because of problems created in the parish that I was serving. It was not until 1987 that I was received into the Church.

A second group of priests followed a different path. They were under the leadership of Father Jim Parker of Georgia. Father Parker subsequently became a secretary to Cardinal Law, who had a special assignment to handle the Anglican issue. Cardinal Law is the ecclesiastical delegate in the United States authorized to bring in married Episcopalians who request to be priests in the Roman Catholic church. The program was approved in 1980. There are eighty or so Episcopal priests who have come into the Roman Church during the past fifteen years. They are working in various dioceses throughout the country.

My greatest surprise since I joined the Catholic Church comes from my background in Episcopalianism. Our laity there were well informed. I was mildly surprised by the lack of understanding by many Catholics of the basics of their faith.

My biggest disappointment, perhaps because of an early naiveté, comes when people don't behave as if they believed the precepts of their religion. For example, when there is pettiness, lack of charity, and unreasonable complaints. That is really not a prime issue in this parish, but whenever you have 4,000 people and 1,800 families, you are bound to have at least one percent who are not happy.

My biggest joy is being intimate with people at times in their lives when they need the healing touch of Jesus. That happens in confession, in counseling, in the visiting the sick, and in the caring for the dying. At those moments I am allowed into the most vulnerable situations in people's lives. It is a real blessing to see the wonderful response that comes out of pain when God, through a priest, is able to reach people at those critical times.

One thing a priest can do for people that members of no other profession can do is to focus on the personal growth and holiness of those he serves. He can also do that for himself. We priests have quiet days, are able to go on retreats and days of recollection, and have opportunities to discover the length and breadth and depth of our soul. That is one of the privileges of ordained ministry.

Everyone wants to make a difference in the world, and I do believe that I have, though sometimes in ways hard to measure. A simple example: I had a counseling session with a woman whose daughter's husband died. She was moving back east to be with the daughter. I gave her some encouragement and a few suggestions. Ten years later I got a Christmas card from her, thanking me for that conversation, saying what a difference it had made. She told me she had never forgotten the words of encouragement I gave her. She had taken them to heart, and they had changed her life. I think of how many others that may have happened to who didn't have the opportunity to write. When I preach a homily to one thousand people I am reaching one thousand sets of ears, one thousand lives. There will be one thousand responses to what I am saying.

I know I made a difference in the lives of the Episcopalians I brought into the Church. Some of the controversy and the publicity was not good. If I hurt people at that time, it was not intentional. But I, like anyone else, must admit to a shadow side of my influence on people. On the positive side, if I have made a difference, it is God's work, and it is often humbling. When I call on someone who is near death or in a crisis and find that person comforted by what I say, I always go away feeling nourished. Often I leave saying I don't know whether I would be that strong or that courageous if I were facing the terrible problems they are experiencing.

I have found celibacy to be a very powerful experience. It allows me an intimacy with people that would not exist to the same extent if I had a personal family. There is a sense in which the people of God are somewhat jealous of their priests. If I am going to be a father to people—a father figure—that means I have a family relationship with them. And the father of a family has to be trusted. He has to know everything that is going on in the family. He is the sign of unity for the family. Celibacy is also a sign of the kingdom; it is countercultural. It can be difficult at times, but there is a difference between being alone and being lonely. There are moments when I feel a tug of the heart.

My crystal ball on the future of celibacy is my reading of the history of the Church. New things are not created out of nothingness. Ordinarily, the Church responds to life. First we have life, then we have law. Something is going on first in the body of the faithful, then we have a description of it, then we have law. In the more than twenty oriental rites of the

Catholic Church, first there is life, there is faith, and from that spring different styles of liturgy and of ministry. There are married priests outside the United States. Within the U.S. there are married priests coming from the Episcopal Church. I think that life among the faithful will unfold in different patterns. In the third world, especially among tribal people, family life is a central value. Monogamy has not been a cultural practice. To live the single life is almost unacceptable. If we are to be honest, we must admit that the practice of married clergy already exists. In time the Church will deal with that reality. I am not at all sure there is going to be an edict from on high suddenly declaring a universal married priesthood. More likely it will unfold in a piecemeal fashion over a long period of time. We will probably have, in the near future, two shades of priesthood. There will be a priesthood that leads to other orders of ministry for the celibate priest—a monastic style of life like our current model. The other model will be the family model. But all of this will only happen gradually.

When hope is in short supply, we can begin to restore that virtue by a return to an authentic spirituality. That means developing the whole person—leave out any part and we become dysfunctional. In terms of the priesthood, we are going to have to deal honestly with our problems. Some priests do not complete their growing up process and wind up as priests with problems. We will have to re-evaluate how we select, train, and ordain our priests. We can't bury our heads in the sand. Externally this is a tough time to be ordained. But for me that makes it all the more stimulating. I would deplore having been ordained at a time when there were no problems to solve, no mountains to climb, no oceans to cross.

I am ecstatic about the gift I have received. My vocation has brought me so many rewards, so many satisfactions that I can't begin to number them. There is no better way, no greater opportunity in my judgment, to become the person God wants you to be than to become a priest.

Louis A. Sigman
Phoenix, Arizona

Father Louis Sigman was ordained in the Episcopal Church in 1957. He is a priest who did not have to choose celibacy but did. His observations about the legacy of celibacy are enlightening. In 1965 he entered the Roman Catholic Church and two years later chose the priesthood, testifying to his joy in serving God and the faithful as a priest. He shares his reflections on celibacy from a historical perspective, and he also evaluates the significance of obedience in a disciple in the words that follow.

Father Sigman is a dynamic, hard-working man, ministering in an area that is exploding with Catholic families. He is the pastor of Corpus Christi parish in Awahtukee, South Phoenix, which serves a number of rapidly growing communities and already lists 3,000 families as members.

I was born in Chicago into an Episcopal family with strong religious convictions and practices. Our parish was staffed by religious priests, the Society of Saint John the Evangelist. All my life I was accustomed to a Catholic religious surrounding. We said the rosary and the Angelus, went to confession regularly, had Benediction every week, and attended daily Mass. I was a regular penitent and communicant.

I thought of medicine, law, and journalism, all of them attractive professions. In grade school I had thought often of the priesthood. I thought of it less often in high school. After high school I studied journalism for two years at the University of Illinois. Although I enjoyed writing and was attracted to the exciting life that journalism could provide, something was missing in my life. Then I came to the realization that a priest is a doctor of the greatest type. Some of my closest friends are medical doctors, and I admire their skills. But they deal only with the body. One friend, a surgeon, was an extraordinary minister of the eucharist. He told me that when he held in his hands the body of Christ he thought that was the most sacred moment of his life, more sacred than even saving someone's life with his knife. A doctor can save a body, but that body is eventually going to die. The task of the priest, his opportunity, is to save a soul for eternity. I also have good friends who are lawyers. Law in the best sense is a reflection of God's love for us. A priest practices law when he preaches the Ten Commandments and when he teaches morality. The priesthood takes the best of all professionals— the psychologist, the doctor, the lawyer, the craftsman—and rolls them into one.

My parish priests advised me to go to the seminary. I was not completely convinced, but they told me that the door is always open and that I could leave at any time. I finished college in a semi-seminary environment, then entered the Episcopal seminary in Wisconsin near Oconomowoc. I completed my study at the Seabury Western Seminary in Evanston and was ordained for the Episcopal Diocese of Chicago.

Throughout my entire training, I felt a strong desire to be a Roman Catholic. I had a difficult time with my Church not accepting the papacy, and an even more difficult time with our not being under the primacy of Saint Peter. Those convictions led me to join the Catholic faith in January, 1956, long before the movement toward ordaining women in the Episcopal Church led many others to the Roman Church. For a while, after I joined the Church, I gave thought to simply being a good Catholic layman. I could be a daily communicant, and so my love for the eucharist would be fulfilled. In the High Church we priests believed in the teaching of transubstantiation and in the real presence in the consecration, but I am not sure all the people did. In the Catholic Church when I saw people receiving communion I knew they were believers in the real presence of Christ. Finally, reflecting on all those years when I offered Mass as an Episcopalian, the thought of not ever saying Mass again was just inconceivable.

I made the decision to enter the Catholic priesthood. I studied at Saint Bede Abbey, then Conception Seminary, in Missouri, and was ordained for the Diocese of Peoria. Because

my parents had retired in Arizona, two years later I came to
the Diocese of Tucson. I served in several parishes before coming to Ahwatukee, which is now in the new Diocese of
Phoenix split off from the Diocese of Tucson.

One of the few disappointments in my life as a priest is the
polarity that exists in the Church now and the lack of respect
for the Holy Father and for the teachings of the Church, even
among priests. To balance those minor disillusionments, there
have been simply unbelievable joys in the priesthood. As
Elizabeth Barrett Browning said, "How do I love thee? Let me
count the ways." Every Mass is a joy. My day wouldn't be
complete without the eucharist. One of the satisfactions and
affirmations of the priesthood is hearing from men and
women whose lives I have influenced in the past. I still get
calls from grown-up boys and girls whom I taught in high
school fifteen years ago. They ask me to witness their weddings and to baptize their children. Or they say to me, "My
mother died, can I come and talk with you?" I am not the one
who has made a difference in their lives. It is the priesthood.
They don't come to me because I am Louis Anthony Sigman.
They come because I am Father Sigman.

I don't care for labels like conservative, liberal, and traditional. When I am asked where I stand on controversial
issues, I reply: "I am loyal." What the Church wants me to do,
I will do. I had no girl altar servers. Then when the bishops
said we could have them, I had girls trained within twenty-
four hours. I like to think I am along the line of people like the
great theologians John Courtney Murray, S.J. and Teilhard de
Chardin, S.J. They waited patiently when their ideas were
criticized by Rome. They kept on studying and praying. But
they were loyal to the core. When Vatican II came along, their
ideas were accepted. Father Rosini was the founder of a
community of priests who work in Peoria, Florida, Ireland,
and Italy. His works were considered, if not heretical, at least
dangerous. He burned his writings publicly. He said there is a
possibility that the Holy See is correct. If that is true, he didn't

want to give scandal, didn't want to lead people away from the faith, and didn't want to be a goad between Rome and the people.

With all the clamor for getting rid of celibacy, my view may come as a surprise. Celibacy was actually one of the things that attracted me to the priesthood. The Episcopal Church did not require it, but I chose that path because all the priests I admired were celibates. During my younger years I began to question celibacy, but as I got older I could look back and evaluate things with greater clarity. It is difficult to divide love between a wife and the Church. I have several friends who are Orthodox and celibates. They see genuine value in celibacy. They realize that their own married clergy must put their wives and families first. Celibacy has an almost intangible sign value. It points to a beauty of single-mindedness and single-heartedness. When I was a young man and would meet priests or sisters walking down a street in Chicago, they radiated beauty, serenity, and a full, complete, and absolute dedication.

As a historian I find that when celibacy becomes elective in any Church, it soon disappears. It has all but disappeared in the Greek Orthodox church: their bishops must be celibate, and all their bishops come from Greece, because there are no celibate priests in any other place, not even a candidate. In the Polish National Catholic Church, which broke from Rome some time in the twenties, celibacy was made optional. Their brightest students were sent to the Episcopal seminary. Celibacy completely disappeared in that Church and it does not exist today. In the Old Catholic Church of Utrecht, which separated from Rome after Vatican I, celibacy was made optional. It no longer exists there either. The Philippine Catholic Church, numbering two or three million, also broke from Rome and made celibacy optional. Likewise, it no longer exists in that church either. Because of that history, I would not favor a married priesthood. We would lose too much of value.

Before the papal pronouncement on the ordination of women, I would argue with fellow priests, more as an exercise of the mind than anything else, that the male priesthood was possibly a cultural thing rather than a scriptural matter even though it was two thousand years old. But Rome has spoken definitively and that closes the issue for me.

I think some of us chose the priesthood when we found an emptiness in our lives that was not filled through any other vocation. We may try college or working in a bank and still find there is something lacking. Father Clements, the vocation director, tells me that is what happened in his case. He graduated from Arizona State University in business, had a fine job, but realized there was something more he wanted out of life, and so he entered the seminary. An airplane pilot is visiting with me now. He makes over $100,000 a year. He is happy, has loved planes since he was six (he is one of the youngest men ever to get a license), but there is something missing in his life and he is thinking of the priesthood. When I talk to him or others, I tell them they will find peace and joy in the priesthood. If they become priests and lead the spiritual life of a priest, the prayer life of a priest, the pastoral life of a priest, they will be happy. There will be times when they are alone, but they won't mind that. Actually, sometimes they will long to be alone and with God after a busy day. Once I was told that a priest is like a sponge. All day long he soaks up the joys, the sorrows, the miseries and the problems of his people. At night he goes before the Blessed Sacrament and squeezes it all out.

When I was preparing for the priesthood I believed in the basic goodness and honesty of people. My life as a priest has not only confirmed that belief but amplified it. The integrity, the beauty of people who receive the sacrament of reconciliation, has been far greater than I ever anticipated, especially with people who have been away from the Church for a period of time. Their sincerity, openness, and total honesty is a revelation to me. It is not only a surprise, but one of the most inspiring things that has ever happened in my life.

Cardinal O'Connor in his excellent tape on vocations says that the Church is at its best when it is persecuted. The same is true for a priest. Cardinal O'Connor says that the Church is persecuted in America today by the media and by society in general. American social life is contrary to everything the Church believes. Poverty is ridiculous, chastity is insane, and obedience is foolishness. And those are the virtues we espouse for the priesthood. America is living in a post-Christian age. That is a great challenge. Challenges create great energy, and from great energy comes holiness. So today the priests we have may be fewer, but they can be better.

VI. Come After Me

Priests Who Conquered

Self-Doubts

AND HE SAID TO THEM, "COME AFTER ME AND I WILL MAKE YOU FISHERS OF PEOPLE." AND AT ONCE THEY LEFT THEIR NETS AND FOLLOWED HIM.

—MATTHEW 4:19

Peter and his brother Andrew abandoned their fishing nets to follow Jesus. At once they left what they were doing to follow Christ. Many Catholics think that men who receive a call to the priesthood answer it in the same way as Peter and the first apostles: clearly, affirmatively, and immediately. Now and then such is the case, but not always. Sometimes men wrestle with their answer before they enter the seminary, and even after they are ordained. The great prophet Elijah felt frustrated and exhausted in his vocation. He walked into the desert, laid down under a tree, and prayed to God for the relief of death. Instead, God sent an angel who told the prophet to get up and eat and drink, and to get going to Mount Horeb lest he not have time to finish God's work (I Kings 19:4-8). This section shares the stories of four priests who relate their experiences of struggling to respond to God's call.

Ned J. Blick
Wichita, Kansas

Benjamin was the youngest son and favorite child of Jacob (Genesis 34:16-20). "Benjamin" is also an affectionate term often applied to the newest members of the clergy. Father Ned Blick, born in Hutchinson, Kansas, in June, 1964, is one of two "Benjamins" included in this book. He was ordained May 23, 1992 for the Wichita diocese, only four years before the interview.

Father Blick's path to the priesthood was more of an ellipse than a straight line. The story of his struggle to reach a decision, up to the very day of his ordination, should be helpful to men who are having difficulty in recognizing and responding to the call to the priesthood.

Father Blick is very candid about his life during the four years since his ordination. He speaks frankly about celibacy, about the need for commitment, and especially about the joy of being a priest. He is enthusiastic about encouraging others to consider the priesthood.

The seven children in our family grew up in a solid Catholic background. We had prayer in the home, daily rosary, and always the rosary in the car when we went on a vacation. The seed of my vocation was planted in the family, first and foremost. My parents did not speak about the possibility of my studying for the priesthood, but you could tell how thrilled they would be if I were to make such a choice. They never spoke unkindly about a priest, nor would they allow us to do so. My brothers and I used to play catch in the backyard and would talk about what we wanted to be when we grew up. One of my brothers said that he wanted to be a doctor. I said I wanted to be a priest. We thought of those as the two greatest professions: one healed the body, the other healed the soul. Both of us ended up being what we wanted to be.

Three of my aunts were religious sisters. When we visited them, I was always impressed at the joyful life they led. They were so peaceful and happy. My uncle, a Benedictine priest in Shawnee, Oklahoma, was like a Santa Claus, jolly and full of laughter.

Catholic education was another influence on my vocation. I attended parochial schools all the way through college. It was taken for granted in grade school that we would attend Mass before classes began. I was an altar boy. When I was in the first grade and we were asked to draw a picture of what we wanted to be, I drew a picture of a priest. Sometimes I tell people that I never made a serious commitment to the priesthood until I was in second grade.

When I got to high school, I met a lot of girls, and my aspirations cooled down a little. During my college years, I talked to my uncle, the Benedictine priest, about my uncertainty. He said, "Just keep your options open. You will need a degree, no matter what kind of life you choose." I thought that was a good idea, so I continued college with a pre-med major. Right after graduation the idea of the priesthood came back, and I entered the seminary at Mount Saint Mary, Emmitsburg, Maryland. I had a college girlfriend with whom I kept in touch, and I lasted exactly one semester in the seminary. I simply couldn't make up my mind. I worked for a while, driving one of my dad's beer trucks, then re-entered college to study engineering.

It wasn't long before I found that engineering was not for me. Again I began thinking of the priesthood, so I took some philosophy on my own at a local college. Finally I realized I had to quit experimenting and make a decision. I applied a second time to the vocation office, told the seminary rector I was ready to go, and was accepted. Yet I was still queasy and uncertain. I was doing volunteer work for the Sisters of Saint Joseph, who taught disabled children. One of the sisters told the kids I was going back to the seminary. I begged her to keep it quiet, because I was again getting cold feet. I went into the chapel to think about it and did some of the hardest praying in my life. Another sister, a very spiritual woman, floated in and knelt beside me. She took my hand and asked me what the problem was. I told her I had a girlfriend on the side and couldn't make up my mind whether I should go back to the seminary. I have never met a person who could tune into my thoughts and needs more deeply than that sister. She prayed with me and actually wept. She said, "If you don't go to study for the priesthood, who will?" I felt that moment that I had my answer and was more sure than ever before. That certainty lasted just two weeks.

Would you believe it? I still had misgivings. The seminary was about to re-open in the fall. I called the rector and told him about my uncertainty and that I didn't want to go back and mess it up again. He told me to stay at home and gave me a week to think it over. To this day I wonder at the patience and understanding of those men. They could have written me off at any point, but they didn't. When I finally showed up at the seminary, I felt good about it, and from that time on the road was smooth.

Well, almost smooth. Guess what happened to me the night before I was ordained? I woke up in the middle of the night, anxious about the big leap I was to take in the morning. I saw a bible on the desk. I had heard stories about people who would open a bible at random and point to a passage that would give them a lead on what God wants them to do. So I opened the bible and with my eyes closed put my finger down in the middle of the page. The passage was Jeremiah 20:14, "Cursed be the day on which I was born; may the day my mother gave me birth never be blessed." That passage kept me up the rest of the night. For a moment I thought of hitting the road. Then I thought, if I went for the road, my mother would find me and bring me back. After all, she had already sent out the invitations. So I shook off my doubts, and didn't look for another scriptural passage to guide me. I think all that struggle was good for me later on. You are never certain until the bishop lays his hands on your head. Sometimes the Holy Spirit, as he did for Samuel, keeps sounding the call over and over.

Having been a priest for only four years, I can't share as many wonderful experiences in the priesthood as an older priest can, but I can tell you it has been a great four years. For three years I was at Saint Francis of Assisi in West Wichita, a large parish with 2,400 families. Now I am at Saint Thomas Aquinas on the east side of Wichita with 1,400 families and a grade school.

I teach in the school and do lots of marriage preparation. I value that work, probably because I was and am so attached to my own family. We have an Order of Christian Initiation of Adults program with a class of thirty who will finish at Easter. I am involved with the Parish School of Religion, teaching the public school students. The majority of students in our parish attend the Catholic school through high school. The high school is inter-parish. I make the rounds of the grades, teaching in each. I reach out to the homebound and visit the hospitals. A busy routine, but I love it.

Often I am asked by grade school pupils going through the lunch line, "Why did you become a priest? You seem like such a normal guy." I usually don't have much time for an in-depth explanation of my motives. Sometimes I tell them I look good in black, or that I lost a bet. By the way, that is true. In college I made a deal with a girl, "If you go to the convent, I will go to the seminary." She is the one who welshed on the bet. Sometimes I tell them I prayed a lot and asked God to let me know how I could do something really wonderful with my life, and he answered my prayer. Or, I tell them how I happened to call on someone in the hospital who had been away from the Church and that person has now returned to the sacraments. And I can say to myself: "I just saved a soul." That of course is an exaggeration, but it does describe how I feel after that kind of an experience. I can at least say I did something worthwhile this afternoon, something I couldn't have done as a banker or a lawyer. I know that bankers and lawyers and business people can also bring people back to the Church, but I have far more opportunities for that kind of achievement than they.

I often tell the students about the value of a vocation to the priesthood. I think when we beat the bushes we will find the vocations. In our diocese we have only ninety priests, but we have twenty men studying in the seminary. We started a weekend discernment program. Every year forty or fifty men take the program. This year we will have somewhere between five and ten men entering the seminary.

I also tell men about the importance of commitment and say that if they want to make a total commitment, become a priest. Young people understand that and respect it. I like working with youth and showing them that in a world lacking in values, we can give up many things and still have a happy life. I call myself a playground priest. I can get more done out in the school yard in an hour than in all the rest of the day combined.

Since I have been ordained, I have been surprised, no, astonished, by the effect on people of things that require such a small effort on my part. I visit people in the hospital and they never forget it. I make a simple phone call and the person I called is so grateful. I give a student a hard time about the Church, and all of a sudden the parents are excited about the Church because I got the attention of their child. I had no idea such small things would be so much appreciated. Why that happens to priests is interesting. It may be because we confront the spiritual dimensions of people, while most other professions do not. People have deep spiritual needs. When they see them met, however inadequately, they respond.

A special happiness for me was the going-away reception my previous parish held for me when I was appointed to Saint Thomas. The number of parishioners who came to tell me they would really miss me and appreciated what I had done for them was an affirmation so warming you couldn't believe it. I was only there three years. The camaraderie of my priest friends brings another joy. We have a group that gets together for lunch, a movie, biking, or a trip to the lake. When I decided on the priesthood, I was afraid that I would be lonely. I have never been lonely because of our priest support group and the many close friends I have in the parish.

Celibacy hasn't been particularly easy for me. I place a high value on families and I often wish I had one of my own.

While that promise has been a burden at times, it hasn't been a stumbling block. Everyone who considers the priesthood will have a struggle somewhere along the line, either before he is ordained or after. I was lucky and graced to have my struggle at the time I did. I worked through it, and things are going pretty smoothly now. For me, the single life has been a blessing. I liked the idea of giving my life to God and the Church. That gift has a romance all of its own. Celibacy actually forces the priest into the chapel to nurture the space that is in his life. That space has to be filled with an intimacy with God. In other words, the requirement not only enables but pushes me to have a deeper relationship with the Lord. I mean that in a positive way. I know that I will find plenty of disagreement with both priests and laity, but I believe celibacy will be around for a long time, and should be. I seriously doubt that celibacy is, in the long term, an obstacle to vocations.

The pendulum is swinging back from the "free love" era, and the time is ripe for people to be touched by the work of a priest. I was in Medjugorje a couple years ago, helping a religious sister climb Apparition Hill. She belonged to the Good Shepherds. The charism of her order is to pray for priests. She started to talk to me, to ask about my prayer life. She said, "Priests have time to play ball, to fish, to golf, but do they have time to pray? You have to pray that hour every day." I thought she was reading my soul. Then she said, "You have to realize the amount of good you do; you are the apple of God's eye. Every day when you wake up, remind yourself of that." People like her know how to put zest back into the life of a priest. She made me do a lot of thinking, and she made me pray a little more.

My life hasn't been all perfect. I have had tough days. My dad was an all-weather optimist. When one of my friends, about to be ordained with me, stayed at our house, Dad said, "The priesthood is a great life." Then I heard Mom say in the background, "But it is a hard life." Somewhere in between is the truth: it is a life for which I thank God every day.

Andrew J. Umberg
Columbus, Ohio

Father Andy Umberg is another relatively "new" priest. He was born in 1963 in Cincinnati and was ordained for the Archdiocese of Cincinnati in 1991. He served as an associate at Saint Dominic's parish for three years, and then was appointed Dean of Students at Josephinum, the pontifical seminary located in Ohio.

Father Umberg is not one of those who immediately followed Christ after hearing the call to priesthood. It could be said that he shopped a while at the vocation mall. He is a young man who has analyzed the value of celibacy, is convinced of its need, and who thinks it should be mandatory.

I am sort of a post baby-boomer. I aspire to some of the same things as that huge generation which came just before me. To put that into context, I started kindergarten in 1968. Nixon was president, and I saw the unfolding of his career. The hippie movement was on, also the implementation of Vatican II. There was confusion and controversy. Yet my early religious training at the hands of my parents and in pre-school religion classes was very solid. Grade school training, from 1970 to 1977, was rather flaky in terms of the presentation of Christian doctrine. In fact, very little doctrine was taught formally. The textbooks were a disaster. They talked a lot about love of neighbor, seldom about love of God. Even at that age I felt there was something wrong, something missing in that sociological approach. There was a lot of non-doctrine. However, a few of the teachers would take the bull by the horns and make sure there was some content in the religious education program. I wanted to know something more about Jesus. It seems my world view was different than what I was being taught in school, possibly because of my father and his style. I took life seriously and was bewildered by those who didn't. It was the golden age of TV, and I was influenced by that, especially by the Norman Lear productions.

The great freedoms that were being preached got to me and began to undermine my religious beliefs. I picked up on the anti-authority stance and associated it with being religious. It was fun to be smart and to be a rebel. My family went to Mass every Sunday and Holy Days; for those living in the house there was no option. I had no problem with that; for some reason or other my rebellion didn't cover the Mass. I knew attending Mass was very important, though I was never an altar boy (probably because we lived a couple miles from the parish and my involvement in sports left little time for other things).

In my freshman year at a Catholic high school I began to attend daily Mass. One of our teachers was a very zealous Jesuit who promoted devotion to the Sacred Heart and critiqued some of the current theology. During my sophomore year I goofed around more and went to Mass infrequently. I began to think of marriage. There was so much talk of sex on TV, and I thought the only proper way to have that experience would be through marriage. I would follow the rules. In my third year I worked at a fast food place thirty-five hours a week and did very little in school. One of my brothers followed the same pattern. We asked Dad if we could switch to the public school for our senior year, and to our surprise he agreed. The school was adjacent to our backyard, compared to a forty-minute bus trip to the Catholic school. One of the reasons why I wanted to transfer was that I was disappointed in the religious education I was getting. Our coaches made fun of religion, of the sisters, and sometimes of the priests. Then I found that the public school was no better than what I had left. The kids seemed so shallow. It was a completely materialistic period, the time of the launching of the "Jordache jeans" mentality. My classmates thought of me as a rebel against their type of life. Yet I drank beer and went to the parties.

But I had my own problems. I was becoming very anti-intellectual. I associated education with literature, and most of the literature that got heavy press during that time was written

by twentieth-century atheists. I didn't realize that good
Christian people wrote solid material. Consequently I saw no
connection between the intellectual life and faith. The only
subjects I studied were languages, which I thought would fit
in with the career I now had in mind. I wanted to be a chef.
My plan was to attend public school one more year, goof off,
and then take the easy way out in a cooking school.

Why such a career? I liked to cook and was good in the
kitchen. I wanted to be a chef, have a restaurant of my own,
get married as soon as I could afford it, and have a bunch of
kids. I had no intention at that time of becoming a priest,
although the idea had haunted me since early childhood. I
didn't want to be a celibate, and I certainly didn't want to
waste my time studying.

After graduation I signed up in a technical school—not a
fashionable culinary school—just an ordinary place. On the
first morning, driving down the highway, I thought, "This is
the beginning of my career. I'll be a chef in two years, get my
restaurant in four, then get married. The Church won't want
me as a priest so I will be safe."

But again I found a shallowness among the students.
Their morals left something to be desired, and they never
talked about anything serious. Suddenly becoming a chef lost
its appeal. I had been interested in European culture, German
music, and creative dishes. But I found no romance in the
school or in the restaurants where we got on-the-job experience. There was no interest in being creative. The goal was to
put out a product and make a profit.

I decided cooking was not for me. I would have to go back
to school and get a degree. But for what occupation? Again
the idea of the priesthood came up. I prayed the rosary for
three days and made a novena to Saint Jude, looking for an
answer. Then my father had a heart attack, a jolting reminder
of how little time we have. The brevity of our existence on
earth has shaped many of my decisions and ultimately was
one of the things that led me to the priesthood. I keep thinking that if I have only sixty or seventy years of life, I had better do it right, because I won't have another chance. I still

wanted marriage, but the priesthood seemed to be what the Lord was calling me to. I decided I couldn't cop out anymore. If I really believed in God, and he kept knocking me on the head, how could I turn down his call? I had to at least try it.

Since I can't conceive of copping out, it is difficult for me that the priesthood is being sold out, even by some of the clergy. Different models of the Church are proposed, some of them with the supposition that the priesthood is dying out. The priesthood is not dying, and it never will. It is changing, and the Holy Spirit has yet to tell us where the changes will lead us. Kids watch their elders, looking for those who are happy. When they see people happy in a particular calling, they are attracted to that vocation. I don't want to be phony with kids, but I do want to show them the positive side of the priesthood. A parent tries to be upbeat with a child who is depressed. I serve as a religious parent for youngsters. The kids gave me a pair of in-line skates, and I take every opportunity to use them. I try to be aware of the music they like, to show them I am interested in their legitimate pleasures.

God has blessed me with great assignments and wonderful friends. In my first assignment, although the pastor and the people were kind and complimented me often on my work, I was lonely. All the men in the neighborhood had wives. I felt I was missing something, and began to feel sorry for myself. Had I made the right decision? Then I found support from friends, especially a few priests who helped me sort things out. They told me not to deny any of the sufferings or loneliness, but to quit focusing on my feelings. I immersed myself in prayer and reading the scriptures. These bouts of loneliness have come and gone. At first they were overwhelming, but each time I built a better strategy to handle them, and now I take them less seriously.

Celibacy, rightly lived, is a gift to the priest and to the world. It is a statement to our hedonistic society that a person can be healthy and normal, yet in control. And I believe the commitment to celibacy makes people take the priesthood seriously. It causes them to reflect on what kind of commitment they should have in their lives. The requirement is difficult, as are all things that are worthwhile. It should be an inspiration to married people to remain faithful to their spouses and to single people to keep their own promises. Commitment to celibacy says that we are putting all our eggs in one basket. It shows we are not in the priesthood for what we can get out of it—reputation, honor, and respect. It shows how much we believe in the afterlife.

If celibacy were optional, and a priest chose that state, people would likely say, "I guess Father just didn't want to get married." They would give him no credit for adopting that life for a spiritual motive. If the Church changed the law, it would seem to be like selling out; like it was too much to ask of priests, even for the sake of the kingdom of God. My choice keeps my job from being part-time, changes it to a total commitment. When I am tempted to goof off and waste my time, I ask myself, "Did you give up the prospect of marriage so you could just hang around?" Celibacy helps me realize how serious my job is and to remember that my job is to spread the gospel. Every priest is in a position to make important contributions to society. In my judgment one of the most significant gifts I can offer is my celibacy. It is a contribution of the first order, because it speaks of sacrifice and zeal and commitment, and it encourages the commitment of people to their marriage, to their faith, and to their friends.

Donald J. Goergen, O.P.
St. Louis, Missouri

There are many paths to the priesthood. Some priests are attracted by the liturgy, others by the prestige of the office, still others by a simple desire to serve people. Father Donald Goergen, a Dominican, was born to be a teacher. Then, from the time he started school, he never wanted to be anything else but a priest. In his mind the best way to become a teacher was to be an ordained priest. He pursued his twofold goal relentlessly, becoming both priest and teacher. From 1985 to 1994, when he was only in his forties, he served as Provincial for the Dominican Friars of the Province of Saint Albert the Great. Currently he teaches at Aquinas Institute in St. Louis.

Father Goergen is also a writer of considerable reputation. In the 1970s he wrote The Sexual Celibate, *examining a topic which at that time had scarcely been touched. The second book was* The Power of Love, *a treatise on Christian spirituality. These were followed by a series of four books on Christology. He has also edited a book on the priesthood and a journal on process theology. More recently his province published a series of letters which he wrote to his Dominican brothers and sisters when he was Provincial.*

Few men express more succinctly and yet more eloquently the unfolding of the paschal mystery in the priesthood— how inevitably linked are joys and pains. Though he is an accomplished scholar, he insists that people don't look for someone who knows about God. Rather, they seek someone who knows God.

Father Goergen was born in 1943 on a farm near Remsen, Iowa, and was ordained for the Order of Preachers in 1975.

From the beginning I always enjoyed school. In fact, partly because I had asthma as a kid, I did much better in school than on the farm. Teaching seemed to me to be a wonderful way of life, and I grew up thinking I would become a priest so that I could teach. During my college years I became interested in philosophy; perhaps I could teach that subject. Then, when I began theology I found it, too, was fascinating, and that probably was where I belonged. As a member of the Order of Preachers (Dominicans), preaching, teaching, and especially theology is what I do.

I was accepted as a seminarian by the bishop of Sioux City, and went to Mount Saint Bernard Seminary in Dubuque, intending to become a diocesan priest. However, because of a misunderstanding, I was asked to leave. I stayed at home for a while, still wanting to be a priest, and then applied to several dioceses, none of which accepted me. After a year and a half I applied to the Dominicans, and they admitted me to candidacy.

I have always had a strong belief in divine providence. When I summarize my life, a phrase I often use is this: God 4, Goergen 0. Many things I planned didn't work out the way I thought they should; yet in the long run they were always for my good. Had I persevered in the diocesan priesthood, I would not have been given permission to enter most of the ministries for which I have talents. Had I remained in the Sioux City diocese, I would have wound up as principal of one of the high schools, and at a certain point I would have felt confined. So I found my vocation through vicissitudes, but also through perseverance. I could have given up somewhere along the line, but I didn't, and so I ended up exactly where I belong. I would never have chosen to be Provincial; however, it happened to be the right place at the right time for me, and I was selected. My story is an example of the paschal mystery. Only through suffering does one reach happiness. Good Friday precedes Easter Sunday.

I really believe that in today's world temporary commitment is to be valued. But permanent commitment is still a strong value for society that ought not be lost. An analogy I often use: it is important for society to have available a number of physicians and a number of farmers. It isn't necessary for everyone to choose those occupations, but society is not well off if it has none of them. Similarly, it is not necessary that everyone be a priest or live the religious life, but a society is healthier if there are some people who are committed to those choices. And those choices do require a longer commitment. A short term commitment doesn't give witness to the depth of some of the values in our lives. We all make temporary commitments in some areas. But what if I were to say I am going to be a chemistry professor for four years, then the next four I will practice as a Buddhist monk and then join the military for the next four? My life might be enriched, but I would never be able at any point to say what it is like to be something through the ups and downs of the paschal mystery. Or if I say that I will be married to Jane three years, Sue three years, and Mary the next three, I will never know what that first relationship could yield, and what it would have been like to go into the depths of that relationship.

Most people should make a long term commitment to something, because that helps to give witness, meaning, and focus to what the person's life is about. Long term commitment isn't simply persevering in some laborious thing that is destroying me. It is rather a declaration that this is the thing to which I am giving my life. It would be sad at the age of eighty, if I were to look back and say, "I regret having given myself to the service of humankind; I regret having taught; I regret having been a priest; I regret my marriage." But it would also be even sadder to get to that point in life and have to say, "I really never gave my life in depth to anything or anyone sufficiently to know whether it was worth it, whether there was any value there." And so in that sense, I do think long term commitment is not outmoded. It is not required of everybody, nor in every area of one's life. We have to respect temporary commitment. But only people who do give their lives to something totally are able to discover what that life is and what it has to offer.

What keeps me in the priesthood, when so many of my confreres have left? When I was out of the seminary, trying to get into a diocese or a religious order, Mimi Vernon, a social activist in Dubuque said to me, "Maybe your vocation is to stay out of the priesthood and keep trying to get in, so that those who are in will realize that there is something worthwhile to stay for." An astute observation. Priests were leaving because they hadn't found something worthwhile to which to give their lives. After I was dropped from the seminary, I went through a number of experiences; at one point I thought seriously of marriage. Even when I joined the Dominicans, I wasn't certain of my decision, but I had to go there and decide whether it was right or wrong. I think God has kept me in the priesthood. Another thing that has kept me here is human companionship and friendship. God has worked in my life not only through prayer, but through the gift of friendship I found among the Dominicans. I have also been supported by my family. Since I was the only son, there must have been some sadness that I didn't carry on the family name; but in all my struggles and in my final choice, both of my parents supported and approved.

Over the past years, seeing the changes in society, in the Church and even in the priesthood, I have done a good bit of reflecting and writing about the role of the priest. Overall, his role is the same today as it has always been. The priest's role is serving people and providing spiritual leadership. He is called in some way to evoke, respond to, and articulate the spiritual needs in the lives of people. But I see the role of diocesan and religious priests as being somewhat different. Diocesan priests, at least those in parishes, are involved in building community through pastoral work in local settings. Religious life, which is the context of my experience, relates to the particular mission of each religious congregation. I see the role of the Dominican as preaching, teaching, theological education, missionary work, and solidarity with the poor. Jesuits, Benedictines and other religious communities have fairly specific roles, depending on the vision of their founders. I see no basic change in these roles over the years, although there certainly have been radical changes in the way some of those things might be done. I see myself as a teacher and preacher.

Teaching comes to me naturally. When I was in fourth grade, I wanted to be a fourth grade teacher; in fifth grade, a fifth grade teacher; in high school, a chemistry or a Latin teacher. Writing came later.

The priesthood has been both a painful and a rewarding life. Some of the pain, most of it really, came from the experience of leadership. A leader enters into the mystery of discipleship on a more profound level. In other words, a leader enters into the paschal mystery in great depth. And that involves both pain and joy. I believe that, for almost every calling, life brings more pain than we could have imagined when we were children. That is as true of marriage as it is of the priesthood. But in both cases there are also rewards that could not have been imagined. One special pain for me in the priesthood has been to see the ideological conflict in the Church itself, aggravated by the ideological conflict in our secular society. Sometimes it appears that a person's deepest commitment is more to the "right" or to the "left" than to the gospel.

I have been surprised how every ministry I entered into, none of which I chose, but which I took on through obedience, was incredibly rewarding and for my own good. I chose to be a diocesan priest; I became a Dominican. As a novice, I was planning to work with a mixed community of women and men on social issues. We were going to live with the poor in Chicago. The day before we were to move, the Provincial said, "No, you can't do that." He didn't want to get into a conflict with Cardinal Cody. So I wound up teaching at Aquinas Institute in Dubuque. Had I not followed the orders of my superior, I would probably never have gotten into teaching and writing. In about 1981 I was invited to teach at the Catholic University. Some of the bishops blocked that appointment because they didn't like my first book, *The Sexual Celibate*. Had I gone there, I might have been locked into that position and likely would never have become Provincial. As Provincial I was able to travel to such places as Central America, Bolivia and Nigeria, where we have missions, and to get in touch with the wider world, an experience that has been very formative in my life. So, everything that I chose for myself ended up not working out. Everything I accepted under obedience turned out to be a blessing and an opportunity to grow. Just recently I was able to go to India, and to experience not only the reality of the poor, but the depth of spirituality of another culture that enabled me to look differently at the utter secularity of our own society. So God has graced me in many ways, and those graces have often come when I was frustrated because I was prevented from doing something I thought would be good for me. Priesthood has been a joyful experience. One of my favorite Pauline quotations is, "Eye has not seen nor ear heard, nor has it entered into the human heart what God has in store for those who love God" (based on 1 Corinthians 2:9). We usually apply that quote to the future life, but it is also true for this life.

One of the personal opportunities for an enriched life in the priesthood is the chance that I have to lead a more "soulful" life. Let me explain what I mean by that term. In our secular society we are often unreflective; the needs of simply sustaining life and making a living are so great that what I call soulfulness fades into the background. We often speak of the body and the soul; that is not what I mean by soulfulness. Rather, I mean a dimension of interiority, of being apart, of being my true self. In a secular, consumer society, people tend to lose contact with that soulful dimension. Actually, people don't often think there is anything deeper within us than the psychic life. But biblically there is a clear distinction between *psyche* and *pneuma*, or spirit; and the depth of our soul is what I would call spirit. Today people don't see a difference between psychological counseling and spiritual direction, and so spiritual direction often takes the form of therapy. But there is a deeper level to which we are called, and the function of religion is to keep people in touch with that dimension of themselves—the soulful or the spiritual dimension, the pneumatic. We live in a therapeutic culture today, and for that reason people can actually lose their souls. Does that make sense to you?

Well, to put it succinctly, in the priesthood I have a daily opportunity to save my soul, to experience my soulfulness.

When I was in Dubuque, I would often spend weekends at the New Melleray Monastery, a Cistercian abbey. Later I made several lengthy directed retreats; three were with the Jesuits. Then I began going to Christ in the Desert Monastery in northern New Mexico for thirty- to forty-day retreats. Recently in India I stayed for a week at a Christian Ashram and a week at a Hindu Ashram. Once I made a Zen Catholic Christian retreat here in the States. These opportunities have helped me come to a level of comfort with myself and to deepen my experience of soulfulness.

People today aren't looking for someone who knows a lot about God. They are looking for someone who has met God; for a person who gives witness to a genuine encounter with the spiritual world, who has tapped into the divine. Every priest is called upon to be that type of person.

One of the rewards of being a priest is the extraordinary privilege of having people let us into their lives, making themselves extremely vulnerable. One of the things I have learned when working with people on such an intimate level is that both priests and those to whom they minister have two great needs: one is forgiveness, the other is hope.

Authority isn't as great a problem for religious priests as it is for a diocesan priest, for the reason that a bishop is superior until he is seventy-five, while in religious life leadership changes frequently. If one superior causes a problem, wait a little because he will move on. I did have a temporary problem with the Holy See when I wrote *The Sexual Celibate* in 1975. It was well received and well reviewed, but in 1980 my Provincial received a request from the Vatican to look into its orthodoxy. The Master of the Order stood behind me and the problem was resolved through a simple inquiry. If I were to write on the same topic today, it would be a different book. But at that time there was nothing written in the area.

Marriage could enhance the spiritual life of some priests, but it could also bog a person down in things not essential to the priesthood. Personally I favor the option of a married clergy for diocesan priests. For members of religious communities, celibacy is a natural part of our lives. Dominicans are bound up in community; that is what we choose. If we had chosen marriage, we would have selected another style of life. Celibacy has opened doors for me in terms of my ability to respond to a wider world. I am blessed with not being tied into the concreteness of the life found in the married state. I can make a forty-day retreat or a sabbatical or visit an Ashram or have solitude during the day. In theory those things are possible in married life, but in fact, often not. Celibacy has also enriched me in the many strong relationships I have established. It is a conundrum to the people in our society. But if you see the Hindu celibates in their Ashrams, or look at Gandhi's experience and at other religious traditions around the world, you find people for whom it makes complete sense because it leaves them free. I think the difficulty with celibacy as we practice it is that it is not freely chosen. However, it has given me a freedom to continue to shape and reshape my life; granted, within certain limits. But I don't see it as a confinement in any way. It is an opportunity, not a noose.

I can remember in my early forties taking a look at religious life itself and at my own life, and asking myself the question, "Is this all there is?" Yes, this is all there is; but now I must get about the business of learning *what* this is, and see that there is more to it than meets the eye. One of our men said to me, "I am old enough to have learned that it is always greener on this side of the fence." In a moment of pain, we think it is greener on the other side. It could be just as green, but not greener. Life is what you make of it.

In the body of Christ there are many gifts. We should use all of them. I have no objection to married priests, nor to accepting back some who have left in order to marry, but the real question will always be what is their depth, what is their quality? I do favor allowing national episcopal conferences to take more charge of how to respond to the needs of their geographical regions. What is good for India is not necessarily good for Ecuador.

The demands on priests will continue to grow. More Hispanics will come to the States and initially they will be poor, as were our immigrant grandparents. At the same time our second and third generation Catholic immigrants have moved into the mainstream and are becoming more wealthy. So we will be faced with a stronger gap between the rich and the poor as well as a more multicultural society. We will be expected to reach out to an increasingly wide diversity of people. There is some talk that there might be a schism in the Church. That is unpredictable. But I believe in the Holy Spirit who is the principle of unity as well as the principle of diversity.

Once I was Utopian. I thought I could change the world. My goals have shrunk since then. But I do believe I have made an impact on the lives of some people, have enriched them, made their lives less painful and more meaningful than before. Some years ago there was a movie titled *Julia* in which two German girls who grew up as friends were separated, then came back together for a visit. When they reviewed the tragedies brought on by the Nazis and reflected on how little effect they could have on that regime, one of them said something that I recall when I think I haven't done enough. She said, "We must do today what we can do today." I walk into a library and am overwhelmed by all the books I should read. Then I remember that sentence and tell myself, "You are never going to read them all; if you read one more than you read yesterday, that's OK."

We are living in a time like that described in the *Tale of Two Cities*—the best and the worst of times. There are ideological conflicts, a lack of direction, considerable turmoil. But it is an adventuresome time, and all these things can be seen in terms of opportunities. If we are open to adventure we must be open to the unpredictable. To be a priest today requires a lot of self confidence; we can no longer rely on the structures to support us. But look at what we have: greater flexibility, an appreciation of diversity not known a few years ago, an opportunity to be yourself, to be creative. The priest is no longer put in a straight jacket. I believe that the amount of pain in life is proportionate to the amount of joy; if we close off our capacity for pain, we close off our capacity for joy. The possibilities today of a priest making a genuine contribution to society are endless.

James A. Krings
St. Louis, Missouri

Father Jim Krings was born in 1945 in St. Louis and was ordained for that archdiocese in 1971. He is in residence at Saint Cronan parish and serves as chaplain of Saint Mary Health Center.

Commitment and integrity are important to Father Krings. His deep attachment to his family is touching. He shed tears when he spoke of his love for his sister and for his gifted younger brother, John. The Krings family's care for John is a story in itself.

What happens to priests who leave the ministry for a period of time to examine their commitment and reassess their life goals? Some of them obtain favorable employment because of their extensive education; some marry. Father Krings' story is of a priest who was able to return.

This year I celebrated my twenty-fifth anniversary of ordination. Ten years ago I had a cancer that was pretty severe and very scary. I didn't expect to see my fiftieth birthday or to celebrate my silver jubilee as a priest. Back to that story later.

Shortly after my birth, my mother was pregnant with twins. The first child, Joseph, was stillborn. Not realizing there was a twin, the doctors didn't act swiftly enough delivering the second boy, John, and he was born with brain damage. The diagnosis was cerebral palsy. Some time later my mother had a miscarriage. When I was in sixth grade, she gave birth to my sister Annie. After the difficulties with John, the loss of Joseph, and Mom's miscarriage, we all looked forward to Annie with great joy. She is just a wonderful sister and has become one of my dearest friends.

When I was in grade school, Father James Finley, a priest in our parish, crossed my path. He is a loving, caring person. He once told me that he barely had the intellectual qualifications to get through seminary. Yet he is gentle and kind, as fine a priest as you will find anywhere. The goodness of his life is a marvelous thing to see and restrains somewhat my own political, social, and theological positions. One day I came home from school and told my mother I wanted to be a priest just like Father Finley.

My parents were an inspiration to me, always willing to put aside their own needs to take care of us kids, especially John. When John was very young the doctors said he probably would not live to be fifteen. When he was in the early teens, they said he certainly wouldn't reach twenty. Then he was twenty, and they said there was just no way he could make thirty. He is now forty-seven. I hope that he will make fifty. He has outlived all the predictions, and it is clear that the reason he lives is the incredible care of our parents. He now resides at Mary Queen and Mother Nursing Home.

John entered a nursing home the year I was ordained. That was a very difficult step for Mom and Dad. What a year for them. They had this wonderful joy of my becoming a priest and the sadness of moving John out of the parental home. I know I can't completely understand their sorrow, but it must have been a heavy burden for them to send him to Mary Queen and Mother. Yet I know that if John were still living at home, his world would be very small. It would be Mom and Dad and TV. Now that he is over the shock of being in a nursing home, he is happy, smiles a lot, can make himself understood, and has excellent care. Perhaps because he is a young person among many senile residents, he has become the center of attention. And so his life has blossomed since 1971. His world is bigger and there are a lot of people who care about him.

The priest's retirement home, Regina Cleri, is located on the grounds of Mary Queen and Mother. When Dad and I go to see John, we walk him up to Regina Cleri. Some of the retired priests who knew John when he lived with the family come out to see him. It is wonderful for him and for us. He is our entrée to the retirement home. If not for John, Dad and I would probably rarely go to visit the retired priests, but now we see them often. And it is such a treat for John. They visit with him and give him their blessing.

John is very much at the heart of the difficult and even unhealthy parts of my life, but also of what has been best about me. When John was about a year old and I was four, I became aware of what it meant to grow up with a brother who had cerebral palsy. I saw how he was shunned, how he struggled with difficulties in speaking and walking. I was there when, time and time again, he was taken to the hospital for surgery. But as a little person I wasn't able to understand those things. He was just my brother. And to this day I think that is where I get my righteous outrage when people are treated unfairly, whether they are homosexuals or African-Americans or Jews or anyone else thought to be different. When you grow up seeing your brother shunned and abused and made fun of, it creates in you a sense of anger at any kind of intolerance.

A second result of John's condition was that I learned compassion from the time I was very young. I changed John's diapers up to his teenage years. My closest friends were very understanding about John. We would bring him in his wheelchair to see our games at Saint Joan of Arc School, and when we did that, there was a part of me that said John was really OK. I grew up knowing that men did sensitive things and chores around the house. Of course men cried. Of course men did the dishes. Of course they did their own laundry.

John's condition affected my life in a third way. Because of the attention he needed, my folks couldn't always spend quality time with me, and so I had to fend for myself. The normal letting go that every first-born has to undergo and learn to accept was accentuated by John's unique needs. And I can remember as a little boy I just loved to be alone. I enjoyed playing by myself, I enjoyed solitude. It was in that solitude that I discovered God's bounty and goodness.

A thread in my life, developing during childhood, went back to that love of solitude. I had been ordained ten years when I became enamored of the Trappist Monastery in Ava, Missouri. I had gone there twice a year for a four- or five-day retreat, and now wanted to try a one year sabbatical, living at the monastery. Looking back, it was like trying to force a square peg into a round hole. I talked it over with Archbishop May and several spiritual directors, and they all questioned its wisdom. They said, "You like the retreats, but a year in a monastery is a long time." Archbishop May reluctantly approved my request, and I went to Ava in early July. Within a week I was miserable. After another week I was depressed. I came back, incredibly embarrassed for having failed. All around the archdiocese the word was out that Jim lasted only two weeks in the monastic life. A wonderful friend of mine, Father Bob Krawinkel, invited me to live at his place. Emotionally, I was beginning to come to terms with the fact that I was meant to be an active ministry person and had compulsively driven myself to another way of life. I hadn't been listening to God through my advisors.

When I was teaching in a high school, there was a woman with whom I served as campus minister. Our friendship continued while I was in the monastery and afterward. I was unhappy with a number of things in the archdiocese and with the Church. She was preparing to become a Maryknoll sister, was unhappy about the religious life, and felt let down by the Church. Our disillusionment with our lives and our mutual attraction led us to fall in love. When I was at Saint Cronan's, she was living on the West Coast, running a household for abused women and giving workshops and retreats. I decided to take a leave of absence from the priesthood to live there and try to be of help to the women, but also to sort through with my friend what our relationship meant and to find out if we really did love one another.

I wrote to my Ordinary, Archbishop John May, in December, 1985, with the intention of leaving in January. It was not a kind or tactful letter. I just told him I was going to take a leave and do some work in Washington. At the end, I said, "If you want to talk to me about anything, I will be available." And he actually called me, not through a secretary, but personally, and said he would like to visit with me. Our meeting was just unbelievable. He sat there with the letter and said, "Jim, I'd like to ask you a question. There is a woman in the picture, isn't there?" I said, "Yeah, how did you know?" "Well," he said, "there usually is."

Then, the archbishop added: "Jim, most people who take leaves don't come back. But I think you might. I will write to you, and I am going to keep you on priests' health insurance." I was stunned with his kindness and understanding. I went west and sent him a quick note. He immediately wrote back. Whenever I wrote to Archbishop May he would write back the next day. After five or six months, I wrote him that it wasn't working out, and I thought I should begin negotiating my return, though I probably needed to do the whole year. He wrote and said, "Fine. No problem. You are welcome to come back whenever you are ready."

The decision to disengage from the relationship with my lady friend had come during a retreat. I became ill. I had been a runner and a biker, and suddenly I couldn't do these things any more. I began to be short of breath and my condition continued to get worse. A doctor examined me and said I had an ordinary case of bronchitis. Yet no medication worked, and I finally realized that something really serious was going on. I had gone on retreat near Seattle with my friend to pray and to see where God was leading us. One day, sitting in the back of the retreat house, feeling worse by the hour, I realized that I was preparing for death. I remember vividly thinking, "How do you want to die, Jim?" And it was clear to me that I wanted to die back in St. Louis as a reinstated priest. Just as quickly it occurred to me that if I wanted to die as a reinstated priest, that must also be how I wanted to live. So I began the process of returning to St. Louis.

I went to St. Louis and checked into Barnes Hospital for an examination. Within a day or two the archbishop was on the phone, and he came to visit me. He said, "We need to put these hospital bills on priests' insurance, because you won't have enough to cover them. And cut down on your visitors so you can conserve your strength." Then we had this marvelous conversation. I asked him what was the protocol for being reinstated. He said, "Well, I don't know. You are the one who said you wanted to quit being a priest. If you want to start again, I guess you just start." I asked him if I could start saying Mass right away." "Of course, and when you are ready for an assignment, let me know." I have never been treated more kindly in my life, and this by someone whom I had often thought was running the archdiocese all wrong.

The doctor decided that open lung surgery was needed, and sent me to the Jewish hospital for more tests. A lung biopsy was taken on a Thursday and the results were to be in on Friday morning. By mid-afternoon there was no report, and I judged the results would be bad. Father Bob Krawinkel came to visit me. Then a half dozen doctors came in and surrounded my bed. I was terrified. I asked if Bob could stay while they gave me the report, and they said it would be OK. They told me that I had lung cancer. It was awful to hear that news. Tears were streaming down Bob's cheeks and mine. His remembrance of the incident was that they were telling me I was going to die very soon. How would I tell my parents? Bob's willingness to take on that task still moves me with awe and gratitude for his love and courage.

The diagnosis had come on a Friday. On Monday, Dr. Peter Weiss came in and spoke about various options that could be pursued. "If nothing works," he said, "we can try an experimental program." When we first began the treatment, Peter, a Jewish physician, said, "Your prayer, the prayers of your family, your communities and your friends, will be as important as the medicine I will be using. My medicine will be minimally effective if you don't pray."

I went through chemotherapy, and the side effects were just awful. But slowly I began to recover, and now I have no symptoms. The doctor has publicly called me his miracle case. One day I reminded him how he had given me hope when I visited his office, and he replied, "Yes, you surprised even my most optimistic hopes that you would be cured."

As normal health began to return and the side effects of my treatments diminished, I began to wonder about my next ministry. Several local Catholic high schools invited me to be on their faculties, but I just wasn't interested in returning to teaching. I decided to explore chaplaincy and accepted an offer of Continuing Pastoral Education residency at Saint Mary's. The archbishop agreed that, since I had a lot of experience with illness, it might be the right time to work in that direction. I have been chaplain at Saint Mary's since 1988.

Years later, Archbishop May had a brain tumor. I felt so honored that he let me visit him at his residence. We talked about his cancer and about what he was facing. I shared with him my own fears when I had lung cancer. And then he was moved to the nursing home where my brother John lives. He was almost in a coma and his motor skills were nearly gone. But my last memory of him is when I brought John into the bishop's room and told him that John was my brother. He couldn't make his right hand work, but he managed to raise his left hand and bless John.

Celibacy has obviously been a problem for me, off and on. I can only speak for myself, but I think there is something within me that lacks the ability to commit to any one person, and my healthiest way to live is with a lot of wonderful friends. I am better off, happier, less compulsive, less driven when I don't have an "in love" kind of relationship. When I sorted through my experiences, I realized that no relationship I ever had with one person had worked. I guess I am not willing to give my heart and soul to one other human being. When I talked to my sister and brother-in-law about the woman in Washington, I told them she was not willing to move back here, nor I to move there. We had both put some preconditions on our relationship. And my brother-in-law said that committed relationships can't have those kind of preconditions and that marriage would not be good for me. He is right. I have no track record that says I could live in the married state. So my associations with women tend to lead in an unhealthy direction, into a blind alley. Celibacy is the right choice for me. Like an alcoholic who says he can't drink any more, I have to be humble and admit that I can't let myself get into a situation where any one woman would become central in my life. It would always wind up the same way, with me leaving the relationship and hurting the woman. Counseling has led me to my understanding of celibacy as I have described it.

I love the scripture passage that says there are different gifts for different folks. I have never been a pastor and have no desire to be a pastor. I did enjoy the work in high schools despite my initial apprehensions. I love being a hospital chaplain. I love writing. I savor teaching Bible classes. I appreciate the chance to do so many different things. I also love the opportunity I have for solitude. Another thing that has been good for me in recent years involves my cycling vacations in Ireland, Russia, and France.

I have experienced a great deal of tragedy. One year when I was teaching school at Dubourg, a teacher and seven students died from car accidents, a homicide, and cancer. Somehow I was selected to announce the first group of deaths. That began the pattern, and I had to continue making the announcements through the rest of the year. In addition, working at this hospital I have experienced many deaths.

I love Vatican II, but I think we have lost some things since then. All the resurrection, empty tomb, butterfly theology is nice, but I think funerals should also include grief and sadness. So I guess my specialty in the area of death is my ability to show compassion, to suffer with people. It is interesting that being in the presence of someone at the moment of death is not nearly as jarring as hearing about a death over the phone. Somebody calls and says, "So and so just died." That hits me harder than when I am in the room and see the person pass away. My experience is that they are not really gone. The heart is not beating, the lungs are not pumping, but the spirit of that living person is still there.

When I was ordained, I thought that the life of a priest would be so easy. I was surprised at how hard it was to make decisions. We need to recognize that life is supposed to be hard. It always involves the cross. I have the impression that we are most happy when we are living the cross faithfully.

But the cross is supposed to hurt. And so the hardness of making decisions and of difficult meetings is just the cross.

With all the difficult times, there have been unbelievable moments of joy in the priesthood. Right now, my greatest joy is just being alive. For my twenty-fifth anniversary, we celebrated one of the regular Sunday Masses at the parish. I invited a few families to come, those who had nurtured me in a special way. But the real party was that night at the ballpark. Four hundred people came in my honor and watched the Cardinals play. It was pure fun. My name was on the scoreboard.

I do believe I have made a difference in many lives. Because of my own perfectionism, I don't think I have made as much of a difference as I should have. But I see some of my students who have made a decision to leave McDonnell Douglas because they were making arms. They learned something in my justice class. In Saint Cronan's, the previous pastor, the present pastor, and I have established a place for disenfranchised Catholics. We are Roman, we are faithful to Church teaching, yet political activists, feminists, gays and lesbians have found a home that is true to their personal beliefs but also connects them to the world Church and to Rome. These are people who would have bailed out of the Church long ago had it not been for us at Saint Cronan's.

There is a young man from my parish right now who gives indications that he would be a wonderful priest. I talked to his family about it. They are cautious because of the times, but I continue to discuss vocation with Sam. If a young man has an inner calling and is met with kindness, compassion, thoughtfulness, and truthfulness, he will go to the seminary.

I can say that it has been a surprise to discover how wonderful is the life of a priest. I have been led by God through difficult relationships and through illness to a delightful freedom. Concerns about my ministry all died on a hospital bed.

VII. I Have Been in Danger

Priests Who Survived Unusual Difficulties

THREE TIMES I HAVE BEEN BEATEN WITH STICKS; ONCE I WAS STONED; THREE TIMES I HAVE BEEN SHIP- WRECKED, AND ONCE I HAVE BEEN IN THE OPEN SEA FOR A NIGHT AND DAY; CONTINUALLY TRAVELING, I HAVE BEEN IN DANGER FROM RIVERS, IN DANGER FROM BRIGANDS, IN DANGER FROM MY OWN PEOPLE AND IN DANGER FROM THE GENTILES, IN DANGER IN THE TOWNS AND IN DANGER IN THE OPEN COUNTRY, IN DANGER AT SEA AND IN DANGER FROM PEOPLE MASQUERADING AS BROTHERS; I HAVE WORKED WITH UNSPARING ENERGY, FOR MANY NIGHTS WITHOUT SLEEP; I HAVE BEEN HUNGRY AND THIRSTY, AND OFTEN ALTOGETHER WITHOUT FOOD OR DRINK; I HAVE BEEN COLD AND LACKED CLOTHING. AND, BESIDES ALL THE EXTERNAL THINGS, THERE IS, DAY IN AND DAY OUT, THE PRESSURE ON ME OF MY ANXIETY FOR ALL THE CHURCHES.

—2 CORINTHIANS 11:25-28

Seldom do those who serve the Lord intentionally seek out hardships or compete with Saint Paul in his difficulties. Yet, those who choose to serve with love often run into obstacles that really challenge them. Overcoming those obstacles can be disheartening. The stories of the next three priests are highlighted for the joyful manner in which they met their difficulties and the relief and comfort they experienced in their struggles.

Raymond B. Kemp
Washington, D.C.

Father Kemp was born in 1941 and was ordained in 1967 for the Archdiocese of Washington, D.C. Currently he is the coordinator of a program known as "Preaching the Just Word," a project of the Woodstock Theological Center of Washington, D.C.

Father Kemp, who has spent most of his priestly life in parishes, speaks in stentorian tones, perhaps to conceal a heart full of compassion for the downtrodden, the misunderstood, and the neglected. His story of the religious and societal conflicts during the turbulent sixties, several of which he participated in as a central figure, recalls with great vividness the heat, anger, and frustration of those heady days.

Once he is convinced the job is needed, Father Kemp is not a man who shirks from the task because it is difficult. He is one who dares to tread where others have not gone before. He is a man who solves problems rather than points fingers. Too, he is one who demonstrates that the priesthood offers opportunities for a man to develop and use his talents in unlimited and unsuspected ways.

I grew up in Saint Michael's in Silver Spring, Maryland. My parents gave generously to the Church, and the parish was the center of their lives. It was their respect for clergy and religious that encouraged me to respond to a vocation. Priests were always in and out of our classrooms and in our home, and I got a sense that they cared about us and were worthy of emulation.

By the sixth or seventh grade I knew I wanted to be a priest. After high school I entered the seminary at Saint Charles College, Catonsville, Maryland. Those were pre-Council days, 1959 and 1960, the days of Pius XII. Priests on the faculty told us about this wonderful new movement called Young Christian Workers. We also heard about the

Catholic Family Movement and Cardinal Joseph Cardijn in Belgium, who taught the See, Judge, and Act program. There was a real sense of hope, of being able to relate to Jesus in life situations. We were convinced that our life as future priests could be very productive.

After two years at Saint Charles I was sent to the oldest seminary in the country for philosophy, Saint Mary Seminary on Paca Street in Baltimore. I was highly impressed by a Sulpician who told us about the development of a new community between Washington and Baltimore called Columbia, and how they were planning to mix races in something of a model community. A lot of things were beginning to happen in the United States, including the Civil Rights movement. At Paca Street, we were in the heart of the inner city, the ghetto. African-Americans lived just beyond the walls of the seminary. The work of Martin Luther King, Jr. and the vision of Pope John XXIII were core elements in my life. Liturgy was being reformed and becoming participative. These things gave me a picture of what a priest should be.

Theology was a mixed bag. We had some professors teaching the old, some teaching what they thought was the new, and others so progressive we didn't know where they were coming from. But it was an electric atmosphere. We saw a relevance of religion, a relevance of the Church. It was an exciting time in our lives. We read, we studied, we talked theological topics at night sessions. We discussed what was going on in the world. We thought we were going to be the ones who would bring about a brand new Church.

Cardinal O'Boyle, Archbishop of Washington, called us all into his office the day before ordination and said, "You guys have learned a lot of things in the seminary. I want you to forget it all and preach the Creed." We laughed. Little did we know that was a shot across the bow that would come into play in about a year when *Humanae Vitae* appeared.

Right after ordination I worked for six or eight weeks in a camp run by the Saint Vincent de Paul Society for black inner city kids in southern Maryland. Then I was assigned to Saint Augustine's. The big mentors in my life there were George

Gingras, the pastor, now deceased, an incredible guy who was on the mayor's Human Relations Committee, and Geno Baroni, an activist from Pennsylvania.

Possibly all of this background resulted in my having a commitment to minorities, especially to African-Americans. There is a great spirit in those engaged in the struggle. Martin Luther King did as much for me as a lot of folks in the Catholic tradition by saying and showing what ministry can be about.

In April of 1968, when I was at Saint Augustine's, Martin Luther King was assassinated. The heart and soul of the neighborhood and of the parish in which I was the junior associate simply blew up. A large crowd, gathered at the Poor People's campaign headquarters just a block away from the rectory, heard the news that King had been shot. When it was reported that he had died, a group of five thousand started to march down Fourteenth Street, a hundred yards from the rectory, heading for downtown D.C. They were really mad. They had fire in their eyes and in their hearts. Stokely Carmichael, an activist at the time, caught them about a block south of U Street and said, "Let's go home. Martin King would not want us to have this anger." He literally turned them around by the force of his speech, but unfortunately he didn't calm them. They marched back up Fourteenth Street toward the church and it was a full blown riot. The city burned for three days.

That night two young African-American teenagers sat up with us. They said, "You think that because you wear the collar you can walk anywhere? Not tonight you can't. We want to see you live till tomorrow." They stayed with us, and we listened to the news reports until 3:00 a.m. Just before dawn, we stepped out onto Fourteenth Street. You would think you were in Dresden. The whole area was on fire. The smell of tear gas was in the air. We thought it was over, but as soon as the sun came up, it started again. The city continued to burn, not only Fourteenth Street, but H Street and other neighborhoods. It was a great eye-opener for Raymond B. Kemp. I learned that even a priest can't be secure inside the church. Jesus worked in the streets. We had to be in the streets. I learned that our influence in the streets can't be measured by what is going on in our church or our school. We have to do something in an organized way for the poorer folks of this parish. I simply got pushed in the direction of starting neighborhood and community organizations, working to help people take control of their own destiny. I spent the summer of 1968 applying for federal and local grants to promote summer programs in our own school and others. We did get substantial grants; people called it refrigeration money; that is, funds to keep the African-Americans cool. We were able to build community organizations that have lasted ten or fifteen years.

In 1968, three weeks after King's assassination, I got arrested with King's associates. A group of us clergy were asked by the National Welfare Rights Organization to attend a candlelight vigil on the Capitol grounds. We joined it and were arrested. I spent a night in jail with the National Welfare Rights mothers. When the pastor woke up, his two associates were nowhere to be found. We had called Father Baroni of the Office of Urban Affairs and told him what happened. He informed the pastor that his assistants were in jail. The pastor said, "Let them stay there a while." But he and Cardinal O'Boyle gave us good support and we were released.

Something else happened in 1968. *Humanae Vitae* was published. I was doing inner city ministry and dealing with the civil rights movement. Then the papal document burst on the scene. It was preceded by some decrees on catechesis about sexuality, including artificial birth control, issued by Bishop Shehan of Baltimore and Cardinal O'Boyle of Washington. A group of seventy-five priests met to discuss those decrees, which seemed to be a trial balloon in anticipation of *Humanae Vitae*. They signed a document stating that they believed people could use birth control conscientiously. A few days later *Humanae Vitae* was published, reinforcing what the bishops were saying. The cardinal contacted the seventy-five priests and told us, "Cease and desist." Forty-one did not, including yours truly. The pressure was on. First I was arrested, then I was with a dissident group of priests who have a brouhaha over a papal encyclical.

O'Boyle suspended the lot of us. The suspensions were at different levels. I and several others were suspended from hearing confessions. Some were suspended from preaching, teaching, and hearing confessions. The two leaders, Father Jack Corrigan, who preached at my first Mass, and Father Joe O'Donohue, who had a brother in Maryknoll, were also suspended from saying Mass. The cardinal restricted my suspension to hearing confessions because, he said, I was young and was probably influenced by the older guys. By that time fifteen or more had already left the priesthood.

After about a year, four of us from the inner city went to O'Boyle and said, "Your Eminence, our parishioners are well beyond the *Humanae Vitae* squabble. They know that we are in trouble because we disagreed with you. Is there some way we can come to a compromise?" We created acceptable language and signed it. Our suspensions were lifted. Twelve other priests remained under suspension, and that was not resolved until the case went to Rome.

A few assignments earlier, when I had helped out at a Josephite parish in Baltimore, I had become acquainted with Fathers Phil and Dan Berrigan, two brothers who were activists against the war in Vietnam. They asked me join them in trashing Dow Chemical Company for making napalm. I resisted because of my ministry. However, the day they poured blood on the documents at Catonsville I did pick up Dan from the D.C. jail at the request of Phil. All in all, 1968 was a pretty wild year.

The Church was not very hospitable at that time, and many of my friends were leaving the priesthood. It seemed like everyone was jumping ship. But a bunch of us decided to stay. I resisted entreaties from the Berrigans to do the Vietnam thing, telling them my call was clear: I was going to work with the poor, with African-Americans, right in the inner city. During that rough, scarred time, two things kept me alive: one was the eucharist, breaking both the bread and the word; the other was looking at the struggle of six generations since the emancipation of African-Americans, and helping them try to make their mark and become equal members of this society.

So I redoubled my efforts in the neighborhood. I knew Saul Alinsky, the community organizer from Chicago. Father Jack Egan, another organizer, was a good friend of mine. However, I took a slightly different road. My interest turned to public education, and in 1971 I talked myself into running for the D.C. Board of Education, which had only been in existence for three or four years. Cardinal O'Boyle called me in and said, "You can't do this. They will kill you. They will kill me. They will kill the Church." And I said, "This is a natural outgrowth of my work in the neighborhood, and I want to do it." He didn't forbid me to run for the board, but his not wanting me to do it hit the paper and gave me more publicity than I would have had otherwise. That may be one of the reasons I won.

Time would tell that the cardinal was right. They did kill us. I was involved in too many things—the neighborhood groups, the public school program, and the parish. The whole thing eventually became too much.

The first two years on the Board of Education were interesting, though. Marion Barry, the mayor of Washington, was chairman. We were trying to save the D.C. public schools, which in 1966 were in abominable shape. We gave one superintendent a rough time. Marion Barry understood better than the superintendent what was going on in the schools. Finally the superintendent quit, and we interviewed applicants for his job. A lady from Chicago applied. Three of us could not see how she could possibly work out and said so. The sister of Whitney Young, former Urban League president, told me that this woman could not be superintendent of anything. I repeated what I heard in what I thought was a confidential meeting. It ended up in the newspapers and, of course, Young's sister had to deny it. The lady got the appointment. Within a few months the board room was like a battle ground. During that time there were pickets in front of my church. At this point church work didn't look so bad after all. I was getting reamed out. City politics were a mess. I was being whipped. The meetings were lasting till one or two in the morning. I was having all kinds of second thoughts.

In 1976 I became co-pastor of the parish and turned my attention to parish work. Two plants, Saint Paul's and Saint Augustine's, had been merged. Ten percent of the parish were over eighty years of age. The place had emptied out while we were doing inner-city organizing. We had to rebuild the parish. We brought in a gospel choir, began to develop the liturgy, and people started showing up again. Word of mouth began to build. The place started to take off.

I didn't know it at the time, but I was burned out. There were temptations to marry; but always the eucharist, always the priesthood, always the picture of Christ kept holding me in. I sought direction and help. I had seen guys leave, had seen what their lives were like after they left, and that was enough to say to me, whatever your troubles, whatever your failings, there is so much that you can do inside this Church. Stay with it.

I had written a book on the Rite of Christian Initiation of Adults (RCIA). In 1978 and 1979 Christianne Brusselmans, a catechist, and Father Jim B. Dunning of Seattle, who was president of the North American Forum on the Catechumenate, enlisted me in speaking to parishes on how to implement the RCIA program. I quickly found a second career in the early 80s, going around the country giving workshops. About that time, Archbishop Hickey, the new ordinary of Washington, created the position of Secretary of Parish Life and Worship and handed me the job.

It was clear that things were turning in the life of the Church, and also that the cardinal was turning. He was getting assignments from Rome, including the investigation of Archbishop Hunthausen in Seattle. The climate was beginning to change. Orthodoxy was becoming the priority. The Josephites left a parish in 1986, and Father Ray East and I were asked to take over Holy Comforter-Saint Cyprian's in the fall of 1986. East is the man who succeeded Father George Stallings when George began the schism with his own black church. (Stallings was ordained a bishop by an Old Catholic bishop.) It was a sociologist's dream, a parish with many alcoholics and drug addicts.

We began to preach about VD, violence, and drugs, and a new kind of epidemic where kids were shooting up and shooting each other. Father Ray East started something there that evangelical churches do, a program built around a symbolic gesture called "opening the doors of the church." It is done during the Sunday liturgy right after the homily. The presider or somebody goes to the microphone and says, "Will the ushers open the doors of the church." It is a symbol that we are letting people and the Spirit in. We are not going to lock the Spirit out. Then the presider or usher says,

> "Some of you who are sitting here are members of this church; many of you are not. Many of you are here for the first time or have been here only a couple of times, but are looking for a church home. Any of you who are willing to acknowledge that the Spirit might be moving you to seek your home here, let the Spirit move you off the pew. Come up into this sanctuary."

When they get there, we ask them their names, and what they want from the Church. It is like an old-fashioned altar call. That simple program has been tremendously successful and changed my whole idea about how effective word and sacrament really are. Through all my travails, I get restored to the priesthood and restored to a sense of the vitality of the Church when I see both young and old people come forward at that call.

In two and a half years we put 250 to 300 people through a twenty-eight-day drug treatment program. We got Catholic Charities to redo their whole operation for the homeless. We began to see ourselves as a supportive community which was helping people in transition from treatment back to the real world. Cardinal Hickey came and read his pastoral on drugs and violence from our pulpit, then encouraged other bishops to attack the problems of violence and drugs in the inner cities. It has been a fascinating experience for me.

At the end of my six-year term, Jesuit Father Jim Connor, who runs the Woodstock Theological Center, asked me to help Father Walter Burghardt coordinate his retirement program, "Preaching the Just Word." I turned him down twice.

The third time I went to the cardinal and asked what he thought. He said, "It is you. Take it." Father Jack Egan also told me to go for it, so I did. We have been all over the country. We've presented over fifty retreats. More than 2,100 priests have made the program.

Now, four years into this program, I'm not sure what is next. But, having seen much of the church in the U.S. and a little exposure in Australia, Canada, and Jamaica, I am terribly impressed by the unstinting labors of very good men who are pastoring and preaching in our parishes. We have a treasure trove of priests. I only hope that my generation and those a few years younger than I can continue to keep the flame alive so that others might be attracted to this kind of ministry.

The real joy of my priesthood is that I can still sit down and say, "Jesus, I am with you." And he will reply, "I am with you, too, regardless of it all, regardless of any infidelity on your part. I want to wrap you in my love and keep you alive for all the possibilities ahead." It is a consolation for me to hear that and to have that idea reinforced by a lot of people who have suffered much more than I have. That picture of Jesus as comforter, as friend, as encourager, stays with me.

We priests have to ask ourselves the question, "What are you doing to encourage people to imitate what you are called to do?" The first time someone asked that of me, I said, "I am afraid I have been whining and griping so much it's easy to see that someone would judge I'm not happy in my priesthood. So I had better stop what I am doing and begin to encourage youngsters." Since I have been assisting Father Walter Burghardt, I have had four young people work for me. Two of the four are now in the seminary. One is studying for the Jesuits, the other is at the North American College studying for his diocese. We are fighting stiff odds these days, with all the swirl we are in. It is hard to sell a male celibate priesthood in a culture that does not value long term commitment.

Another thing we have to do in terms of the crisis in vocations is to involve the laity. Father can't do it all. We have evolved an impossible job description for priests. Priests have to have study time, time away, time for relaxation and recreation. We need to define the job so that it becomes clear how we are to achieve our principal task of giving the message of the gospel.

One thing that has surprised me about the priesthood is this: even with all the media hype telling us that we are under the control of the pope and the archbishop, I have the notion that it is the one job in the whole world where you can shape what you do, in response to what you feel God is calling you to do. This gets some of us in trouble, because we don't know enough to say it's time to go to bed, or to take a rest, or take a day off. But in the priesthood you can pursue your own best instincts about preaching, about organizing people, about how you spend your time. It has been a great joy for me to be able to work with such a variety of persons—city people, university people, chancery people, and the working class. There is no place and no time that a priest can't be in a position to help people.

Have I made a difference? That is a great question, and the answer is yes. When I go to bed at night, I take to bed with me the stories of all the people who have entered my life, for whose lives I have made a difference. I could give you a litany of people who have said I have made a difference in their lives. And that brings me an enormous amount of satisfaction. I can give you a list of kids I had in class, or of priests whom I have touched in this work, and six months later I get a note of thanks saying, "The time spent with you in conversation or in confession was time well spent." Or the guy who says, "You changed my life in terms of how I looked at the priesthood." I don't know a job in the whole world where we can make such a difference, because in this work people open up to us, they are so honest and above board with us. That is why I don't see myself ever doing anything else. If I last long enough to become an octogenarian, I hope I can still be working, and working hard.

My tough experiences have been good for my priesthood. I can look at my vocation as having been saved by African-Americans. I can see it as being saved by the civil rights struggle. I can see it as having been saved by the wonders of getting a parish organized. I can see it as having been saved by developing that therapeutic community which was so full of alcohol and drug abuse. I can see it as having been saved through "Preaching the Just Word" retreats. It is all Jesus Christ. In all the situations I've just described, Christ in his dying and rising has kept me in the priesthood.

Robert L. Marciano
Warwick, Rhode Island

Father Marciano suddenly faced a problem in his work that most of us would find devastating. Through a horrendous error of identification, he was publicly and falsely accused as a pedophile. Shattered by the blow, his reputation in ruins, Father Bob met the problem head-on.

Father Marciano has a surprisingly mature outlook on life. He has balance and poise, a deep commitment to the priesthood, and a delightful sense of humor, all of which he needed when facing the agony of the publicity surrounding his accusation.

He was born in Providence, Rhode Island, and was ordained for the Diocese of Providence in 1983. He was recently appointed pastor of Saint Rose of Lima's in Warwick.

I must say, it was my parents who fostered in me a love for the priests and sisters. They were almost a part of the family and were considered our best friends. My parents had a deep respect for authority, whether civil or religious. They said we were blessed with the gift of faith and should never take it for granted. They said we should never sacrifice our integrity or our honesty. Once you lose those qualities you never get them back. Years later I was to be reminded of that warning. When I was in school, I talked over all kinds of things with my mother. One thing I remember so well, she told me that you never have a license to be unkind. You can be strict or stern, but never unkind.

I went to the Bishop Hendricken High School, run by the Irish Christian Brothers. I admired the brothers deeply and thought of joining them. In my sophomore or junior year, together with five classmates, I signed up for a vocations explorer day in New York. But somehow the day did not attract me. Actually, I was dating steady and had given thought to being a veterinarian. I just wanted to settle down, get married, and have a family. However, I was intrigued by the priests I had met.

I decided to try the seminary. My folks were shocked, but receptive. They thought it would be a lonely life with hard burdens, and they only wanted me to be happy. They said to me, "You choose whatever you feel is right. Just do the best you can and we will always be behind you." The seminary offered an open study program in which you could attend classes at Providence College. I opted for that and was accepted. As I packed my cases my mother was crying. I told her I was only going a few blocks down the street, but she saw it as being a million miles from home. I didn't unpack for two weeks, thinking the idea would pass. It took two years for my parents to finally accept my calling. When they saw how happy I was, they were happy, too. Don't forget they are Italians, and Italians are always looking for at least fifty grandchildren.

I made some wonderful friends in the seminary, but also had a rude awakening. I found that all priests didn't measure up to the parish priests I grew up with. The seminary was in turbulence during the 70s. Some guys were saying Mass on tree stumps in front of the chapel. That sort of thing turned me off. I came to the seminary with the conviction that the eucharist was to be the center of my life. Next thing I knew some of the faculty would say, "If you don't want to go to Mass, don't bother. Stay in bed and say your prayers." At the time I thought there was something wrong with me. I finally realized the guys saying these things were not happy. They were miserable, and it showed. It was a crisis time and the disenchantment experienced by some of the priests splashed over onto the seminarians. I decided not to continue and confided my decision to a classmate. I still remember his saying, "If you aren't happy with what is going on, don't run away from it. Get into it. Be the best priest you can be and change the situation." I decided he was right. I was just looking for an excuse to get away from something I knew I had do to. And so I stayed.

While making a retreat in preparation for the diaconate, I began to have qualms and wasn't sure I was worthy of this calling. My prayer life after all those years in seminary was not the best. I went back to Saint John's and told my spiritual director that I couldn't accept holy orders because I wasn't worthy. He said, "Of course you aren't. None of us are. The day you feel worthy of being a priest is the day you had better get out." That settled me down, and I have never had an unhappy day in the priesthood. Difficult days, yes, but not unhappy ones. I have felt peace at the strangest times, even at the bedside of a child dying with a brain tumor. That was a sad occasion but I was at peace because I knew that as a priest I could help that family survive the crisis in their lives.

When I was to receive my first assignment, the bishop called me in, went over the personnel record and asked what kind of parish I would like. I described it to him, and he sent me to a parish that was the exact opposite. I told him I was obedient and would go wherever he sent me. He said, "I don't hear that word often these days." I am not blindly obedient, and sometimes I react strongly to orders. I questioned authority when I was in the seminary and was asked to do some strange things I didn't agree with.

Besides the obvious influence that my parents and the parish priests had on me, I think the thing that led me to the priesthood was the way in which people let priests into the deepest part of their lives. We are with them at birth, marriage, and death. When a priest first asked me why I wanted to be a priest, I told him that I wanted to help people. He said, "You can help people running a gas station." So I began to rethink my motives and found that what I really wanted to do was to help people toward their eternal salvation. I wanted to spend my life doing something that will outlast me. I knew I had ability and could easily earn a good living. But material things don't last.

I really have a full life. I teach in our school, work with the youth and the elderly, and serve as a military chaplain for the reserves. It's a wonderful experience being in touch with people at all levels. I marry couples, baptize their children, then join them on the road for the rest of their lives. The job of a priest as I see it is to bring to people the human face of the divine. I try to show the happy side of the priesthood. Every now and then a young man will enter the seminary because of what he sees in me, and that gives me a special lift, a wonderful feeling of accomplishment.

I say that I aim to show the happy side of the priesthood, because there is always a rough side. Most of the hard times for me were in the seminary. For a while I thought I was in the wrong church because of the spiritual directors we had. But I tried to keep my balance, and shortly after I was ordained, six boys entered the seminary from the parish where I was assigned. The bishop took notice of that and made me chairman of the vocation board.

I wouldn't say celibacy has never been a problem for me. It is not easy to give up a family, but I realize that is part of the vocation that God gave me. Because it is right for the Church, it is right for me. Once you fall in love with someone, in this case the Lord, no one else quite measures up. The same is true with married life. Once a man meets a woman and truly loves her, it is not difficult to live out the marriage commitment because no one else will measure up. Next week I'll be at a National Guard conference for chaplains. On those occasions the priests and ministers often discuss celibacy. At the last meeting a black minister said to me, "It is amazing what happens when Catholic priests come here and go to the chapel on base. There is an instant affection for them. They have dinner invitations to the homes of people they don't even know." That is true, and I think celibacy has something to do with it. We belong to and are a part of every family.

The roughest time of all came through some allegations made about me in the media. It happened in March 1993, when I was at Saint Kevin's. I had gone to City Hall in Warwick to offer a prayer for Saint Joseph's Day. I came back to the parish to pack my bags and get on a plane to Mount Saint Mary Seminary in

Emmitsburg, where I was to preach a lenten mission to the seminarians. My secretary said to me, "Father, you better sit down. One of the Boston television channels had your picture on the news twice yesterday and again this morning with the wrong name under the picture. It is the name of a priest who was some time ago charged with child molestation." I knew the man. He was about ten years older than I, and his first name was Robert. I always went by Father Bob to my parishioners and the kids, and most of them didn't even know my last name. Calls were coming to the rectory. The school kids were in tears. Father Bob has been arrested. How do you get the feathers back when the pillow has been broken?

It was a nightmare, and it was a case of pure carelessness. The charges had been made against this man back in 1973 when I was in high school. Printed under my picture in the diocesan directory is my ordination date, 1983. When the picture was aired for the first time, a classmate in Boston called the station and told them they had the wrong man. The story aired again, and he called them a second time. It appears they were just churning around old news because they needed filler. They finally stopped the story when my attorney presented them with the facts. We had documented proof that they kept running it after being notified of their error. At first they said they hadn't received the correction. Then they admitted getting the message, but blamed it on an internal breakdown. I talked to our bishop. He advised me to keep it quiet. He said, "If you sue you will just be tarred and feathered all the more by the repeated news stories." I said, "No. I'll take the risk of more publicity. I want my reputation back, and I want a public retraction."

Peter McGinn and his law firm were most helpful. They told me I could ask for anything I wanted, and I would get it. But I didn't want to become a millionaire over someone's carelessness. We began legal proceedings. I asked for three things. First, the station should do several television specials on some good priests. I would pick the priests; they would do the specials. They agreed and did an excellent film on my first pastor, Father Blain, following him around with a camera.

They also did a show about priesthood called "Making a Difference." Second, I asked that the head of the station, not a subaltern, make a public apology. Third, I asked for a monetary sum to be used as I saw fit. We got all three without an argument. During and after the proceedings, the support of the people was just great. I had bags of mail: "We love you." "We would never believe that of you." Yet I couldn't take a chance. My father gave me my name. He is a hard working honest man. He has not disgraced it, nor has my brother. The TV station was not going to disgrace it. I wanted the record cleared.

I believe that a priest today has to be a man of prayer; everything else flows from that. I have to block out time every day, head over to the church, and spend time before the Blessed Sacrament. The priest is the one who calls people to holiness and challenges them to a better life. To do that he first has to be committed to regular prayer. I think we are the last respected voice of morality left.

One of the things I enjoy most about my life is preaching. I take seriously the fact that I have a captive audience every Sunday, and I begin to work on my homily on the weekend before I am to preach. I use stories and try to keep in touch with daily issues. In a previous parish I put a piece in the Sunday bulletin, asking for suggestions on topics people wanted to hear from the pulpit. That worked out well. There are hot issues and they have to be discussed even though they ruffle feathers. I talked on abortion once. A very angry lady came up to me and said, "You have no right to tell me that to be a good Catholic I have to be pro-life." I took off my nameplate and gave it to her and said, "Here, you be the pastor. You talk about the issues important to the Church. That is what I have been doing, and when I stop doing that, you had better get rid of me." She said, "All right, but you were a little strong about it." And I replied, "If you went to a doctor and he said you have cancer, but it is okay, you can keep on smoking, I hope you get a new doctor. If you come to a priest and he says

abortion is bad, but it's OK to do it once in a while, get yourself a new priest." She is my greatest supporter now, and
comes to daily Mass. Abortion, divorce, and other sensitive
topics shouldn't be regular grist for the homily, but they must
be dealt with or we are not doing our job as preachers.

We seem to be on the edge of a huge self-examination of
who we are as Church. I am optimistic about vocations in the
future. In the sixties and the seventies we neglected to invite
men to become priests. Now I see those invitations being
given. Twice a year, in my homily, I stress our responsibility
to encourage vocations. We used to hear that Catholic education was free. It has never been free. It has always been costly
to Catholic families. Years ago families gave not only of their
money, but of their flesh and blood. They gave their sons and
daughters to serve the Church. Now that Catholics have
stopped giving that treasure, we have fewer sisters and
priests to staff the schools, and we need to raise tuition, sometimes, unfortunately, beyond the ability of many to pay it.

News articles tell us there are homosexuals in the seminary;
some even say that the seminaries are full of them. The latter
is incorrect. The former is not a problem. As long as we are
calling human beings to the priesthood, it is inevitable that
some would have that sexual orientation. The Church's teaching is definite: orientation is not sinful, acting out the orientation is. Homosexual celibates have the same obligation as het-
erosexual celibates. I do get a bit tired of the priests who fall
in love with a woman, then tell us that they never really
understood celibacy. Every seminarian has a full eight years
to deal with that question, far more time than married couples give to explore the nature of a lifelong commitment to a
spouse.

What some call a priest shortage appears to me to involve
an identity crisis. Somehow we have lost our sense of self-
esteem as priests. When we get that back, when we are again
proud of who we are and are supposed to be, the vocation
crisis will be largely solved. If priests have two qualities, men

will be attracted to the seminary. First, the priest must be happy in his vocation and proud of it. Second, he needs to preside at the liturgy with reverence, seeing it as a vehicle to the divine. We priests have a chance to be a sign of contradiction to society, to represent Christ. The reason people followed Jesus was because he stood out in the crowd, not because he went along with society. Someone said to me the other day, "I think you priests forget the power you have. We call you to the hospital, to our homes, to pray with us, and we see you as powerful men with rare gifts to represent Christ in our life." I think, too, that we have to make sure the priests already ordained are happy and fulfilled in their work. I would like to see more priests back in the schools. That is the front line for young people and that is where the energy is.

John F. Carney
Tijeras, New Mexico

Father John Carney was born June 25, 1946, in New York City. After attending Catholic schools from elementary to college, all in New York, he spent twenty successful years in the U.S. Army. Following retirement, he studied for the priesthood and was ordained in 1991 for the Archdiocese of Santa Fe. Father Carney is currently pastor of Holy Child parish in Tijeras, just east of Albuquerque, as well as vocation director for the archdiocese.

Father Carney's youthful appearance belies the fact that he has already completed one career. He is a dynamic man who is encouraged about the recovery the archdiocese has made since the nadir of its reputation, and especially about the amazing increase in local vocations during the past few years. The seismic upheavals of the 80s and early 90s involving clergy molestation of youth and sexual misconduct in general found their epicenter in the Archdiocese of Santa Fe, with 150 lawsuits brought against priests. Father Carney tells the story openly and honestly. Archbishop Michael Sheehan, of Santa Fe, adds further details.

We may find it beyond comprehension why a man trained in the military would accept the job of vocation director when his diocese was awash in charges of unspeakable behavior. Here is a dimension of the priesthood that is rarely found and hopefully rarely needed.

My parents, natives of Ireland, came to the States in the late 1920s. They met and married in New York City. My mother is now eighty-five and still very active. She spends her weekends with me in Tijeras, and the people love her. Having a mother in the parish makes the pastor more approachable, I think. And the people are so kind, partly because of her. They bring in all sorts of food after the weekend

Masses. One Sunday my mother said "You must have made the people angry with your homily." I wondered why. "Because they didn't bring you more than a couple tins of rolls this morning."

I was a good student in high school, but did poorly in college, being more interested in parties, beer, and young women, though I managed to scrape through and graduate in 1967. I had begun in pre-med, but found it took too much work, so I enrolled in political science classes where, with my glib tongue, I could talk my way through the exams.

The Reserve Officers Training Corps was a required program, and I fell in love with it. The armed forces were in Vietnam, and I looked forward to serving there in the army. At graduation I was commissioned a Second Lieutenant, Infantry Officer in the regular army, and spent the next twenty years in the service. I went to various army schools: infantry, ranger, airborne, and others. Then I spent a year in Vietnam as a platoon leader in an airborne combat unit. From 1969 to 1971 I served as Operations Officer, Company Commander, and in other positions in Germany before returning to Vietnam. On that second stretch of duty I was an adviser to the Army of the Republic, Vietnam. When the northern part of the country fell to the Communists on May 30, 1972, I wound up in Germany again. Later I was assigned to recruiting duty at the University of Southern Colorado, then to the Command and General Staff College at Fort Leavenworth, Kansas, the school for future battalion and brigade level officers. I graduated there in 1980 and worked at the Pentagon for the Defense Intelligence Agency, together with the CIA, providing information to the War Room (the National Military Command Center). I had the job of briefing people in the government including, occasionally, Casper Weinberger, Secretary of Defense at that time. After a little more than three years, now a lieutenant colonel, I was assigned as an executive officer to a brigade in Korea. For the two years before my retirement in 1987, I was an adviser to a National Guard brigade in Decatur, Illinois.

Although I went to Catholic schools through college, my faith was not central to my life. I was what might be called a lazy Catholic. In the service I had Roman Catholic on my dog tags and always went to confession and communion before a fire fight when I knew I might be killed—just a little extra insurance. But the Lord wasn't that important to me. My interests were in parties, girlfriends, cars, money, and success in the military. When I was about thirty, I finally realized that life was something more than those things, so I began to go to church again. I became active in the parishes where I lived and did volunteer work for their programs. When I came home at night after helping out, I would feel so good. I didn't realize it at that time, but God was using me as a conduit of his grace. He is pretty sloppy with his grace. It splashes all around the place. Everyone gets some of it, even the conduit. Pretty soon I said to myself, "I wouldn't mind doing this all my life, but how? What about being a priest?"

I had always put priests on pedestals. I was aware of my own sinfulness and never gave a thought to my becoming one. I thought you have to be really saintly to be a priest. That image stayed until I met some priests in the army. They weren't bad guys at all, just men. They were sinful men in some ways, but they were good priests and happy in their priesthood. So, it turns out, my models for priesthood were not saints. They were normal guys who had their faults, but who loved the Lord and who loved being priests. I looked at them and said: "Well, since you don't have to be perfect to be a priest, maybe God would accept me." God did, and I give thanks every day for the grace of ordination.

I enjoyed the service, but wanted something more out of life than the military. The priesthood had been in the back of my mind for a long time, a distant second to other careers. But now the idea became more attractive. My sister, mother, and father had moved to New Mexico and loved the state. It is such a beautiful area that I wanted to be there too, so I applied to the Archdiocese of Santa Fe and was accepted.

The Archdiocese of Santa Fe suffered tremendously the last several years. If you asked the Holy Father where is the biggest problem in the Catholic world, not in terms of warfare—that could be Croatia—but in terms of shame, he would probably say with some emphasis, "Santa Fe!" Dozens of our priests had molested children and engaged in other misconduct. We have just settled more than 130 lawsuits, and there are more to come. But we do have a handle on it now. We are facing the music. We have ninety-one parishes in the archdiocese and relatively few healthy priests to serve those parishes. Also, in the last three years we have lost more than thirty priests. About twenty of them have been removed from their jobs and can no longer function as priests. Others have quit because they didn't like the changes made by the new archbishop, especially his demand that we be held responsible for our actions. So, it has been a terrible time. For nearly a year every headline in the Santa Fe newspapers was about the scandals.

When I first thought about the priesthood, I would close my eyes and envision New Mexico, the Land of Enchantment, and would dream of baptizing babies, burying the dead, and eating the chili that people would bring. I would play golf, fish, and enjoy an easy life. After all, I was *retiring* from the army. But the Lord had plans for me that I wasn't aware of. If I had known then what I know now, I would probably not have become a priest. Yet, that would have been a shame. I'm glad I didn't know those things. I would hate to have had anything keep me from the priesthood. God spoon-feeds us at first, then drops the bombs.

My first assignment was as a parochial vicar at Saint Thomas Aquinas in Rio Rancho. Two of us took care of 4,000 families. After one year I was assigned to Holy Child parish in Tijeras—a pastor after only one year! A year later the archbishop asked me to take on the additional responsibility of being vocation director.

Holy Child is bigger than it looks. We have eight churches in this area. One priest and a permanent deacon take care of all of them. I do wish I had a couple of young priests to help out in the parish, not to take a load off me, but to work with the group that so needs the attention of a priest: our teenagers. The area is about twenty-eight miles north to south and twelve east to west. Some of the churches were built many years ago. There was no parish here in the mountains until about 1962, and so each of the little Hispanic communities built its own church. In the old days a priest might come by once a year at fiesta time. He would baptize all the babies, marry the couples, and bless the graves in the cemeteries. Today we have five or six Masses on the weekends, scattered among these eight places. Some have Mass weekly, some only monthly. One has Mass only on its fiesta. Actually it sounds more difficult than it is. Each of the churches is a little jewel; each has a major-domo assigned, a kind of caretaker, who does a wonderful job. When the priest is not there for Mass, the laity conduct the stations of the cross.

Archbishop Michael Sheehan, who had been bishop of Lubbock, Texas, was appointed to Santa Fe three years ago. When he appointed me vocation director, we had only five seminarians in the entire program. Two of them were asked to leave within a short time. Note that this was in 1993, before the misconduct became public. So the scarcity—only three viable seminarians—was not because of the scandals. That is a critical point.

Only three years later, we have twenty-three seminarians, nineteen of them in theology or pre-theology, four are in college. So, at the same time that the stories of ignominy broke, we had a sizable increase in vocations, exactly the opposite of what you would expect. Why? A couple of reasons. First, to be honest, our priests hadn't been encouraging vocations. My predecessor as vocation director had quit the priesthood. He was not a happy priest. He admitted that he did not value his priesthood, even though it was his responsibility to encourage vocations. What a recipe for failure. We were actually chasing vocations away. A second reason for the increase: in times of trouble, good men and women surface. The fact is that those who apply in our archdiocese today are actually attracted by the troubles. Like the Marines, they judge that we need a "few good priests." Several seminarians have said that one of the reasons they come here is because they want to help fix the mess.

The president of Mount Angel Seminary is a fine man who has done wonders. When I began my job as vocation director,

I told him we were going to have thirty-five seminarians in five years. He laughed at me. "Come on, John, don't be ridiculous. Don't set goals you can't possibly reach." I turned out to be wrong. We won't have thirty-five. It will be more likely forty or even fifty.

A great joy I have is seeing those eager guys in the seminary. Two of them are doctors, two are lawyers. We had one doctor, age thirty-seven, who spent a good bit of his time helping the poor. One day he woke up and said, "Why don't I just become a priest, then I can do this work full time?" He retains his license. He will be able to anoint, to give some penicillin, and then tear up the bill. One of the lawyers was about to inherit his dad's criminal law business in the east. But he didn't accept it. He was on the verge of making a fortune, but that was not what he wanted out of life. The other lawyer, a former county attorney, forty years old, is now studying in Rome and tells me he has never been happier in his life. He is glowing. There is one seminarian from this parish; he is forty-eight. A man starting theology today at twenty-eight is considered a young buck.

I challenge every young man who applies to be a seminarian. I brief him on the problems we have had. Once I decide that I have an excellent prospect, I put him to the test. Hoping he won't accept, I suggest that he go to another diocese that has fewer problems. Every time I make that approach, the candidate rejects the idea. And I say, "Are you a little crazy, wanting to study for Santa Fe?" I like the way the man growls at me, "Father, that is exactly why I want to be a priest here. I want to let the Lord use me. I want to be part of the solution. I want to help fix this mess, and I believe I can."

Several of our prospects who are now in law or medical or dental schools are on the brink, but the lure of big money is a powerful attraction for them. The Lord is tempting them, but we are competing with secular values: money, power, comfort. The real point for them to consider is that the gospel will comfort the afflicted. The priesthood gives a joy and peace of heart which I have never found elsewhere, not even when I was much involved with the Church in the secular life. The greatest selling point for the priesthood is a happy priest. People don't want to join a misery organization.

A couple of years ago the religious vocation directors in the United States held a national conference in Albuquerque. Archbishop Sheehan was invited to give the opening prayer, and I attended with him. Most of the people who attended were vocation directors for their religious communities. Because of our location, the motif was Western. None wore the Roman collar, and I got some funny looks for wearing mine. The men had cowboy hats and boots. Women wore Annie Oakley outfits with high boots. The featured speaker was a nun who, judging from her published writing, doesn't like priests. I said to myself, "These are the people who are here to try to determine the causes for a lack of vocations? Look at them. They discourage vocations." So I left. Later one of the men asked me why I didn't stay. He said, "Sister gave a wonderful address."

"Yes," I replied, "and I bet she took the pope apart."

"You bet she did," he said. "She can't stand him, but who does?"

My response went something like this:

No wonder we are having trouble. You guys don't believe in what you are doing. And if you don't believe in it, you're never going to sell it to someone else. Can you imagine an army recruiter who hated the army? Can you picture going to a recruiting station and the guy sitting behind the desk says, "You want to join up? You must be joking. This army is terrible. We can't stand the general. He is a nut. The army is all screwed up." No wonder nobody wants to sign up for the priesthood.

Things are beginning to brighten up in the diocese. We have taken several specific steps. We have a review board with a toll free line. Anyone with allegations is urged to use that line. We hired four investigators to do our own research, and actually sought out victims not yet reported, to try to get them some help. We feel a sense of responsibility for them. The archdiocese was threatened with bankruptcy, but that problem is being resolved.

When times are hard, good things happen. This Church is on its knees. We do our best work when we are on our knees. When we are haughty and arrogant as a Church, we aren't doing what Jesus did: he walked through life on his knees. Things have changed radically in only three years, and I am optimistic. We expect to have thirty seminarians in August. We just finished a discernment weekend, and eighteen men attended. Most of them were in their 20s, 30s, and 40s. We are seeing older vocations, guys who in a way mirror my own story. They started out in one direction and realized something was missing. Now they want to give the rest of their lives to the Church.

When I left the army to go to the seminary, I was sitting on top of the world. I had loved the officers I served with, and thought, now I am joining this elite corps of priests. It's going to be even better. It didn't work out that way. My biggest joy has been getting to know the Lord Jesus, knowing him far better than before I was ordained. I have met him in so many ways through his people. I meet him when I anoint the dying and see the strength of faith they have when they face eternity. My faith has gone out of my head and into my heart. Every day I see miracles of God's strength working with people. That is my joy, to have met the risen Christ through his people, especially through his suffering people.

We priests have a tremendous influence on people, and that is because we act *in persona Christi*. People will tell the priest what is troubling them, the most intimate details of their lives. That is really disarming. It is hard to believe that this man or this woman is telling me things in absolute confidence that they have never told to another human being.

Have I made a difference in the world? The answer is an unqualified "yes." I have been there for people who were dying, have heard their confessions, and given them peace when I commended them to the Lord. Unworthy as I am, I know there are people in heaven today because I said yes to this ministry. I sometimes tell men who are discerning a call to the priesthood:

> "Take your time to make up your mind, but please make it up, because there are people here who are dying without a priest, people who are starving for the bread of life. Every day we don't have a priest for these people, some will be lost. Doctors do make a difference when they save temporal lives. We save eternal lives. Not that we are worthy of it, but God does that through us."

I've had some difficult moments in the priesthood, especially when I see tragedies among my people and can do only so much for them. I just had a funeral of a thirty-seven-year-old woman who died in an auto accident, leaving three young children. I wish I could unblock something and fix it all up. I wish I could take that Lazarus out of the tomb as Jesus did. Wherever there is deep joy in my ministry I am going to find deep sorrow. They go hand in hand.

In my judgment the priest has to make not only a total but a permanent commitment. Surprisingly, living a committed life is the easy way out. If you love something but don't make a commitment to it, then every morning you get up you have to figure out the universe. You are always looking at your navel, constantly introspecting. I am a simple person. I loved the army and was committed to it for twenty years. I loved being a soldier. Now I am committed to something much, much greater. You can't even compare the two. So I think committing to something with your whole soul, mind, heart and strength is liberating. It frees you from the insanity of trying to figure out life every hour of every day.

Celibacy is a gift to me, a gift I can in turn give to my people. There isn't a man ordained who hasn't had the chance to think it over pretty thoroughly. We were confronted with it every week for four years in the seminary. It was the subtheme of every conference on spiritual direction. If you can't handle it, the door is open. I had a great deal more instruction on celibacy than the eighty hours of instruction in Airborne

School before they kicked me out of an airplane. Married people don't have that much training. Of course celibacy is only a matter of discipline, not dogma, but I do hope that in the future we hold on to it at least as an option. Some people say that because of all the sexual misconduct priests should marry. That makes no sense. Most pedophiles are married men. There are more cases of incest in America than pedophilia. So if we had married clergy, we could have other problems to deal with. People who tie the celibacy issue to these disgraces need to be challenged.

I have never had a real problem with the chain of command. Probably that is because of my service years. I sympathize with the guys who are made bishops and the abuse they take. Even our former archbishop, who seemed to have had problems with leadership, was a guy I loved. Someone has to be in charge. Jesus knew human nature, and that's why he appointed one man to head up everything. First he had the seventy-two, then the twelve, then the one. He approved the hierarchical system. I have worked with two bishops and found them to be reasonable men. The two bishops I worked with were not oppressive, never arbitrary or capricious. They were just sincere, hard-working guys. Priests who have a problem with authority might have had bishops who were different from mine.

The great issues of the Church don't seem to matter so much here in the field, where the rubber meets the road. Still, I know there are complicated issues, and I'm not the one to solve them. I defer to the bishops and theologians. Thank God I am not the pope or a bishop. I am just a simple priest, so controversial issues of the Church don't keep me awake at night.

Good things are ahead for the Church. We are going to see the priesthood grow in numbers, strength, and quality. Change takes place more rapidly today than formerly. But if we do have that increase in vocations, I hope we won't ever go back to having priests keep the books, line the baseball field, or supervise dances for the teenagers. When I talk to my seminarians, I tell them, "If the time comes when you feel you are overburdened, take a look at what you are doing, and ask yourself, 'Do I need to be ordained to do this?' If the answer is no, get someone else to do it."

Every parish is loaded with talented people ready and willing to help, so we should never be afraid of burnout. We don't burn out from overwork, we burn out from a lack of healthy work, from a lack of prayer, from the lack of a balanced life, and from a lack of recreation. I have yet to see a priest who prays get burned out.

One thing that helps our program is that success begets success. We have a barbecue at the archbishop's home in August. When the seminarians come, they see a group of men who are healthy, happy, and having fun. Men often express their affection for one another by throwing barbs and jibes. When the seminarians see this done, not brutally, but with a smile, they are seeing men who act like men. The guys now studying for the archdiocese look like American men with all the bumps, bruises, and warts that men have.

People applaud the positive steps the archbishop has taken. They see we have made mistakes, but are honestly trying to rectify them in such a way that they should never happen again. The men who join our seminary need not fear that the image of priests has been so tarnished that people will look down on them. I wear my collar everywhere I go, and no one gives me a dirty look. People were saddened, angered, disappointed by what happened, yet they didn't abandon the Church. Actually, the laity has been easier on priests than priests have been on the laity. I've never been so affirmed in my life. Of course, we have to earn that affirmation. Once when I was preparing for midnight Mass as a seminarian, a priest in the sacristy was complaining about how hard he was working, and that no one loved him. About every five minutes someone would come in the door with a gift or a check. He would thank them and continue complaining. That guy was one of our problems. People want to love the priest, and will if they are given half a chance. As long as we treat people with respect, they will trust us. It is almost scary how the people love and affirm their priests.

Michael Sheehan
Santa Fe, New Mexico

Archbishop Sheehan is the man behind the amazing recovery of the Santa Fe archdiocese. He offered to add some comments to the story told by Father Carney. Though one can sense the incredible strain the archbishop has been under, he shows little outward tension or anxiety. He is a no-nonsense bishop, completely loyal to the Church.

I came to Santa Fe three years ago and found the archdiocese in a very bad state. Scandals of priests involved in pedophilia and other misconduct filled the front pages of the newspapers and were daily fare for the television stations. Morale was at an all time low. There were 150 separate suits filed against the archdiocese, and the amount of money requested through litigation was staggering. The archdiocese was faced with bankruptcy.

The first thing we had to do was to restore the confidence of the public in our administration. We met with the media, discussed the situation frankly, hid nothing. We set up a commission of priests and laity to actually seek out victims and uncover new cases. The commission included people with professional training in law, medicine, and counseling. Gradually the public became aware that we intended to tackle the problem head-on. At the same time we needed to resolve the threat of bankruptcy. The insurance companies were not prepared to pay more than a tiny portion of what was needed to settle the lawsuits. The National Council of Catholic Bishops made available several highly trained bankruptcy lawyers who represented us with the insurance companies and gave us invaluable advice that prevented a total financial collapse of the archdiocese. We obtained help from three other sources. First, we appealed for donations from the dioceses of the country, and many responded wonderfully.

Second, we got some help from foundations. Finally, I met with the pastors of the archdiocese, told them about our financial situation and suggested that if they had any uncommitted funds they could provide a valuable service by making them available. One pastor stood up and said, "Archbishop, I have $100,000 that is not committed; it is yours." That started a wave, and before long our parishes made available nearly two million dollars from their savings.

Already we have settled 137 lawsuits. Probably there will be more. But we are beginning to see light. Amazing things have happened: our churches are full, our collections are up, and the number of our seminarians has doubled each year. The seminarians are all good men, happily uncomplicated Catholics in union with the universal church. How did that all happen? To me it is a proof that Christ founded the Church. If he did not, this archdiocese would have gone down the drain. It is also an indication of how the Church thrives under difficulties. I do believe that our frankness in handling the cases has done a world of good. It has been an extremely painful experience, but also an unbelievable journey of faith.

VIII. Get Up and Go

Priests Who Changed

With New Insights

IT HAPPENED THAT WHILE HE WAS TRAVELING TO DAMASCUS AND APPROACHING THE CITY, SUDDENLY A LIGHT FROM HEAVEN SHONE ALL ROUND HIM. SAUL FELL TO THE GROUND, AND THEN HE HEARD A VOICE SAYING, "SAUL, SAUL, WHY ARE YOU PERSECUTING ME?" "WHO ARE YOU, LORD?" HE ASKED, AND THE ANSWER CAME, "I AM JESUS, WHOM YOU ARE PERSECUTING. GET UP AND GO INTO THE CITY, AND YOU WILL BE TOLD WHAT YOU ARE TO DO."

—ACTS 9:3-6

This account of Saint Paul's dramatic conversion is well-known. Not all conversions are as radical. But often people will experience a dramatic and comprehensive faith experience. Two priests tell of their personal "Damascus experience." Each experience is different, but both priests found in that sudden moment of insight a new approach to their apostolate that radically changed their lives.

Thomas C. Brady
South Beloit, Illinois

Monsignor Tom Brady is one of those priests on whom a bish-
op leans, a man the bishop can call on to handle difficult tasks.
Pile job after job on his shoulders, and he will accept each gra-
ciously and carry it out with efficiency. He has no instinct for
self-preservation and so is incapable of turning down the one
burden that can break him. At least that is how he was until
his generosity almost cost him his health and sanity. Then he
had a conversion experience that turned his life around.

However talented and effective a priest may be, occasional-
ly he fails to recognize that too many tasks obediently accepted
can cause him to burn his candle at both ends. The irony of this
very productive priest is that he exudes such quiet happiness
that other priests often say, "I wish I had what Brady has."

Monsignor Brady was born in Harvard, Illinois on
October 4, 1927, and ordained for the Diocese of Rockford in
1954. He is currently pastor of Saint Peter's in South Beloit,
Illinois.

In retrospect, it all began with my older brother, who always
planned to be a priest and intended to enter the seminary
when he got out of service. I remember serving Mass with my
cousin Phil O'Neill. The associate pastor, Father Fred
O'Rourke, called us aside and asked, "Did you two ever think
about being a priest?" "No," I said. "My brother Bob is going
to be one, though." That night the seed was planted, and I
couldn't get the idea out of my head.

I wrote my brother, who was in the service, to tell him
what I had in mind. The letter was returned. He had been
killed in the Burma, India theater. His death made me more
determined than ever to go to the seminary.

When I finished high school, I turned down a football
scholarship at DeKalb State Teachers College and enrolled at

Loras College, in Dubuque, Iowa. Loras accepted me conditionally because of my poor grades in high school. But now that I had a goal, I studied hard and amazed myself by making the honor roll. I covered four years of Latin in two.

I attended Saint Mary Seminary at Paca Street in Baltimore. The war was on and many of the students were leaving, some to enter the service, some to join the FBI. I was recommended for training in an FBI program. But I stayed at the seminary, and four years later was ordained with my friend from home, Phil O'Neill. Remembering how Phil and I got there, I never fail to extend an invitation to my altar servers.

Before ordination I had doubts about my vocation, but never afterward. I have not once entertained the idea of leaving the priesthood. The night before ordination, I reflected on my life. I knew that I had to make some sacrifices to become a priest. I had dated and had serious emotional relationships with more than one young lady. They were diversions, but dangerous ones. Severing those relationships was not easy. Yet the sacrifice of celibacy was one of the things that had always attracted me to the priesthood. And it has not really been a problem for me. It is so directly connected with my priesthood that I seldom give it a thought. I do love children and sometimes regret not having any of my own and not having someone to cherish intimately. But that evening I pledged my total dedication to the priesthood, and I have never regretted my decision.

After ordination I was assigned to be an associate with my former pastor in Harvard, Illinois; then I served four years at St. James in Rockford. Both were great experiences, and the pastors were wonderful men. I became involved in the Catholic Family Movement, then in vogue. We had twelve groups in the parish. It was an eye-opener for me to see the lay people come alive studying scripture and applying it to their lives.

One day Bishop Lane called. Would I like to go back to school, get a degree, and work with our local high schools? I demurred. "Bishop, I really like parish work, and I never burned up the leagues when I was in school." In my naiveté I didn't realize the decision was already made. "Go down to Notre Dame and register. Classes start Monday." I did go to Notre Dame for a year and two summers and earned a master's in school administration. The bishop invited me to stay on and get my doctorate, but this time I declined more forcefully. I was assigned to Marian High School for four years, where I taught modern European history and religion and was dean of discipline. After two years I was appointed superintendent. Following Marian, I served six years as principal of Boylan Central High School in Rockford.

While at the high schools, I took classes at Loyola University with a man who had a great impact on my life, Father Charles A. Curran, clinical psychologist. He introduced me to a completely new mystical spirituality. Everything I learned about psychology from him was already in the scriptures, and he brought it out beautifully. I took all of his courses. Since my schools were a long way from Loyola, I changed to a summer program and received a second master's degree, this in religious education. In 1969 Bishop Lane appointed me diocesan Director of Adult Education.

I thought all my problems were over, but they were just beginning. Bishop Lane died and Arthur O'Neill, a priest of the diocese, was made the bishop. I told him that whatever assignment he gave me, I wanted very much to also do some parish work. In addition to the jobs I already had, he appointed me Director of Education. I worked on the centralization of the Catholic high school program. I was also appointed Personnel Director, Vicar for Spiritual Formation, and the pastor of a small parish in Rockford, Saints Peter and Paul's. Later I was asked to take on the jobs of Vicar General and director of the retreat house.

I had just given a talk to the major superiors of sisters, had returned and was sitting in the office preparing for a meeting of the senate committee at the Faust Hotel. Suddenly I thought I was having a heart attack. I rested a little, then went to the house and poured a couple of Scotches. The next day I felt worse. My head felt like it was going to blow off. I went to see the doctor and he put me in the hospital. When I was released I was in a state of denial. I couldn't be sick. I had too much to do.

The bishop sent me to Florida for a rest. There I blacked out with hypertension. I began drinking a little heavier and played some golf. Then a phone call came reminding me that I was to give a talk at Offut Air Force Base. The blackout came back. In a panic I flew home and took some tranquilizers. The bishop walked into my office, took a look at me and said, "You are going nowhere. Get a substitute."

It didn't end there. I was up to my neck in work and was constitutionally unable to turn down any job offered to me. I thought I could walk on water. Just past forty, I felt I had only a few years to accomplish whatever I could do for the Church and was going to give it all I had. My condition continued to get worse to the point where I couldn't say Mass. My mother said she would rather see me dead than the way I was. Flat on my back, I began to realize that I had the wrong attitude. I was ambitious. I didn't want anything to jeopardize my career in the Church. However, after the crash, I was ready for the greatest joy of my life—a genuine conversion experience—even more important to me than my ordination. It began innocently enough.

After working with and studying with Father Curran, I had begun to give retreats. In order to broaden my background and training for the retreat work, I enrolled at Loyola for study leading to a doctorate in educational counseling and psychology. Shortly after this time, while giving a retreat, I ran into some priests who were involved in the charismatic renewal. I had many questions about that program. Several charismatic priests in the area had gotten into difficulties, and some had left the priesthood. I thought of them as being a bunch of holy rollers. One night my curiosity prompted me to go to one of the meetings in the area of Loves Park. People got up and talked about Christ being a personal friend, and then prayed spontaneously. I was amazed, a little frightened, but edified. Still, I thought, that's not for me. I was invited to another prayer meeting at a different place. Prayers, singing, speaking in tongues, everyone giving their neighbors a hug. That turned me off, and I walked out. A few weeks later I gave a retreat at the McGuire Air Force Base. After one of the talks, someone came up to me and said, "Father, you must have been baptized in the Spirit." I asked the chaplain what was going on. He said the nucleus of the group making the retreat was charismatic and that when they listened to my presentations they assumed I was one of them.

During refreshments I visited with some of the charismatics and found them to be gentle and kind. I told them, "You people have something I don't have, and if it is good for me and for the Church, I want it." That night they soaked me in prayer, and I began to read their books. When I returned home some lay friends asked if I wanted to be baptized in the Spirit. This time, I said, "Yes." They pulled up their chairs and prayed over me. I expected something powerful to happen, but felt nothing, and was disappointed.

The next morning when I woke up, everything was different. I can't explain it, but I began to realize for the first time how much God loves me. Then I surrendered to that love, and my life has never been the same since. Gradually I worked out of the fog. My charismatic renewal experience helped reduce the hypertension. From that time on I got rid of my ambitions, and nothing mattered but being a priest and a good priest.

Many things were different. I was hungry to read the scriptures. I attended a priest's funeral and I prayed that the celebrant would give a good homily, when before I would sit there and criticize it. It was a deeply felt conversion experience that radically changed me, a mysterious breakthrough that simply can't be explained. I can't give it to others, but I do pray daily that my parishioners will have the same experience. I wouldn't give up what I have now for a winning million dollar lottery ticket. Now everything makes sense to me. I have eyes to see and ears to hear that I didn't have before.

I recall giving a talk at a parish after my charismatic renewal. The pastor who introduced me said, "I wish that I had what Brady has." For the first time I realized that what I had experienced with the charismatic movement had completely changed me.

Later I found there are all kinds of conversion experiences: the Rite of Christian Initiation of Adults, Cursillo, Marriage Encounter, and Medjugorje. All of them can produce breakthroughs. Each of them seems to make us more tolerant of people, more respectful, more kind. Today when I am driving and someone pulls out in front of me, I am tempted to say, "Get out of the way, you @#&!!" Then I realize that person is bonded to me through Christ. Everything that I once knew intellectually has become real for me. The eucharist has so much more meaning. I just want to be the best priest that it is possible for me to be. It may sound corny, but I had to learn to listen to the Holy Spirit and be willing to be the vessel for the directions offered me.

I see many good signs of a reawakening of the traditional values which the Church stands for. I see a change in bishops who don't resort always to canon law, but are compassionate and understanding with their priests and with the laity. We have a young priest who speaks about vocations in our grade schools, something we did long ago, then for some reason discarded. I preach about vocations in my parish. I put a note in the bulletin asking people to fill out a card if they know any youngster who would make a good priest. Then I call on that boy and ask him to think about it not because I judge he should be a priest, but because the community thinks so. When I talk to the students, I tell them if they choose the priesthood, they are getting into an exciting profession, because there have been few times in history when clergy can make such a difference in the lives of people.

Charles Fortier
Los Angeles, California

Monsignor Charles Fortier, affectionately known as Padre Carlos, is a humble, modest man, long on accomplishments, short on recalling them. He is fluent in English, French, and Spanish, and has a working knowledge of Portuguese. He has an accent that is an unusual combination of French, Canadian, and Southern, the latter from working in Louisiana. His linguistic talent has taken him literally around the world, working in various capacities in family life, marketing, and rural life. Monsignor Fortier is an example of a priest for whom every obstacle, once accepted, opened the way for greater service and for unusual experiences.

Those who have not experienced a charismatic conversion may be a bit skeptical of how it changes one's life. Here is the story of a talented priest who became renewed through an amazing conversion experience after ordination.

Monsignor Fortier was born January 2, 1919, near Quebec City, Canada, and was ordained in Louisiana for the Lafayette diocese in 1945. He was named a Domestic Prelate in 1963 when he was still quite young, and now works in the family life office of the Archdiocese of Los Angeles.

After attending the local schools in Quebec Province, I entered the seminary in Quebec City. I didn't do well in classes the first year and the next year stayed at home. I went to business school for a year, then enrolled in a special school called *L'ecole apostolique* at the College of Levis across the St. Lawrence River from Quebec City. When I finished my studies, I applied for the rural Diocese of Amos, where my family was then living. I was accepted and sent to Saint Paul Seminary in Ottawa for theology. After my first year there my cousin, whose ordination I had attended, offered me the chance to spend my vacations with him at Laval University and get a degree in philosophy.

I sent a copy of my cousin's letter to the bishop, but in his reply he said he preferred that I spend the summer with him. It was his opinion that if I went to the big city, I would never come back to the small Diocese of Amos. I reported to his office in Amos, but he was not there nor did I see him the entire season. He had left instructions that I was to cut wood by hand at the Saint Joseph Retreat House throughout the summer. I was very lonely and decided I would look for another diocese as soon as possible. The next summer I worked as a counselor at Lake Androscoggin in Lewiston, Maine, with the Dominican Fathers. I began to learn a little English. At the end of the summer I realized I could work as well in an English section of the North American continent as I could in Quebec, so I offered myself to the Dioceses of Saskatoon and Winnipeg in western Canada. I never heard from them.

Then the rector of the seminary suggested that I write to Lafayette, Louisiana, where the bishop was looking for French-speaking priests. I wrote to Bishop Jeanmard, was immediately accepted, and spent my last year of theology in New Orleans.

Many wonderful assignments followed. My first parish as a pastor was at Our Lady of Prompt Succor, south of Lafayette. Two weeks after the appointment the bishop asked me to take care of *Catholic Action of the South*, a paper published in the Archdiocese of New Orleans and shared by various other dioceses. From 1949 until 1954 I was the local business manager. I was also appointed pastor of Saint Genevieve's. A short time later I was asked to serve as Director of the Information Center and Director of Radio and TV for the diocese, and to be in charge of cemeteries. Quite a mixed bag!

In 1965 Archbishop Cody of New Orleans asked for volunteers to organize a service of cooperation between North and South America. My bishop gave me permission to apply for this position, and I was accepted. On June 15, 1965, I resigned all my duties in the Diocese of Lafayette and drove a rented car with all my possessions to New Orleans. That night over the radio came the announcement that Archbishop

Cody was appointed Archbishop of Chicago. My new job was eliminated. With the rug pulled out from under me, I left with a longtime friend, Father Al Sigur, to visit the Vatican Council and find out what was the temper of the times.

While in Rome, I enrolled at the Gregorian University. The ink on my application form wasn't dry when Bishop McGrath, of Panama, offered to send me with Father Pablo Steele, a Scarboro missionary from Toronto, to teach cooperatives and to recruit students for an institute to be financed by the U.S. Government in Panama. I did that for seven months, then returned to Philadelphia and began working with the Academy of Food Marketing of Saint Joseph College, now Saint Joseph University. I helped establish a school of marketing at Rafael Landivar, a Jesuit university in Guatemala City. While on that job I visited all the countries of Central America.

Three years later, in 1967, I spent several months in Bihar, India, working with the Jesuits in a school of international labor relations, establishing a school of marketing. In 1971 I returned to Notre Dame Seminary in New Orleans. I taught there while working on a doctorate in continuing education at Louisiana State University in Baton Rouge.

The director of the seminary was Monsignor Al Sigur whom I had known since 1944. We were as close as brothers. We owned a plane together and even piloted it to Cuba. Of course that was before Castro took over. We flew all over America, to Canada, and Mexico. Al was a powerful preacher and a charismatic leader. One of the principal needs of a priest is to relate well with his confreres. It is important to have a close friend, a confidant, who serves also as a spiritual director. For me that lifeline was Al. I saw him just a few months ago. His health is failing somewhat, but he is the same friendly, encouraging man of our younger days.

I list all these jobs and all these moves to make a point. Every obstacle I found in my way as a seminarian and as a priest has turned out to be the greatest blessing that ever came into my life. The oppositions I faced could have soured me, but they didn't. Each time a superior stepped on me or sent me some place I didn't want to go, new and wonderful opportunities opened up. When Bishop Desmarais treated me as he did in Amos, I found an occasion to work in Louisiana under the finest bishop I have ever known. When Archbishop Cody told me we couldn't start the Institute we had planned for over seven months, I had a chance to go to the last session of the Council and discovered opportunities in Latin America and at Saint Joseph College in Philadelphia. When I was in charge of continuing education for New Orleans, Bishop Schexnayder removed me from my parish. Because he did, I was free for two years to coordinate a program for the U.S. bishops in rural areas. Each time I accepted a decision that was unpalatable, my acceptance opened up a new phase in my life. Often we hear of priests letting authority get them down. If these priests accept the decisions of their superiors, they may be surprised and delighted by what happens to them in their new appointments. Certainly it was that way for me.

In 1978 I went to Des Moines, Iowa, with the National Catholic Rural Life Conference to establish a program for priests, sisters, and leaders in the rural areas of the country. A year later I began working with Worldwide Marriage Encounter, principally in Spanish. That year alone I gave sixteen Spanish weekends in the Los Angeles area. I left the Rural Life program in 1980 and moved to Los Angeles to work with Marriage Encounter full time. I was appointed Associate Director of Family Life for the archdiocese, working especially with Hispanics in marriage preparation. In recent years I have worked principally with Engaged Encounter and Retrouvaille (a similar program for the divorced), while continuing with Marriage Encounter. Because of my facility with languages, I was privileged to give weekends in fourteen different countries as well as training weekends in Spain, Australia, New Zealand, Canada, and the countries of Central and South America.

Few priests have had the privilege of traveling to as many places as I have. I just returned from Canada where I gave a training session in French for leaders of Retrouvaille. This month I will give similar sessions in La Paz, Bolivia, and Central America.

I may seem to overrate Marriage Encounter. Maybe so, but I know what that movement has done for my priesthood. When I came back from India and made the Marriage Encounter weekend, for the first time I realized that I had strayed pretty far from my vocation. I had been teaching and marketing, and not really officiating as a priest. I said Mass daily and was doing a lot of administrative work, most of which could have been done by any competent lay person. I wasn't living what I would term a priestly life. When I met those wonderful couples on the Encounter weekends and saw their commitment to one another and to the Church, I began to reevaluate who I was, what my vocation was, and what I should be doing to serve Christ and his people. If I am a good priest today, married couples are to a large extent responsible. I had been pretty arrogant, always so sure of myself, so proud of my accomplishments. I used to be the one who taught others. Now I permit people to teach me. And I have learned so much from them.

Experiencing the generosity of the laity has certainly been one of the genuine surprises of my priesthood. I thought I knew people well, but I changed my mind when I got into the Encounter movement. The willingness of couples to give of themselves and to become apostles for Christ is almost unbelievable. (Contrast this generosity with the general selfishness that characterizes our present culture.) When I celebrated my fiftieth anniversary as a priest in 1995, I went back to the Lafayette diocese. There I met the children and grandchildren of couples whose marriages I had witnessed. Another celebration was held in Chihuahua, Mexico, where I established Retrouvaille. We had a Sunday evening Mass, and fifty children of those who had made the weekend with me came in, each carrying a rose. Another celebration was in my home parish, Saint Isidore's of Dorchester in Quebec, and still another in Los Angeles, organized by Mrs. Joan Vienner, my boss at the Family Life Office. It was magnificent. There are a lot of joyful moments in the life of a priest, but little in life can compare with the joy of his jubilee, surrounded by those whose lives he has touched in a special way and by people who love the Church and value the priesthood.

In 1995, together with twenty-seven other priests from Los Angeles, I made a pilgrimage to the Holy Land and to Rome. During a papal audience the pope, who had been informed of my work, said to me, "I want to bless you and the couples who work with you in your very special calling. Working with families and couples is the most important apostolic work in the Church today."

Looking back, I see Vatican II as one of the most positive things that has taken place in this century. But change is not easy to deal with, and unfortunately some of our priests and sisters, even some of our Catholic newspapers, have misread the intentions of the Council. Add to that the continuous bickering and the criticism of anyone in authority, and the result has been the loss of a tremendous number of priests and sisters. No one except the Holy Spirit knows what will eventually be the solution. Celibacy has been blamed for that loss, but I'm not at all sure it should be. If a priest is honest with himself, he will admit that celibacy is not the problem. Some have proposed the ordination of married men. I have no trouble with that idea. In my work I have seen the sacrament of marriage become a forming influence on many men, leading them to become apostles for the Church. For the same reason, if women should ever be ordained, I would much prefer that they be married women. I would favor the return of many of our married priests. Some could do beautiful work, perhaps special work in prisons. Each returning priest would have to be evaluated on a personal basis. But while we are doing that, we should also evaluate the working priests of our dioceses and religious orders. Some of them can't function as well as those who have left the priesthood. Corporations and the armed services evaluate their personnel on a regular basis. It wouldn't be a bad idea for the Church to do the same.

When I talk to kids about becoming priests, I tell them that it is a tough calling. When I entered the seminary, the priest was a privileged person. Now he is a humble servant. I tell men that if they have the right intention, if they want to spend their lives helping people, if they are able to love and care for those who are the poor of the world, then perhaps they have a vocation.

I remember giving an Encounter weekend in Brazil. There were four religious sisters on this weekend and the local bishop attended. He was surprised that I had invited the sisters to attend. He told me that perhaps they shouldn't be on the weekend. He said they could become so wrapped up with the couples that they would all want to get married. On Sunday afternoon the sisters shared with all of us the fact that the weekend had been the greatest boon to their vocation. They told how wonderful it was to experience the love of these couples and how it encouraged them to share their love with their students. The bishop changed his mind about religious sisters being on the weekends. He shared with us that there were 150 priests in his archdiocese, and he regretted that he never told a single one that he loved him. That bishop changed his relationship with his priests after the weekend.

Can anyone wonder why I stay with the Encounter Movement? What a gift it has been to my priesthood! What a gift the priesthood has been for me!

IX. That Your Joy May Be Complete

Priests Who Would

Do It All Again

I HAVE LOVED YOU JUST AS THE FATHER HAS LOVED ME. REMAIN IN MY LOVE. I HAVE TOLD YOU THIS SO THAT MY OWN JOY MAY BE IN YOU AND YOUR JOY MAY BE COMPLETE.

—JOHN 15:9, 11

With great regularity the priests whom we interviewed spoke of the incredible joy they find in their vocation, whether in the day-to-day work of the pastor, or in the work of an unusual ministry. They discovered that giving themselves to the Lord brings more joy than they could have imagined. Listen to their words. Read between the lines. The lives of five priests are highlighted here, but the same joy, expressed at times in more subdued tones, is in all their stories.

John V. Sheridan
Malibu, California

Monsignor John V. Sheridan is a priest of the Archdiocese of Los Angeles. As an associate pastor he took a special interest in organizing young people and dealing with gang activities. He is an expert in the various areas of communication. As director of the Catholic Information Center in downtown Los Angeles, he developed radio and television programs, conducted a lecture schedule on contemporary theology, wrote a newspaper column, and authored ten major books. He now lives in retirement as pastor emeritus of Our Lady of Malibu parish, home of many Catholics in the entertainment business. The walls of his study are covered with awards and citations from the president of the Unites States, the state of California, and the city of Malibu. He was once named Man of the Year in the city of Los Angeles.

As interesting as Monsignor Sheridan's story is and as learned as he is, we should not lose sight of the relationship of his brush with death to his enhanced ability to counsel the sick and his compassion which permeates his speaking and writings. He has a realistic evaluation of commitment in contemporary society. Monsignor Sheridan ends on a note that says much about the priesthood.

The fact that I am alive today is one of my continuing surprises. Not simply because of my age, but because of what happened to me more than sixty years ago. In September, 1933, I enrolled in a college level seminary in Ireland. In April of the next year, I came down with pleurisy. I recuperated in the college infirmary and returned to classes for my second year of college in September. In December of the same year I was suddenly hospitalized for what was diagnosed as tubercular peritonitis. Initial surgery was successful, but I fell victim to a series of intestinal complications which were considered fatal. That was the biggest crisis in my life.

I recall my dad and the hospital chaplain standing beside my bed. They were sent there by the surgeons to let me know that I had only three days to live. How they struggled between their tears to give me the doctors' verdict. To be told at that stage of my journey that I was about to die, when everything around me was aglow with life, was impossible to absorb. The sheer necessity of facing death, immediate death, with my senses sharpened if anything by the morphine that had begun to alleviate the terrible physical pain, was something I can never forget. The doctors' message was, "Poison and obstruction are tearing asunder his intestinal tract that up to a few days ago seemed redeemable." That was it. The medics had done all they could.

The priest suggested that I prepare to offer up my young life once again to God. My father, always melancholy, remarked, "How blessed you are to escape so many of life's hardships, to join the company of heaven and help your family and friends here below." Often over the years I have looked into my own heart for the words or silence that would carry the weight of what was being conveyed to me that afternoon, words or silence that would complement my presence to people caught in the same churning vortex. Waiting at the bedside of a dying person, I have searched for the right words and have found *there are no words*. Just be present. That is everything. Only a week ago I saw the face of an old man transfigured as he was anointed with the oil of the sick, with no words spoken except the sacramental ritual. We priests commonly experience that sense of final acceptance, that fundamental hope as it replaces doubt and confusion. But to this day I know that I have never spoken with the faith and the effectiveness of the words that came from my dad and the chaplain in that hospital, sixty years ago. At that moment I accepted death so completely that I can never fear death again, nor can I ever be better prepared for the beginning of a new life than I was that day.

However, I was not to die yet. After eighteen months of hospitalization, an unhealed intestinal lesion, several surgeries, and a confirmed morphine addiction, I was allowed to go home to die. The doctors were convinced that my recovery was medically impossible. On a Sunday morning in 1937, while my family was attending Mass, I got on my knees and asked God directly for a sign of his will that I should or should not entertain the idea of continuing to study for the priesthood. My intestinal wound had been draining for almost three years. The sign I asked for was that the lesion should heal within one week, which, indeed, it did. On the following Sunday there was no more drainage, no more need for dressings and bandaging.

Within the month I wrote to the seminary rector and asked to be re-admitted. Astonished with the news of my recovery, he asked that I furnish him with a certified confirmation from my doctors that I was well. The doctor who signed the certificate enclosed a personal note to me. It read,

> John, I am convinced it was someone greater than all of us who brought you this far. You really should not be here. Your intestines were literally jelly. If this is not an answer to prayer, then prayer is meaningless. Be grateful, do God's work, man, and pray for us.

But, to go back to the beginning. The rural area of the Irish midlands in which I was born and raised was not far from the Sheridan place of origin. Our family was ancient and easy to trace, and it included priests in every generation that we could identify. My family chalice is dated 1769. Uncles, granduncles, and great-great-granduncles celebrated Mass with that chalice, often on the 'mass rocks' of Ireland, or in the hiding places where they were chased by the priest hunters, agents of the bitterly anti-Catholic government that ruled the island for centuries.

Like so many of their compatriots, a number of my parents' family members came to the States to work and to continue their education. My uncle, Joseph Sheridan, a New York accountant, studied for the priesthood at Emmitsburg. He died as a pastor in Birmingham, Alabama. My father worked for the Old Brooklyn-Manhattan Railroad (horse-drawn) and studied at Fordham. My aunt Margaret, the youngest of the family, joined the Carmelites in New York.

Several members of my family went to Rockwell College in the south of Ireland, run by the Holy Ghost Fathers. Two of my brothers studied for the priesthood and joined that congregation. Thus my immediate family of five brothers and two sisters continued a long Sheridan tradition, having three priests and a nun.

Despite all of this religious background, I believe the influence of my mom was what oriented us to the priesthood. Scarcely a week went by that one of the local priests did not visit us or have tea in our home, almost always at the invitation of my mother. Dad, a widower before he married Mom, was much older than she. He was a private man, of very high intelligence, with a deep sense of God's presence, an abiding humor, and a strange melancholy. Mom was totally different. She was exceedingly generous, outgoing, and enthusiastic. Our home was hardly ever without a guest. Dad called her "God's special gift, the ideal wife and mother."

The people among whom I was reared loved and respected the priest. They were quick to forgive their pastor's human foibles and frailties. My parents were delighted when three of their boys became interested in the priesthood but put no pressure on us in that direction. They warned us individually about the danger of becoming a priest and then being unhappy. Years later, my brothers and I often wondered if they might have known some padres who left the priesthood or were discontent with their lives.

As a youngster, I instinctively wanted to be a farmer. The horses, the cattle, the plowing and mowing, the crops, meadows and trees, the conversations among adults about the breaking in of horses, cattle breeding, and agricultural fairs all spelled out the kind of life that a reasonably happy child in our farming milieu would relish. Yet the Church and priests were very much a part of our lives. Our priest taught a class in school, visited our homes, and baptized our baby brothers and sisters. Young as we were, we noticed his kindness to the elderly, to the sick, and to those with special needs.

Our school used to invite missionaries, mostly men who grew up in our neighborhood, to speak to the upper grades.

We kids were impressed with them and would talk about going to China, Africa, the Philippines, or even France. These were the influences that lured me away from my idealized life as a farmer to that of the priest.

While the other members of my family went to boarding schools, I attended a Latin school, the majority of whose students went on to the priesthood. When I graduated, I had already made up my mind that I had a vocation, or at least I would try out at a seminary which would make the final judgment on the genuineness of my call.

After my near-fatal illness, I re-entered the seminary. A couple of years later I came to California where I studied theology and was ordained in Los Angeles in 1943. The years I spent in the inner city and in a downtown chapel and information center are memorable. I reached out on so many fronts to countless thousands: press, radio, TV, conferences and lectures, adult education classes, counseling, confessions around the clock, seven daily Masses. It was an endless ministering to executives, file clerks, alcoholics, occasional murderers, for whom the sidewalk confessional was the image of Christ holding up a big sign, "Journey begins and ends here."

Now in my eighties, I can say that never once, not for a solitary moment, have I regretted being a priest. I have never allowed myself the luxury of living in alternative or unreal worlds. No really committed human being can afford more than one radical lifestyle. Of course I have thought of other ways of life, but I cannot imagine any other that would be more attractive, more fulfilling, more soul satisfying than that of the Catholic priest. I know no other way of life in which I could have a clearer sense of being needed or a deeper realization that I have been an instrument of untold blessings and consolation for countless thousands. This despite my sinfulness, my weaknesses, my endless failures to be what I want to be. I realize my incapacity to reach the level of sanctity achieved by many among the humblest of my flock, but like Saint Paul I am never without hope, never without an awareness and acceptance of God's unconditioned love. That is what I preach every Sunday.

The concept of commitment has radically changed today, not only toward marriage and the priesthood, but in every covenant relationship. I see couples breaking up every day, and I have great sympathy for them; yet vicariously I can understand it. We have been conditioned sociologically and philosophically to temporary commitments, and the situation will not change unless we can recondition ourselves to accept the basic capacity of the human being to make a decision and keep it. I know this is inimical to contemporary existentialist thinking, but I think it is correct. The Alcoholics Anonymous . people give us an example to follow; they renew their commitment daily. It seems to me that any commitment that is to cover the balance of one's life is the kind of decision that has to be dealt with on a daily basis.

The inability of people to make long term commitments today is not a reflection of selfishness. It is due to a societal change in which we no longer view a permanent commitment as necessarily good. There has been a change rather than a decrease in people's values. They have been given a different perspective. We used to place a high value on staying with a job or with a company for life. One of the societal realities today is the fact that modern technology changes so rapidly that within a few years one is better off taking another job.

Let me tell you of an experience I had about twenty-five years ago. I was bottomed out, completely fatigued, psychologically and spiritually depressed. A retreat was needed, and I went to Menlo Park. During the retreat I asked to speak to Tom, a friend of mine and a priest psychologist. I poured out my soul to him. He gave me a book, titled *As Bread That Is Broken,* by Peter G. Van Breemen, S.J. The central issue of the text is the need to be rooted in hope; it changed my whole approach to life. I came back a new man, engaged in writing my book on death and dying, *And When It Is Dawn*. I literally found myself transfusing its every chapter with a new level of trust in the unconditional love of God and Christ. That book has gone through several printings, and has been recommended by hospice and cancer associations throughout the

United States. At times a conversion experience like this puts us back on track and helps personal commitment to make sense once again.

The role of the priest has changed a good bit since I was ordained. We used to have very cohesive ethnic and religious communities, like the Germans and the Irish, where we would have a sociological unit with which we could easily identify. Today there is a great deal of individualism. We are developing a new tribalism in place of the old ethnic groups. And so today while theologically the role of the priest is the same, we must by force of circumstances be more of community builders and facilitators. The central call of priests today is to liturgy. By that I don't mean rubricism, but liturgy at its deepest level, the work of the people. I wish that the sacramentals in the traditional sense were emphasized more, for liturgy is more than the seven sacraments. It is deeply involved in life. It should lead us to a new relationship with our environment, with the people around us, and with ourselves. We should at the same time emphasize incarnationalism. The new emphasis on the presence of the Holy Spirit is a collateral development.

We talk a lot today about the youth being of major importance. Of course they are important. Some of us, myself included, were even agnostic for a while when we were young. We all went through those stages, and we don't really expect youth to absorb an enormous amount of doctrine. The place where I see a great need for special attention is among young adults, especially those faced with crises: jobs threatened, health impairment, the strain of spousal relationships. The stages of life that they go through lend themselves nicely to the sacramental approach. One thing that makes it more difficult today to deal with youth is the fact that the gang has usurped not only the place of the family but even the place of the Church. Yes, I see the ones most in need of help today as being families and those going through the transitions of life. On our side is the fact that people come to priests when they will not go to others for spiritual direction even though others may be more competent in different ways.

Homilies are extraordinarily important in the life of a priest. We are asked to be brief in our expositions. Unfortunately, with the lack of Catholic schools and the limited time that people have to explore their faith, we need more expository homilies: they are crucial, and they can't be given in just a few minutes on Sunday. But even if we fall short in exposition, we find that people are hungry for comfort and for hope, and that is what we can give them in the homily.

Life's ambiguities bring a surprise; God's presence, for example, in the opaqueness of the whole human and cosmic condition. His presence is my abiding surprise. I have met people whom I thought had no faith who surprised me by their faith. I have met others whose faith I thought was shallow, and they became pillars of the Church. At some of my celebrations I have met people who said, "Oh, Father, the wonderful things you did for us." They were things I couldn't even remember. I have developed a habit of thanking God every morning for life as a gift. Generally speaking, that attitude brings with it a constant surprise and awe with the wonderment of it all. I am surprised at being in touch with God and being enthused by God.

Let me give you an example of a powerful experience I had with a brother priest. He had fallen madly in love; she was a strong and beautiful girl. They came and discussed it with me. I spent a good bit of time with them, and finally I was able to get through to him and show him what he would be missing by leaving the priesthood. He stayed and is now doing a wonderful job for the archdiocese.

Among the many good things going for us is the fact that we as Church are entering the ecumenical age. And we are doing this without diluting or neutralizing the basic realities of our faith—incarnation, redemption, and the sacramental expression of our relationship with Christ. Eventually we will have to come to terms with the Orthodox Church, a move that will not be that easy. We emphasize the legal side of things; they emphasize the mystical side of spirituality. One of our problems is that we have by force of history institutionalized spirituality and religion, and people just don't want to belong to an institutional church. Of course we must have an institution—there is no way out of that—but I think we are approaching more of a world church, one that will embody different cultures. For example, the incarnation can apply as easily to a culture that has produced Hinduism and Buddhism as to a culture that operates out of a legalistic framework, such as Judaism. We have to develop an increasingly global, inclusive vision of God's world. This doesn't mean that we should repudiate our basic western axioms. It means we need to be open to the beliefs of others.

Let me be clear on this: the Church is not badly wounded today. People haven't really lost their faith. Maybe they have lost confidence in the institutional church. In the past we were so hidebound, always looking behind our backs for heretics. All that is changing and that is why I think this is a wonderful time for a young man to think of the priesthood. There are great challenges facing the Church, and great opportunities for collaborating with people of other faiths. Yes, we have had scandals, and they hurt. But do they hurt as much as we assume? An Irish bishop with a drinking problem seemed beaten down by the media and by the community. He called a press conference and told the media, in effect, to go home and examine their own consciences. "You are tearing apart the Church that educated you," he said. Despite the scandals, people seem to know the good priests and trust them. They say, "Yes, I know doctors who cheat, but not my doctor. I know lawyers who negate the law, but not my lawyer. I know priests who have been unfaithful, but not my priest."

Father Bill Kerze, the pastor of the parish here in Malibu over which I presided for twenty-five years, said to me recently after our evening Mass, "John, it has been a busy day for me, but a good day." He had officiated at a baptism, two weddings, a funeral, and a memorial service. All of this besides his individual counseling. We have thousands of priests,

I am quite sure, for whom life is as busy, as contemplative, as satisfying as that of Father Bill's. There are countless thousands who, if they really knew the priest's life as we have known it, would join our ranks right now.

Pope Saint Gregory the Great (c. 540-604) faced, not a shortage of priests, but a deficiency of priestly dedication in his time and lamented:

> Look about you and see how full the world is of priests, yet in God's harvest a laborer is rarely to be found. For although we have accepted the priestly office, we do not fulfill its demands.

Who will say that our priests and our Church are not a thousand times better off now than they were in the days of Gregory? So, let's rejoice. Be glad. Tell the good news of who we are to all we meet.

Francis J. Smith
El Paso, Texas

Monsignor Francis Smith was born in 1935 in Chicago and was ordained in 1967 for the Diocese of El Paso, Texas. He is pastor of Saint Raphael's, one of the largest parishes in the diocese. With over 3,000 families, he works with three associates: a Filipino, a Mexican, and a recently ordained widower with eleven children. In residence is a fourth priest from the Philippines.

Monsignor Smith served as Vicar General for his diocese for thirteen years. He works out three days a week to keep fit for the strenuous demands of his parish.

Monsignor Smith comes across as boldly confident. Upon getting to know him further, we find that he is a kind, successful, gentle, articulate, well-balanced and happy priest who has a good grasp of priestly spirituality. The following testimony offers proof of Monsignor Smith's love of the priesthood and of his kindness to his fellow priests.

I came from a wonderful, loving family. They were not superlatively holy, just ordinary, but the Church was important to us. When there was a problem, we went to church and prayed for that intention. My dad was a steel worker. He had his own special devotions, and Mother had hers. I have no sisters, which is probably why I am so outspoken. Sisters tend to make a brother more subdued. My parents, especially my mother, saw to it that we got to Mass every Sunday. When I told them I wanted to study for the priesthood, there was affirmation and support, but no urging and no pressure.

I was born and raised on the South Side of Chicago, in Saint Justin the Martyr's parish. Every newly ordained priest seems to have been assigned to that parish. The priests there were outstanding men. One of them, Jack Egan, was active in the Chicago social programs. Another was Francis Spellman, with whom I still keep in touch. It was the example of the priests I met, especially the associates in our parish, that made me want to be a priest.

My early education was nothing out of the ordinary, but the Church was the focal part of our student lives. In grades five to eight we went willingly to Mass before school. Four out of our graduating class became priests, three of them in religious communities.

My pastor in Chicago, a close friend of Bishop Metzger of El Paso, had suggested that I come here and work with the diocese to discern my vocation. I did work in the diocese for two years, then I went to Saint Bonaventure University in Olean, New York, finished my schooling, and was ordained in 1967.

Four years later I was named pastor of a parish which had converted an empty Baptist church for its use. This diocese is seventy percent Catholic; the city is seventy-five percent Catholic. Several times we have transformed Protestant property into new parishes to ease the burden of funding. Seventeen years and another pastorate later, I was appointed to Saint Raphael's.

We have a large congregation. The church seats 1,500. At the Saturday evening Mass, more than 1,850 are in attendance. On Sunday there are six liturgies. One is comfortably filled, the rest, standing room only.

During the week we can touch only a tiny portion of those who come here. I see the Sunday homily as our best way, really our only way, to reach them all. Preaching is a tremendously important part of our ministry. We don't have to preach long, usually fifteen to eighteen minutes. But we have to prepare well so that when the people leave, they have something to hang onto, something that will make a change in their lives and in the lives of the members of their families.

I am very surprised how well those in the pews actually listen to us, even when they don't seem to respond. We have more influence on people than we realize. A couple came to me a few weeks ago and reminded me of advice I had given them years ago. They said, "You were absolutely right. We should have done then what you suggested." Others have said, "Why didn't you tell me this before?" Or, "I guess our pride kept us from admitting we were wrong."

We have six or seven classes of first communicants every year. When I preach to them, I still repeat the homily that Monsignor Jack Egan gave in my home parish in Chicago when I received my first communion. He told us a wartime story that went something like this:

> A young man, an only son, was called into service. When he was leaving, his father said, "Son, stay close to the general." The boy didn't know what that meant till later, when he found that in combat the general was always behind the lines. The moral: stay close to God and you will never get into trouble.

I would say that people expect pretty much the same from priests today as they did when I was ordained. They want guidance, spirituality, and answers to their questions. The people of this parish are fairly liberal in their thinking. Yet, no matter how modern they become, in the spiritual realm they stay with the basics.

The youth, especially those in grades six on up, are very much in need of the attention of priests today. The grown-ups are already committed to a way of life; the young people are just beginning to make their decisions in life. We have a three-day retreat for those preparing for confirmation. It has a powerful impact on them. They have begun to see the importance of their faith. At the retreats they suddenly realize what their parents have been trying to do for them. Parents call and tell us that after those three days their children returned changed youngsters.

A special group that needs our help, affirmation, and friendship is our own fellow priests. We lead a lonely life, often experience a lack of appreciation, and sometimes wonder whether it is all worthwhile. That's when we need a priest friend. I try to always remember the needs of a fellow priest. I have helped a few just as some have helped me. Recently a priest came to me and frankly told me what he was planning to do. I laid it on the line and said, "No, this is what you are going to do." He was stunned, but he accepted my recommendation. Today we are close friends, partly because I wasn't easy with him. I told him to stand up and be a man. And he did. I look with awe at every priest. He may lack a talent or two. He may make some mistakes. But he is special in the eyes of God, and I always call him Father. Just this month I wrote a letter to an elderly former professor of mine who is inclined to forget the wonderful things he has accomplished. Here is part of what I wrote:

Dear Pete,

Most of the time I forget that life is short and what I wish to say is either postponed or forgotten. Every time I call you and we reminisce, I hang up feeling better for having spoken to you. I remember so well the seminary days. I chose the priesthood because of the example of men like you, Martin Porter, Bishop De Palma, Bill Nolken, Brother John, and others. I can't think of them without recalling their faithfulness and closeness to God. They were a cut above other men, though they didn't know it. They are great human beings. While they are imperfect, their holiness overshadows any imperfections. I think we don't realize how much encouragement we can be to one another in the priesthood, which can be lonely at times.

You may think that because of your physical ailments and all the encumbrances brought on by fighting the good fight, you cannot give much. Let that thought be farthest from your mind. You are still a teacher, a promoter, a source of encouragement to all those with whom you communicate. Your spirituality, wisdom, and love identifies you as a modern patriarch. You have the ability, through humor and joy, to uplift others and that is what we need today in our mad scramble.

I hope you know the esteem I have for you and for many others who have touched my life. God gave you the gift of being able to affirm others.

One of the solutions frequently offered for the shortage of priests is that they be allowed to marry. Part of my family is Ukrainian Byzantine. I have met several married priests in that rite and saw nothing in their lives that would be detrimental to a faith community. They were very spiritual men. I have never found these men lacking in their attention to their congregations. A priest friend of mine at Saint George Syrian Orthodox church has a family of eleven children. We often talk about marriage for the clergy. We see both pros and cons.

Obedience is probably a greater burden for me than celibacy, because in bowing to authority I am being deprived of a piece of my will. Yet I have to realize that there is always someone over all of us. Even the pope has God over him. Once in a while we find ourselves under a superior who loves to ride herd on people. When that happens we had better have a well-developed spiritual life and a sense of humor.

I am convinced that no matter how many programs we develop to promote the priesthood, vocations really start in the home. Today when a son or daughter wants to enter a particular profession, it is typical for parents to estimate their potential gross income for the first year. In major golf tournaments the announcers spend a good deal of time examining, not so much how many tournaments a top golfer has won, but how much he has earned. Corporations analyze their success on the basis of the bottom line. We are obsessed with money, and no priest worth his salt gives a hoot about his salary, as long as his needs are taken care of. We need to find young men who realize that happiness is not measured by the buck. The attractions of other callings are sometimes too much for young people. But I think they forget that genuine happiness in life comes when you are doing exactly what you like to do, whether you are in medicine, law, business, or any other profession. When I was in the seminary a senior priest who had been in a Nazi concentration camp came to talk to us. He saw the wealth of this country and all the possibilities for material success, and told us how much he admired people who were willing to give up those attractions to serve Christ. It was a talk I never forgot.

I really believe the potential for a priest to accomplish things is greater now than it was a generation ago. We have so many more tools at our disposal. I receive daily faxes from Rome; they are the first thing I read after the morning paper. They are like getting a daily paper about the Church. Communications have developed to the point that I can disseminate into the community in a few minutes information that used to require weeks. But even having those tools at our disposal is not enough. A priest can't be a workaholic. We have to stay psychologically and physically healthy. We must take time off, have some hobbies, enjoy them, and then come back fresh and ready for the job.

Last Sunday when we brought in the catechumens of the RCIA program, I was really touched by their faith. It was a day of happiness for them, joy for me. I think of the small recognitions we get from the bishop or from people in the pews, of administering first holy communion and seeing the faith and happiness of the innocents, or of being able to help someone who has lost a loved one. Helping people overcome some of their difficulties without expecting anything in return is very rewarding. We don't send a bill. We don't turn on a timer to estimate a charge for our work. There is nothing greater than the satisfaction of having done something worthwhile for a person *gratis*.

One final thought. Those who are chosen to be bishops today must be men of great spiritual depth. More than that, they should be understanding, supportive and affirming of their priests. They must see them as brothers. There are a lot of vocation programs today. Let me suggest one that will top them all. Choose bishops who love their priests, who are kind to them, who respect them and want only for them to grow in their relationship with Christ. Bishops who extend themselves to their priests and who show them support and kindness will be well-known, and the word will disseminate. And vocations will come.

Edward Ramacher
Breezy Point, Minnesota

Father Ed Ramacher, born September 5, 1917, grew up in a Minnesota family of 13 children.

When he decided that he wanted to study for the priesthood, funds for his education were minimal. So he attended the Pontifical College, Josephinum, at Columbus, Ohio, where all expenses are paid by the institution. While at Josephinum he accepted every extra job offered to him: photos were needed — he became the seminary's official photographer; the extensive seminary grounds needed care—he took over the duties of grounds keeper; the seminary was searching for funds to establish a new program—he raised the money; classmates wanted their hair cut—he became a barber. His extracurricular work not only taught him a great deal beyond the classroom, but also provided him with tools that were to be useful in later life. He was ordained March 10, 1945, for the Diocese of Saint Cloud.

Father Ramacher continued his widespread range of activities after his ordination. His skills with people led him to become a marriage counselor, working with Hollywood celebrities, including the Lennon Sisters, Dennis Day, and Pat O'Brien. Legendary Notre Dame football coach Frank Leahy came to Minnesota to assist Ramacher with benefits and fundraisers. He continued his photographic interest by shooting photos of the California missions. As St. Cloud diocesan director of fund-raising, he spearheaded a ten million dollar campaign for diocesan programs and parochial schools. Barbering was about the only talent Father Ramacher developed in the seminary that he has not pursued after ordination.

Father Ramacher has an obvious love for the priesthood and could have given the entire interview to that topic. However, he was urged to begin by mentioning some of his awards.

Since you asked, let me relate some of my achievements. I was chosen as Outstanding Man of Minnesota in 1949, probably because of the work I was doing with youth at that time. I built two large winter playgrounds and furnished all the skis, toboggans, and skates for the kids. My idea was that if I could get the young people interested in something the Church provided, the parents would follow. And they did. During Minnesota's centennial year I was chosen one of the "100 Living Great of the State" for the work I did. *Country Beautiful* magazine was my love for six years. We wanted to publish it to show how much God has blessed this country with such wonderful resources and to urge their preservation. The magazine continued until someone spent a lot of money they shouldn't have spent, and we couldn't keep it going. President Kennedy wrote a whole chapter for the magazine, on our commitment to the future.

A friend of mine, Father Huebsch, and I made seventy-six color broadcasts for KSTP-TV in Minneapolis on the life of the Church, the home, and other features. Later we did twenty-six broadcasts for a convert series that was so successful KSTP-TV played it for two years instead of one. Much of my spare time has been spent in fund-raising, an activity for which I seem to have a talent. I raised money for the National Catholic Rural Life Conference, but mainly the fund-raising has been for my own diocese. I have two projects going at the present time. I am trying to raise money for Saint Michael's in Morongo Valley, the retirement home for priests near Palm Springs. Priests who can't afford the downtown prices but who would like to visit the area can stay there for eight dollars a day. My second project is the Saint John's boys choir. I will raise a half million dollars for an endowment fund for that wonderful group.

It seems to me that in the past the ones who promoted vocations were parish priests. My pastor asked me to think about the priesthood, and without his prodding I wouldn't have even thought it could be possible. Most of my friends had the same stimulus. Parents are the other important factor. I don't believe they have ever been a primary source of vocations, but today they are one of the biggest obstacles to vocations. Too often they want their sons to rise to the top in the professions and in business. Despite the respect they have for the priesthood, somehow they don't see their own sons as being "successful" unless they are heading for the big time. That is understandable. I don't criticize it. I simply say it is a fact of life.

I think the biggest surprise in my life as a priest has been the reverence and respect that people still have for the priest in spite of the scandals that fill the media today. I felt that respect the moment I was ordained. I could sense it not just in the church and school, but on the street, in the cafes—everywhere. The vast majority of priests are doing wonderful jobs: working hard, giving good homilies, visiting the sick, preparing couples for marriage, and all the hundred and one things a priest is called on to do. They are out on the firing line in parishes, hospitals, prisons, high schools, and colleges. They give up family and big salaries because they love people, because they love children, and because they love Christ. I believe that people realize the need for priests to carry on the work of the Church, and that they respect their responsibilities.

I recently celebrated my fiftieth anniversary as a priest. I told the people who attended my jubilee that I had been a completely happy priest and never wanted to be anything but a priest. In fact, I couldn't conceive having any other kind of profession. I've had a very fulfilling life. I've received all kinds of awards and recognitions, but none of them can hold a candle to the joy I experience when, after going through the long, careful process of instructing a convert, I see the happiness on the face of that person when he or she receives the body and blood of Christ for the first time.

I love the priesthood. I know that ordination puts me in a position where I can do an enormous amount of good and bring something worthwhile to people's lives. I realize I could help people if I were a lawyer, a doctor, or a businessman. But for priests the possibilities are simply unlimited, if we live our promises, if we are men of prayer, and if we really are convinced of the goodness of people.

Patrick J. Waite
San Diego, California

Father Pat Waite was born June 1, 1927 in Winner, South Dakota, and was ordained for the Diocese of Sioux City, Iowa, in 1954. Father Pat is a retired Navy chaplain, and very proud of his roots and upbringing in rural Iowa.

Father Waite selected the Marriott Hotel on the outskirts of San Diego for his interview. It soon became apparent why he picked that venue. Every waiter, waitress, and clerk knew him personally and gave him a "high five" as he walked by. Whatever his successes may have been in the Navy, he has obviously achieved a quiet notoriety among the laity of San Diego who look upon him as their special padre. The obvious joy he feels for his priesthood infects everyone he meets.

When I was in first grade, Sister Gilbert, a Sister of Christian Charity, made a deep impression on me and caused me to think about what I would become as an adult. At that early age she had the ability to interest me in a devotion to the Sacred Heart, to awaken my conscience, and to leave me with a sense of the reality of sin. The sisters would encourage us to think about the priesthood, and I did give it serious consideration during grade school, though the attraction seemed to fade in high school.

My parents were convinced of the value of Catholic education. Whenever my parents moved, they would first check into the availability of Catholic schools. The family always provided an altar for the home, and for some reason or other it was placed in my room. I would act as the priest, my sister would decorate the altar, and my two little brothers would be the servers. My folks had been through the drought and depression years of the Dakotas and the crash of 1929, and saw the devastating effects of that period on priests. When the Franciscans invited me to go to a minor seminary after the eighth grade, although my parents loved and respected priests, they demurred and sent me instead to a Catholic boys prep school in Sioux City, Iowa, run by the Society of Mary.

Right out of high school, in the spring of 1945, I joined the Navy. It was the end of World War II. I spent a year on Eniwetok in the Marshall Islands, and while there began to think again about the priesthood. Arriving home in 1946, I used the G.I. Bill to attend the Evangelical United Brethren College in nearby Le Mars, Iowa. I fell in love and nearly married. Again the priesthood entered my mind, and I thought that if I were ever going to deal with this urge and make some kind of a decision, I had better get to a Catholic college.

In the fall of 1947 I wound up at Loras College in the seminary program. Originally I had thought of joining either the Maryknoll missionaries or the Franciscans. My roommate, who was in the seminary program, asked me, "What's the matter? Isn't Sioux City good enough for you?" And so I began to think of becoming a member of the diocesan clergy.

At the Immaculate Conception Seminary in Conception, Missouri, I had a wonderful confessor, Giles Zaramella, O.S.B., who later became the abbot of San Giorgio in Venice, Italy. During my second year, when my resoluteness to continue was waning, Father Giles suggested that I take the epistles of Saint Paul, which we had already studied in our first year, and read them again, this time looking for the character and personality of Paul. That study was a revelation to me and encouraged me to continue.

After ordination my assignments for the next few years were to teach in both grade and high schools and to serve as an associate pastor in the small, rural parishes of Iowa. I thoroughly enjoyed working with students. I also coached basketball, football, and spring track. They were demanding roles, but very fulfilling.

In 1958, when I was stationed in Bancroft, Iowa, I met a priest who was to have a significant impact on my development, Monsignor Bob Quinn. Bob was a chaplain and commander on the USS *Kearsage*, a Naval aircraft carrier. He returned to Bancroft, his hometown, to celebrate his twenty-fifth anniversary as a priest. Three years later I applied to the bishop to be assigned either to the missions in South America or to a chaplaincy in the armed services. He asked what branch of service I would be interested in, and I said I wasn't sure. With his elephantine memory he said, "Well, you were in the Navy before, weren't you? Do you want to go back?" I said, "Yes." So on December 22, 1961, I was sworn into the Navy. The following month I went to the Naval Chaplains School in Newport, Rhode Island. Then began the first of sixteen assignments as a chaplain.

The Navy was one of the highlights of my priesthood. For twenty-six years I served overseas and in stateside assignments on both the East and the West Coasts. There was a lot of work, a lot of danger, but also much camaraderie among fellow chaplains in the Navy, Air Force, and Army. The Marines always treated us with special fondness, calling us *Padres* as distinct from chaplains, and we formed deep friendships with them. I had four tours with the Marines, four with the Navy Air, and one with the U.S. Coast Guard. I had about the same number of tours on various large bases, stateside and overseas. We were often assigned to bases that had large concentrations of families, and that gave us a wide variety of experiences in pastoral work. The most exciting of all my tours was aboard a carrier, the USS *Randolph* (CVS-15).

When I left the Navy in June 1988, I was given permission by the Sioux City bishop to stay in San Diego and continue to work with the military. I take care of Marine recruits and handle night coverage at the Naval Hospital, anointing the sick and the dying. When active duty priests are not available, I have the burial detail for veterans and spouses of World War II, Korea, and Vietnam at the National Cemetery. I also officiate at weddings of military and civilian couples. Even my work in military retirement has been an active and joyful experience.

I had many enriching experiences during the course of my Navy career. In 1973-74 I was sent to postgraduate training at the Graduate Theological Union in Berkeley, California. It was a wonderful opportunity to update my training in theology and sacramental expertise and in applied theology. At the same time I had my first introduction to Marriage Encounter. I made the weekend and was intrigued by the possibility of using that program for service personnel. I made my Deeper Encounter, a weekend enrichment for team members in Los Angeles. That proved to be an eye-opener for the rich potential the Encounter movement had for enhancing married life. I gave Marriage Encounter weekends in the San Diego area. Then I began to work in Engaged Encounter, in conjunction with the diocesan program headed by Father Bill Ortmann, formerly a Sioux City pastor. This fall I taught a small group of second graders who were preparing for their first communion. First communion day turned out to be held on the forty-second anniversary of my ordination. What an experience that was to teach young children after teaching high schoolers, sailors, and Marines!

My most recent work has been with Project Rachel, offering sacramental confession and celebrating the Mass of the Holy Innocents for women recovering from abortions. The Mass takes place on Sunday evenings after a charismatic weekend of working through the years of grief, guilt, and remorse. For me it is an enormously rewarding apostolate. Every weekend marriages are convalidated and people are restored to parish life.

Like most young priests, I wasn't confident of myself in the beginning. I enjoyed preaching, but struggled with it. In the military I grew in my speaking ability. I still spend a good deal of time preparing my homilies. It is a real challenge to distill the readings, reflect on their meaning, and apply them to daily life. The word and the eucharist are central to the life of any priest. I hope that I will never get to the point where I feel I can walk into the pulpit without a thorough preparation, including a lot of prayer.

One surprise for me in the ministry has been the profound difference between serving in a parochial setting and in the Navy. In service, everything is transitory. Both the people served by the priest and the chaplain himself might be moved at any moment, and so there is always pressure to get things done without delay. I really enjoy the work I am doing now with the Marine recruits. They are youngsters just out of high school. I have been their confessor for the last eight years. Many of them have been away from the Church for some time, and it is a special joy to see them return.

One of the duties of chaplains is to make Casualty Assistance Calls in cases of death. We accompany the squadron commander or the base commander, usually to see the widow. These are very difficult calls, but they afford an opportunity to help people through the stages of crisis. The negative side of the calls is that sometimes the widows, in their depression, put us in the role of their deceased spouse, and we can quickly become over-involved. Situations like that are almost impossible to deal with. We have to be kind and considerate, but those very qualities are easily mistaken for affection. It was a problem for me in the late 1960s. However, in 1969 the Navy developed a marriage program to help us better handle those types of situations, and the danger was lessened.

I still have a strong attraction to the opposite sex, and as experience shows, they have to me. I think our vow of celibacy sometimes presents a challenge to some women, and it becomes almost a dare to attract us. We cannot and must not disparage or dump celibacy. It is too precious, and it is a charism. We have to be careful to preserve it. I do believe that it should be voluntary. Once the kids in my second grade class asked how many sacraments they could receive. I said to them, "Your co-teacher is married, and she will probably never receive the sacrament of orders. I am ordained, and probably will never receive the sacrament of matrimony." The kids groaned, and I said, "Well, maybe by the year 2020 we will have married clergy, but by then I will be 110." One of the kids replied, "Gosh, Father, at 110, I hardly think you will be attractive to any woman." Out of the mouths of infants. . . . !

I encourage men to think about a vocation. I ask them "Do you see yourself having the ability and the courage to study for the priesthood?" I try to plant the idea and let it grow. I do have to be careful not to give the idea just to a few bright kids and not make the offer to some who seem less bright, yet might turn out to be the modern Saint Jean Vianney. I am sure my presence with the second graders is meaningful. I recall Father John Curry, a Franciscan, coming into our first grade room, reaching for his catechism in the back of his cowl, and saying, "Children, if you study this your whole life, you won't understand all that is here." That left a profound impression on me. There is something in the priesthood so special that it takes a lifetime of study.

Theodore M. Hesburgh, C.S.C.
Notre Dame, Indiana

One of the best known and highly respected Americans is the President Emeritus of the University of Notre Dame, Father Ted Hesburgh. Though he "retired" as president in 1987 after thirty-five years on the job, he remains at the university and continues as coordinator of several centers which he helped to establish.

Father Hesburgh is an outstanding leader in both religious and secular fields. He was an advisor to seven presidents and several popes. He served on fifteen presidential commissions and was a member of the Presidential Clemency Board after the Vietnam War, charged with reviewing 15,000 applications for clemency for servicemen who evaded the draft or received dishonorable discharge from the armed forces. He has offered Mass in Anarctica, set a world speed record flying past Mach 3.35 in an SR 71 Blackbird, preached to Russians in their own churches, and received 120 honorary degrees.

Despite all his accomplishments, Father Hesburgh emphatically says that he would be glad to give them all up if they threatened in any way his most cherished achievement: his ordination as a priest.

Father Hesburgh's office is located on the fourteenth floor of the university library, named in his honor, in quarters that could be described, with one exception, as modest. Adjacent to the office of his secretary there is a magnificent gathering room for visitors and special groups. Along the wall are dozens of awards and honors given to Father Hesburgh over the years. On a large table in the center of the room albums filled with pictures of his achievements are displayed. A big-screen television in the far corner transforms the space into a entertainment area for guests, especially on football Saturdays.

In an office to the rear of that special room, still working a twelve-hour day and still envisioning dreams for a greater Notre Dame, is the former president, a man whose career, like his institution, is a legend in America. He was born in Syracuse, New York, on May 25, 1917, and was ordained a priest at Notre Dame in 1944. Father Hesburgh is a member of the Congregation of the Holy Cross.

Yes, perhaps the best known American priest is the very one who sums up his entire life and accomplishments in one word: PRIEST.

I guess I have always wanted to be a priest. I was exposed to some wonderfully good priests in our home parish, Most Holy Rosary in Syracuse. The assistants were very close to us kids, one of the best being Father Harold Quinn, who trained the altar boys, gave us retreats, and was our regular confessor. It was quite a remarkable parish, and in the first thirty years of its existence it produced thirty-four priests and twenty-eight sisters. We were taught by the Immaculate Heart of Mary Sisters. It was a good place to grow up, and from the earliest days in school I never wanted anything else than to be ordained. I have been asked, if only one word could be put on my tombstone, what would I choose? My answer was, "Priest."

I have been ordained for more than fifty years, and it has been a wonderfully fulfilling life. I have met and made a host of friends, men and women, in almost every country of the world. Much of what I have accomplished I could not have done outside the priesthood. I have been able to touch people's lives at the most crucial points of both their joys and sorrows. And you know what, surprisingly, I have come close to so very many people because of celibacy. People were not impressed by the fact that I didn't have a bank account, nor by the fact that I had a vow of obedience, because like it or not, most people have an obligation of obedience to their company, to the military, perhaps even to their spouse. But something about celibacy seemed to grab people. They saw that I was still "normal." I had a great rapport with the wives of diplomats, ambassadors, even presidents. Occasionally the husbands would come to me and ask, "How is it that all our wives gather around you and like you and are comfortable with you, and that is not true of any other guy in this group?" My answer was always, "Very simple. I am not a threat to them. They can relax with me." And they all called me Father without embarrassment. Whether they were Catholic, Protestant, or Jewish, it was always Father Ted. Somehow they knew I was willing to live this kind of life so I could belong to everybody, and was ready to help anybody who needed me.

Celibacy has been enormously helpful to the priesthood, because of the kind of life we lead, the places we have to go, the things we have to do. If I were starting all over again, I would still want to be a celibate priest. And I simply deny that priests who may have gotten into difficulty in the sexual area did so because of celibacy. I do believe that celibacy is important for the religious priests because they live in community. But for diocesan priests, especially those who live in distant missions, I think it might be better if they could be married.

From what I hear, there are quite a few young men who won't go to the seminary because of celibacy. Yet I am convinced there are enough out there willing to commit to both priesthood and celibacy. It is not an easy commitment. It is like climbing a sheer rock face; we all come close to falling off at times, except for the grace of God. I really don't have a great hang-up on celibacy though. For the secular clergy, loneliness may be an insurmountable problem. I have seen priests up the Amazon going to seed. I have seen rectories where a woman's touch is needed. Greek and Russian Orthodox priests do marry, and they are good men. The same with the Anglican priests. Yet I don't believe the married priesthood is the answer to everything. Marriage requires every bit as much commitment and hard work as the priesthood. It demands fidelity. Nor do I subscribe to the proposal that you could sign up for five years, then drop out. You can do that in the Navy. I'm not sure you can do it in the priesthood, where the commitment is too deep and too personal. For myself, I can honestly say that I have seen great value in celibacy and have worked at it hard. And I hope I can make it to the end. If I do, it will be because I tried to be faithful to things like the breviary, daily Mass (I have missed only two or three days in my life), the rosary, and meditation.

The priesthood is a wonderful vocation. If you have it, thank God on your knees and pray to God that once you are ordained you will stay a priest, because it is not an easy life, and the temptations are many.

The priest performs a key function in society. His role today is the same as it was when Jesus chose his disciples. He told them to go out and teach, baptize, and bring to people the grace of salvation. That task doesn't change in any basic way and is relevant to every society, culture, and geography. In 1995 when the Holy Father came to the States, he came not as a diplomat but as a priest. He said Masses for thousands, preached to them, blessed them, talked to the United Nations about human rights, peace, and freedom. The world today needs those functions of the priesthood just as they did in the time of Jesus.

The priest performs a key function in society. Priests are badly needed in every element of society. I know that every group is important—kids in elementary and high schools, young married people, the elderly facing death. But if I had to pick one group that is crucial, I would say it is those of college age, the group I have been working with most of my life. They have advanced beyond the age of simple faith; right or wrong is no longer a childish thing, but something very serious. They are becoming adult Christians, facing commitments and problems that will affect the rest of their lives—marriage, a profession, faith. They are laying a foundation that is going to be around for a very long time. I want to help them make good choices in those critical years.

Preaching is a crucially important function of the priest. I do my preaching mainly at the Masses in the residence halls, all thirty of them. I see the result of good preaching in the faces of those youngsters. They react positively to a good homily. But I had better be prepared, because if I just try to wing it, they will come right out and tell me that wasn't one of my best. I never use a report card for my homilies. When I give a poor homily, the students have no compunction telling me that I was way off target. And when I give a good one, they tell me so. My preparation is twofold: first, I study the readings carefully; second, I pray to the Holy Spirit. I think the Holy Spirit is vastly underused by most Christians, not to mention a lot of priests. That is my ace in the hole. The Paraclete never fails me. Preaching is crucially important. It is half the mission of the priest. But don't forget that one's life is the best homily of all. We all fail at times. But if people know we are working hard to be what we profess to be, that is our most effective preaching. A friend of mine, Father Charlie Sheedy, used to say, "Religious life gets down to one thing: showing up. Don't be an absentee priest. Be where you are needed." Those are the two halves of a priest's mission, bringing the word of God and the grace of God to people.

I guess the biggest revelation for me has been how good people are. When I was first ordained, I thought that I would be disillusioned by what I heard in the confessional; it has been just the opposite. I found people humble in confessing their sins, yearning to be good, honest, genuine. That was a delightful surprise.

I have often reflected on what special contribution a priest can make to society, and I believe it is simply to be an *alter Christus*, "another Christ." Jesus wants to be present to people everywhere, and one of the ways he can do that is through his priests. We make him present first by delivering his message. To be effective, that message must be adapted to current times, made real for people to whom it would otherwise be just words. Jesus could do that in his day; he can't do it now. He needs someone to convey his message to people of every century in a form that has meaning to them. Second, the priest dispenses grace, officially through the sacraments, but often by just being there. Cardinal Suhard of Paris, one of my early heroes, had a wonderful expression, *l'apostolate de la presence*, the "apostolate of the presence," just being there. He was saying the same thing as Father Sheedy when he spoke about just showing up.

Every once in a while I look back on my life and recall occasions when something happened that seems to make it all worthwhile, when something good happened that probably would not have happened unless I was a priest. I have had many of those moments. Sometimes those events take place simply because I was the only priest there. My beat, apart from being at Notre Dame, has been on the outer fringes of Christianity. You don't find many priests in the Antarctic or in the Kremlin or in the United Nations or in the company of people like Gorbachev. Let me pull one incident out of the hat. We were at the University of Vienna one night with academic people and scientists, attending the International Atomic Energy Meeting, a program of the U.N. Atoms for Peace. The head of the Russian delegation, a professor of metallurgy in Moscow, gave the opening talk. He said, "There are a lot of people here, scientists, Nobel prize winners, professors from great universities. But there is only one person here I trust completely, and that is Father Ted, because he has never told me a lie and I have never told him one." That was a moment I have treasured.

One of the great satisfactions for any priest is to realize how he has made a difference in people's lives. Let me give an example that may seem to be out of the normal purview of the priest. I made a difference as a member of the Commission on Civil Rights for fifteen years, the last four as chair. In the Omnibus Civil Rights Act of 1964, we literally changed the face of America. We took an apartheid as bad as South Africa and got rid of it through that bill. President Johnson has to get the credit for its passage. Kennedy could never have pulled it off, nor did he try. But Johnson got the act approved and put the law into being. It was a good feeling to give equal rights to people who came here as slaves more than two hundred years ago. Much of the meat of that bill involved a simple realization of the need for justice for minorities. When we were meeting in the South, occasionally some of my secular friends would give me a hard time. One of the commission members would lean over and write on a yellow pad, "Give them a little theology, Father." Then I would talk about the Christian point of view. Afterward they would say: "You took unfair advantage of us. We know you are right, but our way of life is hard to change."

The priesthood is a wonderful life, but it does have problems, just as any other way of life. One of them is loneliness. We are living in a world where everyone around us has a wife and kids, and we don't. I go back to that lonely room in Corby Hall near the garbage cans, and it is not exactly a great place for human companionship. But we have to see that as part of the price we pay. We can't really belong to one person if we belong to everyone. Loneliness is real, yet it can be sublimated in the fact that we have so many friends. I have kissed several thousand women, usually on the cheek. I am far more free in that way than if I were tied to a wife and family. It is what I call an open friendship in which we trust everyone and hope everyone trusts us. It is a friendship that leads to a kind of human communication that is quite sacred.

I am optimistic about the future of the Church. We are growing very fast in this country. Here at Notre Dame where we are about 85 percent Catholic, we have twenty-one youngsters studying to join the Church. In every age we Catholics have faced special problems and in every age the Church is somewhat reflective of the times. When Europe was in the Dark Ages, so were we. During the Communist regime in eastern Europe, we were in suppression. We had a tough time with the Roman Empire. When we were finally accepted, all the regalism of the empire got into the Church, and we became a kind of petty kingdom presided over by bishops and cardinals. I did my doctoral thesis on the idea that people are mandated to the apostolate through baptism and confirmation. They are metaphysically empowered to take part in the liturgy and to bring Christ to others. Actually I believe the Holy Spirit is leading us toward that concept of the laity through the current shortage of priests.

Is this a good time to be a priest? I think any time is a good time. If I were born in 1150 or 1600 or 2000, I would choose to be a priest. If anyone wanted to really hurt me, they would tell me I could no longer offer Mass, perform the sacraments, or preach, because that person would be saying I am no longer going to be a priest. Don't forget that one word I want to be inscribed on my tombstone.

Afterword

The stories in this book lend no credence to the negative comments splashed about in the secular and Catholic media. The surveys of the *Los Angeles Times* and the National Federation of Priests' Councils and the conclusions of Father Andrew Greeley based on those surveys suggest that what you have read here is typical of most of our Catholic priests. The interviewed priests are proud of the work they do. They see in their work an opportunity to reach their full potential. They believe the teachings of the Church. They repeatedly maintain that what they do contributes to the peace and salvation of those whom they touch. And they are quick to recommend their life to others, the ultimate measure of job satisfaction.

Finally these stories make us realize that we, all of us, can contribute to the ministries of the ordained priesthood by encouraging vocations, by affirming our priests, and by giving more credibility to the power of the Holy Spirit. From what these priests have said, we can happily agree with Robert Browning in Rabbi ben Ezra:

> Grow old along with me!
> The best is yet to be,
> The last of life, for which the first was made:
> Our times are in His hand
> Who saith, A whole I planned,
> Youth shows but half; trust God: see all, nor be afraid.

Acknowledgments

In our two-year endeavor, more than two hundred wonderful people gave us advice, encouragement, leads, time, and financial aid. Without their support we would never have come to closure. Our inability to list them does not reflect our lack of appreciation.

We give special thanks to:

- several priests whose understanding of the priesthood helped to shape and give direction to the book: Frederic F. Curry, Timothy L. DeVenney, Robert L. Ferring, Daniel E. Flores, Louis H. Greving, Joseph L. Hauer, James E. Hayes, Joseph P. Herard, Douglas J. Loecke, Thomas Naughton, S.J., William J. Ortmann, Paul L. Weis and Archbishop Jerome G. Hanus, O.S.B.;
- the officers and members of the Dubuque Serra Club for their constant support and financial assistance; and
- the authors of the Forewords: Virgil DeChant, Supreme Grand Knight of the Knights of Columbus, and Raymond F. Mohrman, President of Serra International.

Finally, because of the extraordinary number of hours of time, effort, and suggestions generously offered, after reading several revisions of *Extraordinary Lives*, we must list four dear friends:

Sharon Cruse	George Freund
Freda Reynolds	James White

About the Authors

MONSIGNOR FRANCIS P. FRIEDL was born November 26, 1917, in Waterloo, Iowa. He was ordained for the diocese of Dubuque in 1943. Monsignor Friedl has a Doctorate in psychology from the Catholic University of America. Serving in a variety of ministries in his many years as a priest, including college professor, college president, public relations director, and pastor, Monsignor Friedl currently gives retreats and workshops throughout the United States.

Monsignor Friedl would like your comments on *Extraordinary Lives*. He can be reached on e-mail at dbqfriedl@impresso.com.

REX V. E. REYNOLDS (M.A., J.D.) retired in 1994 as a professor of speech communication and law from Loras College, Dubuque, Iowa. He is the editor of several books and articles and the author of two books, *China's New Romanized Alphabet* and *Missalet* (Russain, 1993). Rex and his wife, Freda, have a daughter, three sons, and two grandchildren.

Rex Reynolds would also like to hear from you regarding your comments and reactions to *Extraordinary Lives*. His e-mail address is frryn@mwci.net.